Strategic Rebellion

NATIONALISMS ACROSS THE GLOBE

VOL. 5

PETER LANG
Oxford · Bern · Berlin · Bruxelles · Frankfurt am Main · New York · Wien

Pavlos I. Koktsidis

Strategic Rebellion

Ethnic Conflict in FYR Macedonia and the Balkans

PETER LANG
Oxford · Bern · Berlin · Bruxelles · Frankfurt am Main · New York · Wien

Bibliographic information published by Die Deutsche Nationalbibliothek.
Die Deutsche Nationalbibliothek lists this publication in the Deutsche Nationalbibliografie; detailed bibliographic data is available on the Internet at http://dnb.d-nb.de.

A catalogue record for this book is available from the British Library.

Library of Congress Cataloging-in-Publication Data:

Koktsidis, Pavlos I.
Strategic rebellion : ethnic conflict in FYR Macedonia and the Balkans / Pavlos I. Koktsidis.
p. cm. -- (Nationalisms across the globe; 5)
Includes bibliographical references and index.
ISBN 978-3-0343-0148-0 (alk. paper)
1. Macedonia--Ethnic relations. 2. Balkan Peninsula--Ethnic relations. 3. Macedonia--Politics and government. 4. Balkan Peninsula--Politics and government. I. Title.
DR2173.K63 2012
949.703--dc23
2011044865

Cover image © NASA/Goddard Space Flight Center Scientific Visualization Studio

ISSN 1662-9116
ISBN 978-3-0343-0148-0

Hochfeldstrasse 32, CH-3012 Bern, Switzerland
info@peterlang.com, www.peterlang.com, www.peterlang.net

Printed in Germany

Contents

Acknowledgements

I wish to thank Professor Adrian Guelke, Dr Debbie Lisle and Professor David Chandler for their valuable comments on my original thesis. I am especially thankful to Caspar Ten Dam for all the time he has spent proofreading this book and for the valuable and inspirational discussions we have shared over time. I would like to thank Theodoros Tosounidis, Liljana and Andrej Sevchenko and Zana Bozinovska for their help during my fieldwork trips. I must also express my appreciation to the numerous people who shared their expertise and support during the field-research activities and to those who took part in the interview sessions. This book would not have been possible without their precious contribution. I am deeply thankful to Christine Huber, Ioannis Janakos, Yolanta Kogianni, Evangelos Aspiotis, Alexis Makridis and Giorgos Polymeris for their meaningful companionship and support. I would also like to express my gratitude to my parents Ioannis and Eleni for their solid support throughout this venture. Finally, I wish to thank Christabel Scaife and Peter Lang publishers, as well as the book series editors Tomasz Kamusella and Krzysztof Jaskulowski, for giving me the opportunity to have this work published.

Abbreviations and Acronyms

AKSH / ANA	*Armata Kombëtare Shqiptare* / Albanian National Army Armata
ARM	*Armija na Republika Makedonija* / Army of the Republic of Macedonia
ASNOM / ASNOY	*Antifašističko Sobranie na Narodnoto Osloboduvanje na Makedonija* / Antifascist Socialist National Organization of Yugoslavia
CYP	Communist Yugoslav Party / *Komunistička Partija Jugoslavije*
DPA / PDSh	Democratic Party of Albanians / *Partia Demokratike Shqiptare*
DUI	Democratic Union for Integration / *Bashkimi Demokratik për Integrim*
EU	European Union
EUPOL PROXIMA	European Union Police Mission in FYR Macedonia
EWR	Early Warning Reports
FBiH	Federation of Bosnia and Herzegovina
FYR	Former Yugoslav Republic
FYROM	Former Yugoslav Republic of Macedonia
IMF	International Monetary Fund
JNA	*Jugoslovenska Narodna Armija* / Yugoslav National Army
KFOR	Kosovo Force (NATO)

KLA / UÇK	Kosovo Liberation Army / Ushtria Çlirimtare e Kosovës
KPC	Kosovo Protection Forces / *Trupat e Mbrojtjes së Kosovës*
LCM	League of Communists of Macedonia / *Sojuz na Komunistite na Makedonija*
LCY	League of Communists of Yugoslavia / *Savez Komunista Jugoslavije*
LDK	*Lidhja Demokratike e Kosovës* / Democratic League of Kosovo
LDP	*Liberalno-Demokratska Partija* / Liberal Democratic Party
LKCK	*Lëvizja Kombëtare për Çlirimin e Kosovës* / National Movement for the Liberation of Kosovo
LPK	*Lëvizja Popullore e Kosovës* / People's Movement of Kosovo
NATO	North Atlantic Treaty Organization
NDP	National Democratic Party / *Partia Demokratike Kombëtare*
NLA / UÇK	National Liberation Army / *Ushtria Çlirimtare Kombëtare*
OFA	Ohrid Framework Agreement
OSCE	Organization for Security and Cooperation in Europe
PDK	*Partia Demokratike e Kosovës* / Democratic Party of Kosovo
PDP	Party for Democratic Prosperity / *Partia për Prosperitet Demokratik*

SAP	Socialist Autonomous Province / *Socijalistička Autonomna Pokrajina*
SDSM	*Socijal-Demokratski Sojuz na Makedonija* / Social Democratic Union of Macedonia
SYR	Socialist Yugoslav Republic / *Socijalistička Republika Jugoslavija*
UCPMB / LAPMB	*Ushtria Çlirimtare e Preshevës, Medvegjës dhe Bujanocit* / Liberation Army of Presevo, Medvedja and Bujanovac
UDB / SSA	*Uprava Državne Bezbednosti* / State Security Administration
UNDP	United Nations Development Programme
UNMIK	United Nations Interim Administration Mission in Kosovo
UN – OHR	United Nations Office of the Higher Representative in Bosnia-Herzogovina
UNPREDEP	United Nations Preventive Deployment
UNPROFOR	United Nations Protection Force
USA (US)	United States of America
USSR	Union of Soviet Socialist Republics
VMRO – DPMNE / IMRO – DPMNU	*Vnatrešna Makedonska Revolucionerna Organizacija – Demokratska Partija za Makedonsko Nacionalno Edinstvo* / Internal Macedonian Revolutionary Organization – Democratic Party for Macedonian National Unity
VMRO – NP / IMRO – PP	*Vnatrešna Makedonska Revolucionerna Organizacija – Narodna Partija* / Internal Macedonian Revolutionary Organization – People's Party

Glossary of Ethnic Terms

Albanians	All people of Albanian origin/ethnicity/consciousness.
Albanians in FYR Macedonia	Albanians in the Former Yugoslav Republic of Macedonia.
BiH	Bosnia-Herzegovina.
Bulgarian-Macedonians	Bulgarians from the region of Macedonia.
Greek Macedonia	Part of the geographic region of Macedonia in Greece.
Greek-Macedonians	Greeks from the region of Macedonia.
Macedonia	The geographical area incorporating today's Former Yugoslav Republic of Macedonia, the Greek northern province of Macedonia and the Pirin region in Bulgaria.
Macedonians (Ancient)	An ancient branch of the Hellenic people whose civilization developed mostly within the existing borders of Greek Macedonia/Northern Greece.
Macedonians	The native inhabitants of the geographical area of Macedonia, of all ethnic/national affiliations and origins: Greeks, Bulgarians, Serbs, Turks, Albanians, Jews etc.
Macedonian-Albanians	Albanians in the region of Macedonia. (The term denotes mainly those Albanians who reside within FYR Macedonia.)
"Macedonism"	The doctrine that a separate Macedonian nationality exists independent of ethnic affiliation.

Serbs	All people of Serb origin/ethnicity.
Serbians	Serbs and the Serb authorities of the Republic of Serbia.
Slav Macedonians	The native Slavic Macedonian population of the Former Yugoslav Republic of Macedonia.
Yugoslav	Citizen of Yugoslavia.
Yugoslav Macedonia	The geographical area of Macedonia under Yugoslav rule.

List of Tables

Introduction

Ethnic conflict and associated political violence is one of the contemporary world's most significant, and often seemingly persistent, political problems. Contemporary security analysts have counted numerous states directly affected by armed conflicts, while many other regions continue to suffer from conflicts that remain in a state of limbo. Today, the vast majority of societal conflicts contain a strong ethnic dimension and contemporary wars are mainly fought between ethnic or religious factions within the boundaries of a state. A major outburst of such identity-based societal conflicts coincided with the end of the Cold War. Although the frequency of ethnic conflict during the 1980s and 1990s has increased at only about one-third of the level of increase that characterized the 1950s and 1970s, ethnic wars continued to multiply as separatist movements attempted to take advantage of the vast changes in political arrangements that accompanied the transformation of the post-Cold War world system. Ethnic conflicts tend to persist even though the general frequency of violent conflict onsets in the global system continues to diminish in total magnitude. This is largely because societal conflicts are suffused with non-negotiable identity and sovereignty issues, which make these conflicts less susceptible to settlement and more prone to violence (Monty and Benjamin, 2009). Hence, ethnic conflicts tend to continue despite the apparent decline in the frequency of newly erupted conflicts since 1996.

Yet most of these conflicts are neither new nor purely ethnic. Nearly all of the armed conflicts that crossed the threshold to serious warfare in the late 1990s involved an escalation of a long-standing dispute. The recurrence of serious warfare in the late 1990s appeared mainly to happen in areas known for their ethnic complexity and political instability such as the Balkans, Africa and the Caucasus. The ferocity of these ethnic disputes prompted analysts to study the sources and parameters of violent ethnic conflict more carefully. As a result, the study of ethnic warfare became a hot topic during the early 1990s, as a virtual cornucopia of these seemingly intractable societal conflicts exploded onto the world scene, capturing the public eye.

The continual resurfacing of ethnic conflicts throughout the 1990s provided scholars with an additional incentive to inquire further into the causation and wider implications of ethnic warfare. On the one hand, the dramatic collapse of numerous autocratic regimes across Europe and Eurasia revealed a range of deep socio-economic inequalities among different and often rival ethnic groups. The long-standing grievances held by many ethnic groups were finally exposed, while deprivation intensified and expectations increased. There is little doubt that the oppression and social discrimination endured by subordinate ethnic groups created a sense of deprivation, which in turn strengthened in-group identification and provided a basis for political mobilization along ethnic lines. On the other hand, the removal of previous restrictions set by the collapsing socialist regimes coincided with fresh opportunities in the new strategic environment. Numerous disenchanted ethnic groups, influenced by the changing geo-strategic environment and the economic opportunities this new environment created, intensified their attempts to pursue their separate destinies in a world of elusive prosperity. Indeed, the existence of comparative disadvantages among different groups created new opportunities for power-seeking ethnic entrepreneurs to mobilize the aggrieved masses against rival groups. The occurrence, continuation and complexity of many conflicts well into the new century have blurred distinctions between frustration leading to violence and strategic opportunism as motivations of violent conflict. To this day, analysts have reached no clear consensus on whether ethnic groups are motivated by genuine grievance or pure greed.

In the post-9/11 era, the advent of the "war against terror" gave a fresh impetus to the study of ethnic conflict. The subsequent military interventions in Afghanistan and Iraq unleashed a new wave of old-age rivalries, which had been laying dormant for decades, while a series of tribal and religious conflicts in Africa (Sudan, Somalia, Nigeria) attracted international attention. The resurfacing of intrastate conflicts in Iraq and Afghanistan inaugurated a more complex chapter in the study of ethnic conflict, one in which ethnicity intertwines more closely with religious and tribal fractionalization. At the same time, the revival of conflict-related atrocities in Chechnya, Ingushetia and the Middle East (Lebanon, Israel-Palestine) demonstrated the ongoing dangers to global and regional stability posed by the persistence of ethnic conflict. There is no doubt that the great majority of conflicts around the globe today involve some degree of organized violence in the form of terrorism or guerrilla warfare, and often contain degenerate characteristics that many regard as criminal. Analysts and policymakers are continually challenged by the new methodologies employed by groups participating in ethnic warfare and they are prompted to survey more carefully the linkage between ethno-nationalism, religion and insurgent violence. International policymakers are equally burdened with the task of devising appropriate and suitable concepts and policies for responding to the phenomena of ethnic warfare. Policymakers have only recently realized that military coercion by governments and international organizations has been costly and inefficient. The cases of Iraq and Afghanistan, as well as the earlier cases of Bosnia and Kosovo, clearly suggest that military coercion and forceful diplomacy can generate more problems than solutions. Thus, increased efforts towards the effective containment of ethnic conflicts, using the emerging doctrine of non-military strategic coercion, became part of a global agenda in reducing forms of violent conflict.

The present book takes into consideration these major concerns in the study of conflict and challenges dominant explanations regarding the emergence, violent transformation and perpetuation of ethnic conflict. Two major accounts seem to have dominated explanations on the emergence of conflict: these are the theories of grievance and greed (Gurr, 1970, 1995; Gurr and Moore, 1997; Collier, 1995, 1999, 2004, 2006; Fearon and Laitin, 2003). These two major accounts have sparked serious debates between analysts on the motivation and sources of conflict, and until recently many analysts were keen to adopt one exclusively and reject the other. However, new theoretical insights have steadily refined and gone beyond these classical distinctions between greed and grievance (Horowitz, 2001; Kaufman, 2001; Sambanis, 2002; Fearon and Laitin, 2003; Paquette, 2002). The systematic study of identity, strategic mobilization, power-politics, group entitlement, political manipulation and criminalization has certainly stimulated the rethinking of formerly irreconcilable viewpoints regarding the emergence of conflict. However, these studies have still not been able to fully supplement the dominant theories with an adequate alternative account that fully explains the roots of conflict. As a result, classical views of greed versus grievance still predominate, while analysts carry on researching what lies beyond these two competing explanations of conflict.

This book challenges such incompatible interpretations of conflict and argues for a synthetic approach, one that combines the essential theory of relative deprivation (Davis, 1999; Gurr, 1970, 1993) with the realist contours of strategic thought (Ballentine and Nitzshke, 2003; Paquette, 2002; Vasquez, 2000; Horowitz, 2001). The book provides a critique of the greed vs. grievance debate and examines the adequacy of alternative accounts. The analysis also links the basic tenets of the relative deprivation theory with strategic analysis, using fresh empirical data to produce cohesive policy suggestions on ethnic politics and ethnic warfare. This study is intended as an innovative contribution to a field characterized by generic debates between advocates of equally rigid explanations of ethnic conflict.

More analytically, the competing arguments suggest that one cannot fully understand the factors affecting the violent transformation of ethnic conflict without adopting a comprehensive approach. This book presents a selected number of conflict-generating factors and explains how these factors interact with the strategic parameters shaping the decision of ethnic groups to use violence. The major question is whether relative deprivation can sufficiently explain the decision to engage in violence. The book explains that although conflict may be the result of targeted socio-economic and political deprivations, violence may erupt only when strategic opportunities supplement existing deprivations. Hence, the decision to use violence depends not so much on the levels of deprivation as on strategic conditions such as available resources, political organization, and regional constrains and incentives. Therefore, strategic conditions determine the violent transformation of conflict i.e. the decision to move from non-violence to violence.

We therefore present a new theoretical approach that helps to clarify the phases (emergence-escalation-settlement) and parameters of ethnic conflict. The fusion of relative deprivation with strategic considerations brings into play the notion of "strategic rebellion". This emerging concept explores the development of an insurgency by underprivileged members of ethnic groups acting under auspicious conditions. Strategic rebellion is a composite term used to describe a calculated violent reaction against a status of long-standing disaffection by a group of people. "Rebellion" suggests an act of disobedience stemming from resentment towards authority, while the term "strategic" points to the calculated or rationalist rather than impulsive or instinctual nature of such an act. In past years, rebellions or revolts were most often associated with unsuccessful attempts to overthrow a regime. Instead, the term revolution refers to the conduct of a usually successful popular uprising, resulting in a major radical change such as the overthrow or renunciation of one government or ruler and the substitution of another by the governed. Yet the far-reaching and often devastating consequences of a revolution make the term unsuitable for describing revolts or tactical uprisings that usually bring about changes of a more limited scope. The term rebellion or insurgency is more appropriate for describing the occurrence of violent group responses to a perceived lack of status, without at the same time suggesting any of the ethical premises and normative connotations of a revolution. Nevertheless, this study highlights the idea that rebellions of any scale and type are typically rooted in long-standing grievances regarding a perceived or real deprivation. Parallel to this, the notion of strategic rebellion emphasizes the importance of reason over emotion to indicate the deliberate and calculated character of modern-day insurgencies.

The book also goes beyond the reasons that explain the outbreak of violent conflict and calls into question the expediency of coercion, offering thus an assessment of the parameters shaping the termination of conflict. It suggests that international actors and governments favour the employment of multiple coercive methods in the regulation of violent conflict. Starting with the distinction between military and non-military coercion, the analysis highlights the major turn from the former to the latter and puts forward evidence suggesting that coercion is effective only for the short-term management of violent conflict. The book argues that strategic coercion is a risky and unstable method to settle complex ethno-political conflicts that have turned violent, and points to the idea that coercive settlements can generate long-term resentments and backlash effects. Consequently, the entire argument leads to the general conclusion that the conflict-generating potential of relative deprivation is conditional on the influence of strategic conditions, and the perpetuation of conflict is largely contingent on the degree and type of coercion used in the regulation of conflict.

In order to develop a consistent research analysis, the book provides empirical data on the conflicts of South-Eastern Europe, placing particular emphasis on the conflict in the Former Yugoslav Republic of Macedonia (FYROM). The deadly conflicts of Yugoslavia were characterized by ethno-political antagonism, political entrepreneurship and aggressive chauvinism, taking advantage of long-standing patterns of inter-ethnic inequality. Observers were stunned by the atrocities perpetrated among former partners, neighbours and relatives, and strenuously sought for an answer that could explain the forces driving these ferocious confrontations.

The eruption of violent conflict in the former Yugoslavia was not just the result of centuries-old feuds coming to the surface. The surge in ethnic tension and unrest came alongside the gradual though clumsy liberalizations of the fading Socialist regime. Major political and economic changes brought an unprecedented sense of insecurity, which in turn played a crucial part in determining the ways in which ethnic groups acted. On the one hand, the ultimate collapse of Socialism in the Balkans created opportunities for individuals and ethnic groups, but on the other hand, this development signalled the emergence of new threats stemming from the new global patterns and local alliances that were created in a rapidly evolving strategic environment.

The asymmetric developments in the Socialist Yugoslav economy exposed the wide gap between the privileged and the poor, and the unequal socio-economic resources of different regions within a single state. The global retreat of Socialism intensified disillusionment with the ineffective political system, and provided groups and their leaderships with an additional incentive to rally around alternative political (i.e. separatist) aspirations and projects. As a result, ethnic nationalism came to replace Federalist Socialism and provided people with the opportunity to share their anxieties and seek protection.

At the same time, the complex allocation of ethnic groups across the entire region posed a major difficulty in the fulfilment of aggressive nationalist projects. In fact, Steven Sowards has accurately explained that one cannot understand the Balkans without understanding its ethnic groups, and one cannot understand the ethnic groups and their history without knowing the influence of the region's geography. The Balkans, or what many analysts prefer to call South-Eastern Europe, is a mosaic of cultures, languages, religions, traditions, alliances and values. More importantly, South-Eastern Europe is home to several dozen ethnic groups, which are often concentrated in small enclaves, or live as neighbours next to each other in territories without clear majorities. These dispersed ethnic minorities provided the spark, and the alibi, for igniting a chain of deadly wars in the 1990s.

Analysts have only recently realized that the conflict in FYR Macedonia is an exemplary paradigm of such an ethnic conflict, including the role of relative deprivation, the influence of strategic conditions, and the effectiveness of diplomatic, military and strategic coercion. FYR Macedonia is a multi-ethnic state that is segregated along ethno-political lines. The two major ethnic groups in the country are the majority of Slav Macedonians and the large minority of Albanians. Its ethnic groups are distributed across overlapping ethno-territorial domains, in which Albanians and Slav Macedonians maintain different cultural, social and political spheres. The role of territory and ethnography – and the determining role of history and culture – obviously shape inter-ethnic perceptions, and influence the policies and reactions of the two groups towards each other.

In 2001, an explosive mixture of accumulated grievances, growing repression and mutual suspicion instigated a round of hostilities between the Slavic Macedonian government forces and Albanian rebels. This turn of events attracted an armada of international mediators who rushed in to prevent a conflict that would plunge the entire region into chaos and violence. International policymakers attributed the conflict to the state's discriminatory policies against the Albanian minority, and hastily projected the mediatory role of the international community as a paradigm of timely conflict prevention. However, the questionable effectiveness of the internationally sponsored peace process that led to the so-called Ohrid

Accord raised major concerns about the precise sources of conflict, and exposed the inadequacies of outside coercive interventions in the management and resolution of conflicts. The Albanians complained about ongoing social deprivation, while the Slavic Macedonians accused them of greed and ultra-nationalism. The international community considered that the conflict was the result of state-sponsored discrimination and oppression against the Albanians, and promoted institutional remedies for integrating the Albanians into the political and social structures. The Western policymakers largely interpreted the Albanian uprising as a outcry against oppression and deprivation. Furthermore, they saw coercive crisis management as necessary and appropriate to discourage the government from responding violently, and compelled politicians to make undesirable political concessions. However, the minority demands continued and intensified well after the Ohrid peace accord, which in turn radicalized many of the majority Slavs. This development exposed the questionable effectiveness of the peace treaty (and the coercive conflict management that led to it), raising major concerns in relation to the sources of conflict.

The book is divided into six chapters. The first chapter explores the theory of ethnic conflict, with particular emphasis on the influence of relative deprivation. The theory of relative deprivation is presented, analysed and evaluated against other theories in an attempt to explain the origin and emergence of violent conflict. In the same chapter, we present and discuss the theory of strategic coercion or coercive diplomacy as a means of containing violent conflicts. The second chapter analyses, from a relative deprivation perspective, the socio-economic and political factors that led to the disintegration of Socialist Yugoslavia in the early 1990s and the consequent oppression suffered by the Albanian community in the Socialist Republic of Macedonia, and describes how this helped to radicalize many Albanians. The third chapter analyses and measures the continuing levels of perceived and real deprivation among the Albanians in the Former Yugoslav Republic of Macedonia throughout the 1990s. This chapter emphasizes the accumulating sources of discontent up to the moment of crisis in 2001. The fourth chapter looks into the emerging strategic opportunities and conditions produced by the collapse of Yugoslavia – for separatist leaders and opportunists among the Albanians, particularly those in FYR Macedonia.

The fifth chapter addresses the major phases relevant to the emergence, escalation and settlement of armed conflict, and accounts for the coercive methods with which governments and international organizations responded to the violent crisis in FYR Macedonia. This part of the book reveals the interaction between militants and external actors and provides a number of lessons for the containment and resolution of armed insurgencies. Finally, the last chapter recapitulates the implications of coercive settlements for stability and peace.

CHAPTER 1

Ethnic Conflict from a Strategic Perspective

Ethnic conflict is a particular kind of dispute about political, economic, social, cultural and territorial issues (or a combination of all these) between two or more ethnic groups characterized by distinct strengths and weaknesses in a constant struggle for survival and strategic advancement. Amongst a multiplicity of theories attempting to explain the emergence and violent transformation of ethnic conflict, we distinguish the predominant theory of relative deprivation due to its interpretive depth and empirical rigour, as well as for the constant and intense criticism this theory has attracted.

The theory of relative deprivation brings in an enduring account of what many people, – regardless of ethnic, racial, or social background, – may feel, or think of their personal lives and fortunes. In many instances, people's feelings and reactions are based on perceptions that the circumstances of their lives are not providing benefits to which they feel entitled. Such perceptions may equally apply to relatively privileged individuals or members of groups who may believe that they deserve a better treatment or future. Today most analysts are convinced that these perceptions of discontent, no matter if accurate or flawed, are typically created and measured in comparative perspectives and determined by subjective expectations and capabilities. In fact, the depth of deprivation and the intensity of frustration it creates are often determined by comparing one's own position to another's (Runciman, 1966:15). Basically, the theory presumes that the more individuals or groups compare themselves to others, the more likely are to create new grievances or reinforce existing ones.

Essentially, relative deprivation constitutes the negative discrepancy between value expectations and present actualities. More analytically, the theory signifies the perceived gap between what people think they ought or deserve to get and what they actually get (Gurr, 1970:24). As a result, people develop and sustain grievances in relation to their subjective needs and unfulfilled wants and grievances often create an intense feeling of frustration. This frustration generated by the inability to gratify these subjective expectations may eventually cause aggression and stimulate collective violence (Gurr, 1970:36–37). The possible failure to fulfil expectations may very well lead to the development of psychological frustration, anxiety and aggressive behaviour. This study of ethnic conflict illustrates the psychological transformation of frustration to aggression and looks into the expected utility calculation by an ethnic group seeking to improve its comparative political and economic standing in relation to the available opportunities and conditions. In contrast to other theoretical accounts of conflict, the theory of relative deprivation links socio-economic principles and psychological perspectives into a coherent framework that explains the aetiology and development of conflict. This theory provides a satisfactory basis for explaining the emergence of conflict, but the theory still requires further elaboration when it comes to explaining the transformation of non-violent conflict into violent aggression. The theory of relative deprivation represents a typical grievance-based account of conflict. For this reason, it continues to attract criticisms by those who regard conflict to be the outcome of predatory or criminal dispositions, resource capacity, identity-manipulation or mere economic (wealth-maximizing) motivation i.e. greed (Collier, 1997; Kaldor, 1999). Yet the theory of relative deprivation provides an enduring conceptual understanding of the reasoning behind the activation and perpetuation of aggressive responses in ethnic conflicts.

Aggression and Relative Deprivation

It is crucial to start with an analysis of aggression and clarify its vital role in collective human behaviour. Three distinct explanations exist on the primary sources of human aggression: instinct, learning and frustration. Thomas Hobbes was among the first social contract theorists to suggest that humans are inherently destructive, selfish, competitive and aggressive ("state of nature"). According to Hobbes, humans are egoistic and conflict-prone creatures, and conflict is a natural human (instinctual) activity driven by the competitive human impulse of self-preservation (Rosen and Wolff, 1999:10–14). The impulse of aggression is for Hobbes as natural as any other human trait. Based on this atavistic interpretation of human nature, Hobbes thinks it absolutely necessary for society to have an overarching, repressive, absolute authority (*Leviathan*) with the agreed right to maintain the exclusive control over the use of violence in order to regulate or punish acts stemming from innate human aggression. His pessimist idea about human nature coincided with Machiavelli's unembellished political account of governance in a complicated world of utter deceit and self-interest. Niccolò Machiavelli (1469–1527) views aggression as a natural result of human greed; he has based his entire political analysis on the presupposition that "all men are evil, fickle, hypocritical, and greedy of gain, as they are always going to act according to the wickedness of their spirits whenever they have free scope ..."(Machiavelli, "The Prince", 1515). Just like Hobbes, Machiavelli appreciates the necessity of promoting a fear-inspiring sovereign body, the Prince, ruling over an unreliable mass of citizens characterized by conflicting interests.

Instinctual accounts on the roots of aggression can be also traced in classical Freudian psychoanalysis. Freud explains that the externally destructive tendencies of humans reflect instinctive aggression as an innate force of human nature (*Thanatos*). Freud locates the activation of that instinct in an inherently human desire for destruction, which is most usually constrained by *Eros*, the desire, or love of life. Freud thus views conflict as the result of an instinctual rather than learned reaction, based on the aggressive instinct for survival. He emphasizes the selfish nature of humans and highlights the *instinctive* rather than calculated reaction to external stimuli (Einstein and Freud, 1939). In principle, Freud understood human conflicts of interest to be resolved by the recourse to violence, and saw parallels of this process in the animal kingdom (ibid.). For Freud and his successors, the use of violence is a mere expression of conflict, which in human societies is restrained or repulsed by the superego i.e. the fear of punishment and the rule of law.

In later years, socio-biologists elaborated on the internal-stimuli of the aggression instinct, and related aggression to human survival. In his 1966 book *On Aggression*, Konrad Lorenz related aggression to Darwin's notion of the struggle for survival. Lorenz observed that animals would become aggressive when defending their territory, when protecting the young and defenceless, and in search of a female. Respectively, Lorenz regarded human aggression as a means of clarifying social order, and as a way of protecting the advanced social life of one group. Modern socio-biological research has concentrated on the evolutionary perspective of aggression. According to such accounts, group aggression and violent impulses rely upon egoist cooperation through altruist behaviour. Contrary to Freudian accounts, social biologists emphasize the human need of survival, which often makes human communities confront one another in order to maximize their chances of well-being. Hence, aggression manifests survivalist human behaviour (*inclusive fitness*).

Another group of social psychologists has challenged the instinctual accounts of aggression, arguing that aggression and violent behaviour are learned rather than natural responses. These scientists claim that violent behaviour is purposive and rational, geared towards the achievement of certain aims (Bandura and Walters, 1963). In fact, eminent political theorists of the Enlightenment already articulated the learned response-argument prior to the emergence of modern social psychology. Thus, the French political philosopher Jean-Jacques Rousseau (1712–1778) regards humans living in a state of nature as equals to animals, their acts being neither good nor bad. However, he warns that society transformed *amour de soi*, the instinctive human desire for self-preservation, into *amour-propre* or pride. For Rousseau, this passage from "nature" into "society" transforms human aggression, since humans are no longer acting for self-sufficiency. Society corrupts human aggression into a pride-seeking response, encompassing elements of vanity, idleness, wickedness, jealousy and luxury. Nevertheless, he never ceased to believe in human reason, advocating the construction of a civic society whereby moral judgements replace human instincts through learning and education.

In a similar fashion, the English political philosopher John Locke (1632–1704) believes that human beings in the state of nature have freedom to act selfishly according to the laws of nature (*survival of the fittest*). However, Locke condemns any aggressive action that went beyond the limits of righteous conquest. Aggression violates civil rights, unless one is first victimized or attacked, especially when the acquisition of legitimate property is at stake. Yet Locke believes that human nature, although innately selfish, is nevertheless characterized by tolerance and the capability to think rationally, and believed that a social contract would create stable societies by regulating human relations and thus constraining tendencies towards violence.

The Learned Response theory is in line with modern behavioural accounts in psychology. Behaviouralists argue that aggressive responses are part of a learning process, and determine the socialization of individuals. They contend that aggression is a calculated, imitative and instrumental response by individuals or groups for the accomplishment of self-serving goals. Collective aggression represents a rational or rationalized response by largely dispassionate actors who expect to gain through violence. This mechanical interpretation of collective aggression fails to appreciate the intensity of psycho-emotive reactions such as anger, hatred, rage, anxiety and discontent, responding to defined stimuli.

As Galtung suggested, external conditions leading to aggression probably have to pass through the minds of individuals and form into perceptions with a high emotive content before they are acted out as aggression (Galtung, 1964:95). In many occasions, individuals and groups seem to resort to violence against all odds i.e. with little chance of success. Protest rallies, national resistance movements, revolutionary organizations, small-scale rebellions, or even wanton forms of hooliganism are often driven by emotions that seem illogical or pay little heed to rational cost-benefit and risk calculations.

Deprivation theorists proposition that aggression is a predictable reaction to defined stimuli. Some of them believe there is innate aggression, whereas others regard external conditions as stimuli and regulators of aggression. In a classic treatise on the subject, Dollard et al pinpointed that the occurrence of aggressive behaviour always presupposes the existence of frustration and that the existence of frustration always leads to some form of aggression (Dollard et al., 1939). He defined frustration as "an interference with the occurrence of an instigated goal-response at its proper time in the behavioural sequence" (ibid.:7). For example, the husband that comes home from work to find dinner not awaiting him, the employee who does not get a promotion she feels she deserves, the child who is excluded from a game on the school playground.

Despite the existence of numerous exceptional cases, most analysts and authorities today regard aggression as a response that ultimately originates/arises from some form of frustration (Berkowitz, 1980). Yet early critiques insisted that not all forms of frustration lead to aggressive responses. Berkowitz, for example, asked whether every frustration leads to some form of aggression (ibid.:126). In order to shed some light on the possible modifications of frustration-aggression, Berkowitz utilized two intervening variables: anger and interpretation. Although he agreed in principle with Dollard et al., he viewed the functioning of anger and interpretation as a regulatory mechanism of aggression. This finding suggests that angry responses can be tamed and repressed, depending on the interpretation individuals give to certain frustration-generating events (ibid., 1980).

Ted Robert Gurr explained and defended the mechanism of frustration-aggression in his seminal work *Why Men Rebel* (Gurr, 1970). Gurr applied the psychological formulation of frustration-aggression to explain aggression and violence on a group and societal level. He regarded the frustration-aggression mechanism as the primary source of the human capacity for violence. Although frustration does not necessarily lead to violence, the anger induced by frustration disposes men to aggression irrespective of its instrumentalities: "men who are frustrated have an innate disposition to do violence to its source in proportion to the intensity of their frustration" (ibid., 1970:37).

While Berkowitz claimed that interpretations regulate the degree of frustration, and determine the level of aggression, Gurr spotted the source of frustration in the "actor's perception of discrepancy between their value expectations and their value capacities … conditions of life to which people believe they are rightfully entitled" (ibid., 1970:24). During the Cold War, most security analysts followed the premise that *deprivation*, the lack of needs ranging from food and water to political and socio-economic rights, drive people to rebel against the state. As a result, many rushed to embrace

Ted Robert Gurr's concept of relative deprivation (RD). In simple terms, so-called "deprivationists" believe that groups of people who think they can do or deserve to do better produce violent conflict.[1]

Central to the theory of relative deprivation is the nexus of frustration-aggression, which is thought to affect the emergence of conflict. The theory's essence is located in the gap between people's perceptions of what they are rightfully entitled to obtain, and what they think they are capable of getting, or what a group feels it should be able to achieve. Those who are conscious of their comparative disadvantages (real or perceived) can feel deprived. The theory is in stark contrast to generalized accounts of absolute deprivation where relative levels of wealth and social status are compared based on objective differences rather than subjective self-assessments (Fisher, 2008; Duclos and Philippe, 2002). In the simplest view, relative deprivation reflects the gap between what a groups wants, what it gets and what is capable of getting (Rummel, 1977). Very often, current conditions, usually determined by third parties, fail to meet expectations, while groups think they are capable of obtaining a better social positioning. As a result, the inability to gratify perceived interests in accordance to perceived qualifications creates a sense of frustration. This frustration creates the potential for collective aggression and for the violent rectification of injustice. To some extent, groups weight their rights and privileges against their given qualifications. For example, theorists have empirically found that when a population that is relatively rich or well educated is confronted with a repressive and autocratic regime it is likely to act aggressively or turn violent.

1 Caspar ten Dam has been one of the first to explicitly use the terms "deprivationism", "depredation" and "depredationism" in the greed vs. grievance context. See his "How to Feud and Rebel: 2. Histories, Cultures and Grievances of the Chechens and Albanians", *Iran and the Caucasus*, Vol. 15, No. 1–2, June 2011, esp. pp. 237–241. Also see Paul Collier and Anke Hoeffler, *Greed and Grievance in Civil War*, World Bank Policy Research Paper 2355, 4 January 2001 (Washington D.C.: World Bank, 2000; archive <http://www.worldbank/org/research/conflict>); Paul Collier and Nicholas Sambalis, "Understanding Civil War: A New Agenda", *Journal of Conflict Resolution*, Vol. 46, No. 1, February 2002, pp. 3–12; James D. Fearon and David D. Laitin, "Ethnicity, insurgency, and civil war", *American Political Science Review*, Vol. 97, No. 1, 2003, pp. 75–90.

This has been encountered in differing forms and severity in for instance Croatia, the Basque Country, Catalonia, Flanders and Quebec.

One of the most common deprivationist claims is the observation that violence is related to the GDP per capita (Davis, 1999). At very low levels of income, groups and individuals, although poor, are not conscious of deprivation. However, at middling levels of income, they become aware of the potentialities created by greater levels of income and so become discontented (ibid.:12) Hence, political violence may increase when people become relatively well educated, but fail to receive a commensurate level of income. Thus, relative deprivation predicts high levels of political violence in societies where the population has low-income levels relative to their level of education. Violence is also likely when any kind of basic need, which has come to be routinely gratified, is suddenly removed (ibid.:247).

In this way, Gurr substituted interpretative accounts of frustration with a capability to assess expectations and conditions. The vitality of self-interest and profit-maximization is an essential part of the frustration-aggression nexus, one that overcomes any relativity in interpretation. According to Gurr, interpretations of discontent cannot constitute fixed mechanisms of anger-management (Gurr, 1970). For Gurr, when collective groups feel that their rights are explicitly denied, then aggression becomes a natural reaction in protection of given interests. Relative deprivation attributes the emergence of conflict to unfulfilled expectations held by groups, but, crucially, it also explains the emergence of collective violence by the reaction of groups determined to obtain, protect or further their perceived interests. The higher the intensity and scope of perceived unfavourable conditions, the higher the frustration, and consequent propensity to violence (ibid., 1968:255). Perceived deprivation is not only a trigger of frustration, but also the primary source of the human capacity for violence (ibid., 1970:36). Gurr thus regards deprivation – a feeling of injustice – as a much stronger motivating force than economic greed.

Based on this account, Gurr developed a framework defining a set of operative variables that hypothetically generate and structure violent political unrest. These variables hypothetically determine the degree and severity of aggression, and relate them to the feasibility and significance of the objective sought. Firstly, civil violence presupposes that at least some segments of a group feel relative deprivation. Secondly, the degree of aggression and the severity of violence are varyingly relevant to the intensity of commitment to a certain goal, and to intensity of the effort invested to the achievement of this goal, and to the feasibility of the goal or condition sought. Thirdly, the strength of aggression is directly related to the perceived legitimacy of the goal, the environmental opportunities, the magnitude of retribution for participating in violent acts, and the availability of institutions for nonviolent responses (ibid., 1968:245–278). However, Gurr does not look at certain indicators of deprivation, and does not define the severity or level of relative deprivation required to generate violence. Though the extent of deprivation may be subjective, some internal norms, standards, or benchmarks against which to assess deprivation are still required (Rummel, 1977). Hence, in our analysis of the deprivation-frustration-aggression nexus we utilize the flexibility of Gurr's theory by setting a number of social economic, political and institutional indicators in order to carry out a case study measurement of indicators that are appear to have provoked violent conflict.

Donald Horowitz's group entitlement theory refines the basic tenets of the relative deprivation theory (Horowitz, 2000). Horowitz suggests a synthesis of elements from competing theories on the origins of ethnicity and conflict. In addition, he exposes the multidimensionality of ethnicity, and the failure of these theories to differentiate between rationality and passion (ibid., 1998). Horowitz argues that conflict is the outcome of some kind of deprivation and relates grievances to inter-ethnic or horizontal inequality. He authored a detailed empirical study showing that mistrust encourages oppressive ethnic stratification, which in turn creates a sense of deprivation, frustration and violence. A legacy of mistrust institutionalizes inequality through oppressive patterns that subjugate the opponent group by creating a dichotomy between backward and advanced groups. This stratification provokes a violent reaction of subjugated groups against those regarded as responsible for the lack of or reduction of their rights and prosperity (ibid., 2001). This ethnic oppression or ethno-political oppression signifies repeated or periodical systemic domination, reproduced in the major economic, political and cultural institutions by one ethnic group against another. Oppression varies in intensity, ranging from tyranny to discriminatory treatment. Oppressive structures generate grievances, giving rise to feelings of deprivation (Davenport, 1996, 2004; Horowitz, 2001; Regan and Norton, 2003). Discriminatory practices, human rights violations, torture, police violations, and denial of political participation and rights are absolute deprivations that characterize political stratification and ethnic subjugation (Davenport, 2004). Interestingly, Freud was among the first few who addressed the security fears driving the ethnic stratification of society:

> the object of the conflict remained the same: one party was to be constrained, by the injury done him or impairment of his strength, to retract a claim or a refusal. This end is most effectively gained when the opponent is definitely put out of action – in other words, is killed ... another consideration may be set off against this will to kill the possibility of using an enemy for servile tasks if his spirit be broken and his life spared. Here violence finds an outlet not in slaughter but in subjugation. Hence springs the practice of giving quarter; but the victor, having from now on to reckon with the craving for revenge that rankles in his victim, forfeits to some extent his personal security. (Freud, 1932:84)

According to Horowitz's original account, the result of ethnic subjugation is relative deprivation in so far as that ethnic groups become accustomed to position themselves accordingly, and compare themselves to others in various ways, giving rise to ethnically ranked systems (ibid., 2000). While in ranked systems conflict emerges as a reaction to domination, in unranked systems, competition and group worth is projected as a means to dominate or avoid domination. In both systems, a social identity is derived from membership in groups. Members that fail to enhance their self-esteem by belonging to a group, or fear and face extinction, may choose to become aggressive against those who deprive them. Therefore, their self-esteem is raised, or their survival ensured, through the decision to opt for aggressive for self-defence. In this way, ethnic groups project their relative group worth and link it to the group rights they are entitled. Horowitz's structural grievance-based account of ethnic conflict through assertive social identity that enhances group-worth and survival enhances our understanding of the conflict generating conditions in many areas of the globe.

Similarly to Horowitz's ethnic stratification, Susan Woodward emphasizes the pre-eminence of economic inequality as a grievance generator i.e. creator of a sense of deprivation: "ethnic conflict is positively associated with domestic socio-economic inequalities" (Woodward, 2005:1). She elaborates on Horowitz's observation that some conflicts can arise from dominant groups determined to protect their privileged position by force. Indeed, inequality may just as easily provoke a revolt of the rich as a revolt of the poor (ibid.:20). In a similar fashion, Fawas Gerges argues that socio-economic and political conditions like poverty, unemployment, disenfranchisement of large segments of population and political oppression render a social environment susceptible to violent movements (Gerges, 2002).

Essentially, deprivation theorists argue that asymmetries in economic development and social welfare are strongly interrelated. Competition for scarce and inequitable socio-economic resources constitutes a potential source of violence, when viewed through the prism of expectations and capabilities. Threats to societal and physical security exacerbate when targeted socio-economic and political discrimination undermine a society's collective identity. Such selective discrimination ranges from the suppression of free expression to interference with the ability of a specific group to reproduce itself across generations, which may even amount to genocide. In sum, the theory of relative deprivation goes beyond the purely instinctual or behavioural interpretations of violence. The theory puts forward a psychological interpretation of aggression relying on responses against subjective socio-economic and political perceptions. Relative deprivation theorists accept that violence is a largely innate psychological response to real or perceived grievances, but reject the idea that aggression is an entirely learned, habitual or solely instinctual reaction. Instead, the theory proposes that violence arises from accumulated grievances based on sensible perceptions over what people expect and what people actually get in real life.

Relative Deprivation or Relative Depredation?

The theory of relative deprivation attributes the causes of ethnic conflict to a combination of grievances capable of arousing a sense of intense frustration: the more disadvantaged a minority group vis-à-vis a dominant group, the more frustration it will carry, and thus the more aggression it will direct towards the source of its frustration. Deprivation theorists believe that higher political standing and socio-economic improvement may lead to fewer feelings of exclusion. Increased political status and access to essential socio-economic resources, such as education, social security and employment, can foster nonviolent outlets for minority group demands and reduce the likelihood and intensity of ethnic violence.

Yet the causal mechanism for relative economic standing is more complicated. It is believed that higher relative economic standing leads to less discontent and resentment of the dominant ethnic group by the minority ethnic group, which leads to a lower likelihood and intensity of ethnic violence. However, higher relative economic standing may also lead to an increased capacity to resort to and sustain violence, and this might cause more intense ethnic violence. Given such violent tendencies by comparatively wealthier ethnic groups, an economically (dis)advantaged group is also expected to be politically (dis)advantaged. Therefore, relative economic disadvantage alone does not explain the emergence of violence.

After the end of the Cold War, a new depredation-cum-greed school of thought developed by Paul Collier, Anke Hoeffler, Nicholas Sambanis and others took centre stage.[2] This group of analysts argued that it is not

2 See Paul Collier, "Rebellion as a Quasi-Criminal Activity", *Journal of Conflict Resolution*, Vol. 44, No. 6, December 2000, pp. 839–853; Paul Collier, *Economic Causes of Civil Conflict and their Implications for Policy* (Washington D.C.: World Bank, 15 June 2000; archive <http://www.worldbank/org/research/conflict>); Paul Collier and Anke Hoeffler, *Greed and Grievance in Civil War*, World Bank Policy Research Paper 2355, 4 January 2001 (Washington D.C.: World Bank, 2000; <http://archive www.worldbank/org/research/conflict>); Paul Collier and Nicholas Sambalis, "Understanding Civil War: A New Agenda", *Journal of Conflict Resolution*, Vol. 46,

deprivation and grievances but depredation and greed that motivate violent conflict. Paul Collier and Anke Hoeffler were amongst the first to argue that political and social variables that are most related to grievances have little explanatory power (Collier and Hoeffler, 2004). Grievances, including political repression, exclusion and economic inequality are often misperceived, whereas opportunities for conducting viable and profit-maximizing rebellions seem to have a stronger advantage (ibid.). The existence of grievances is ubiquitous across most countries facing the risk of conflict and as a result, violence breaks out when economic opportunities open up. Greed theorists relate opportunities to the availability of financial sources, the costs of rebellion, the capacity to recruit rebels, the geographical terrain, and the relative operational advantage one group has over another. Collier and Hoeffler found that these proxies for opportunity have had a significant impact on the outbreak of violence, and their impact was much more substantial (i.e. statistically significant) than the proxies for grievances, with the exception of the existence of ethnic dominance (ibid.).

The greed thesis was further developed by James D. Fearon and David D. Laitin who analysed 127 civil wars in 161 countries between 1945 and 1999 with proxy grievance and greed variables similar to Collier and Hoeffler's, and came up with similar results (Fearon and Laitin, 2003). In particular, Collier regards opportunities as equivalent to the greed motivation, instead of seeing them as favourable circumstances allowing grievances to be violently manifested (although he admits that rebels are not criminals when grievances are sufficiently widespread to be common across societies and time). In fact, in his 1999 work *Justice-Seeking and Loot-Seeking in Civil Wars*, Collier concludes that: "the motivation for instigating a rebellion war may commonly be a blend of an altruistic desire to rectify the grievances of a group, and a selfish desire to loot the resources of others, both balanced against the costs of rebellion" (Collier, 1999a:15).

No. 1, February 2002, pp. 3–12; James D. Fearon and David D. Laitin, "Ethnicity, insurgency, and civil war", *American Political Science Review*, Vol. 97, No. 1, 2003, pp. 75–90.

Moreover, Collier seems to understand opportunities as economic agendas and benefits, without considering much the existence of opportunities stemming from strategic calculations and political developments (Collier, 1999b:1–8). Collier further insists that objective factors, which might contribute to grievance, such as income and asset inequality, ethnic and religious divisions and political repression, do not seem to increase the risks of conflict. By contrast, the combination of large exports of primary commodities, low education, a high proportion of young men and economic decline drastically increase the risks of armed conflict, and he ultimately concludes that greed seems more important than grievance (Collier, 1999b:14).

In order to elucidate what greed is and how it can be measured, Collier has created an opportunity model that includes variables, which although they seem to have little bearing on what is known as greed (i.e. wish for wealth-maximization), they at least seem to be independent of grievances. These variables included the existence of valuable primary commodities (oil, gas, wood, diamonds etc.), social fractionalization, proportion of males in the population, geographic dispersion and the role of diasporas (Collier, 2004:573). However, the same variables may equally influence the decision of aggrieved rather than greedy groups to take up arms. Therefore, the extent to which these variables can and do manifest and thereby measure greed is questionable. Hence, greed theorists prefer to speak of opportunity rather than greed in response to criticism that individual rebel motivations are hard to determine (Collier and Sambanis, 2002:4).

Collier seems to allow for grievances only to the extent that grievances are being exaggerated and manipulated in order to maximize the legitimacy and profits of militants (ibid.). Yet a more cynical faction of greed-theorists, also known as "depredationists", posit that individuals engaging in violent conflict are predators of primary commodities like diamonds, cocaine and timber, and of secondary commodities like money and food through plunder, robbery, extortion and kidnapping (Grossman, 1999; Kaldor, 2001; Fearon and Leitin, 2003). In an attempt to account for the role of grievances, depredation analysts hold that militant opportunists invent or manipulate grievances as revolt pretexts by imposing negative externalities on other groups and appropriating their resources (Hechter, 1995:61).

This rather blunt economist view of conflict outlines the crude materialistic motives evident in many rebellions and confrontations, particularly in Africa and Asia, but downplays the intense political and socio-economic nature of many other conflicts around the globe. The greed-based conceptual framework fails to explain the reasons why ethno-political dissidence and violent secessionist movements often emerge in economically better off regions, and fails to provide a differentiated explanation from that of socio-economic deprivation and need, to account for what instigates greedy behaviour. Greed theorists also have difficulty accounting for the religious drives that inspire violence, as well as for the brutal methods adopted by numerous fundamentalist and ethno-nationalist groups in ethnic conflicts. The profit-seeking viewpoint relegates behavioural rationalism and social mobilization into a quest of looting, destruction and profit making.

The greed theory, however, loops back to very basic tenets of deprivation, by assuming that the very roots of loot-seeking behaviour and profit-seeking practices by warring factions are caused by generalized levels of poverty and demographic growth (Fearon and Leitin, 2003:88). The proposition that conflict is principally instigated and sustained by opportunistic groups craving for power and riches is plausible but empirically limited, and reflects only one aspect of the emergence and development of conflicts. Greed analysts tend to downplay or overlook institutionalized socio-economic stratification and overlook the mass-hatred in armed conflict. Instead, they emphasize the role of politically isolated yet cunning, trigger-happy and greedy militants, mafia-gangs or bandits who manipulate and exaggerate popular grievances for their own ends.

The greed theory focuses on socio-economic degeneration, but fails to account for the sources of economic decline and the burgeoning social discomfort evident in many political systems. Surely, the greed theory may very well explain some of the most decadent phases of a violent conflict and account for obvious corrupted practices during those phases. It identifies some motives of peripheral interest-based disputes in war-torn areas. It regards expected aspects of collateral behaviour, encountered in most ethnic conflicts, to be the prime motives of conflict. In short, the greed theory, as developed so far, constitutes an empirically plausible but theoretical incoherent approach that captures only one facet of conflict. Hence, due to its rather narrow scope, describing only one of many types of conflict-generating motives, the theory cannot provide a firm and all-encompassing basis for explaining the emergence of conflicts.

In an attempt to update the theory of greed, Mary Kaldor articulated a variant of the greed theory known as the New Predatory War theory. Kaldor, using the war in Bosnia-Herzegovina as her model, arrived at a number of observations regarding the emergence-motivation of contemporary violent conflict, which she labelled "New War", although there is little new to it. First, Kaldor asserts that wars tend to be about identity politics rather than ideology or territory (Kaldor, 2001). Second, Kaldor points to the fact that combatants increasingly rely on guerrilla methods to move or eliminate ethnic rivals from land rather than on conventional battles to conquer territory (Kaldor, 1999, 2001).

Kaldor rightly observes that traditional politico-ideological distinctions have ceased to influence conflicts in the same ways as they did during the Cold War. Indeed, classical ideological divisions, such as Communism versus Capitalism, have ceased to determine the onset of insurgent violence. However, major environmental and security constrains continue to play a significant role in the formulation of ideological principles. The foreign policy choices and positioning of states and ethnic groups clearly reflect these principles within the global arena.

Yet the idea that territory and power are irrelevant to the development of conflict is generally flawed. In almost all ethnic conflicts, territory and the resources it contains are vital to the strategic positioning of groups. This is evident from their persistent political demands for territorial autonomy and self-rule. The acquisition and consolidation of a clearly defined territory helps to ensure the survival of an ethnic group. The possession of land gives ethnic groups a degree of political ownership and economic self-rule, provides access and control of its valuable resources, helps them to evolve culturally and grow demographically, and finally, sustains a sense of historical continuity and belonging; hence, the idea of a homeland emerges. In most ethnic conflict, ethnic rivalries tend to develop within or about a specified territory, i.e. relate to some type of territorial acquisition or autonomy. For this reason, territorial settlements (autonomy, federalism, new state formation, etc.) represent the most common routes for resolving or managing such disputes (e.g. Bosnia, Northern Ireland, Kosovo, Basque Country, Iraq, Georgia, etc.).

Be that as it may, Kaldor, stressing elements of violent conflict related to crime, greed and looting, points towards the increasing criminalization of violence (predatory war/depredation). In line with classical greed-based accounts, Kaldor argues that organized crime and paramilitary groups pursue their own selfish goals by manipulating identity grievances, rather than political and socio-economic grievances as in greed theory, and espousing exclusionist, nationalist policies. Identity is a tool to mobilize and unify groups whose interests are at stake (Kaldor, 1999). Yet some/other analysts challenge the proposition that ethnic conflict is becoming increasingly interwoven with forms of crime as being a simplistic interpretation of modern conflict. The idea that ethnic conflict may lead to criminal practices cannot function as a sincere explanation of the sources of violent ethnic conflict, unless we regard common crime to be the sole and supreme motive for violence. Yet there is nothing to suggest that criminal objectives constitute the driving force of armed conflict, and nothing indicates that present-day conflicts have become increasingly indistinguishable from organized criminal forms of violence. Naturally, criminal practices do tend to flourish in situations of war and disorder due an evident lack of the rule of law. Indeed, crime generally constitutes a bi-product rather than a major incentive of conflict. Kaldor seems to pay little attention to research on earlier wars (Kalyvas, 2001:99). Indeed, the way in which Kaldor elaborates on earlier conventional wars and compares them to contemporary paramilitary and irregular wars is evidently highly selective. Unconventional ethnic, religious and other wars have existed in abundance throughout history, and the atrocities, killings and looting committed during such wars were often equally or even more gruesome than contemporary ones.

Kaldor's theoretical design shares a lot in common with another theoretical account, which rose to challenge the pre-eminence of deprivation and contest the accuracy of greed. Analysts belonging to the theoretical school of Constructivism came to explain conflict by identity manipulation and political entrepreneurship, without attributing motives to either deprivation or greed. Just like Kaldor, constructivists believe that identity is the primary stimulator of conflict, but unlike Kaldor, who contends that greed is the major motivation, they regard both grievances and greed as having little to do with the actual objectives of conflict. Such motivating forces, constructivists argue, are insufficient for activating violent conflict without the interference of political influences. Constructivist critics argue that grievance and greed approaches emphasize the role of interests and social positioning, but neglect the prime role of cultural identity formation in the emergence of conflict (Enloe, 1980; Taras, 1998; Rousseau, 2006). Constructivists basically hold that meanings are coproduced in the human interaction process, and that experiences cannot be objectified but only subjectively constructed. Constructivists believe that if we strip ethnic groups of their hostile attitudes and actions with a socially attributed meaning, by debunking the myths and false perceptions driving them, there will be little ground for violent confrontation. The socially engineered process of conflict, indeed of any human action, and the perpetrators of violence are manipulated and misguided agents, who act through stereotypical perceptions and therefore adhere to the "truth" served to them by superior agents, i.e. their respective elites.

Stuart J. Kaufman, in his *Modern Hatreds: Symbolic Politics of Ethnic War*, explains that myths, ethnic fears and the opportunity to mobilize are the preconditions for ethnic war (Kaufman, 2001). Although he considers the potency of opportunities, he is not convinced that groups seek opportunities through internal wars in order to escape deprivation and oppression. In interstate wars, nations do not go to war simply to maintain or increase power or because they can, but because elites propagate myths and manipulate symbols so as to instigate and mobilize the masses. As an example that reflects a constructivist view, refers to the kissing by General Franjo Tudjman of the Croatian flag – symbol of the fascist anti-Serb Ustashe state in the Second World War. In his opinion, this act ignited ethnic hatred between Serbs and Croats and helped to instigate a war between the two ethnicities in Croatia.

For Kaufman, symbolic politics rather than real grievances explain the emergence of ethnic war. Constructivists like Kaufman attribute war to the practices of leaders, and their distorted images of the "other". Yet they overlook the often-observed fact that ethnic masses rally around leaders not because of their symbolic gestures but because of material grievances, unfulfilled aspirations, lack of realistic prospects and severe oppression that reduce their security and pride. Indeed, economic and social grievances, whether or not (mis)used by "political entrepreneurs", can affect ethnic identity, pride and self-perception, to the point of ethnic conflict. However, the deterioration of conflict into identity politics can mask the underlying political and socio-economic grievances for a long time without producing (political) violence.

Hence, empirical constructivism downplays a wide array of structural conditions that may lead to war. The clash of perceived interests often moves contestants to distort or demonize the opponent's image in an attempt to rationalize their hatred. The idea of treating identities as social constructions, and regard these as the actual sources of confrontation, fails to draw a coherent account on the motivations of conflict. Political convictions and socio-economic conditions can shape ethnic identity just as much as cultural, linguistic and religious attributes. Indeed, both external and internal perceptions and characterizations of any ethnic group are usually defined and articulated in terms of political, social and economic status and dominance. For this reason, ethnic groups relate to real or perceived insecurities and injustices. Hence, constructivists fall into the trap of substituting interest for cultural identity per se. Thus, they erroneously project ethnic confrontations and violence as ethnic constructions of identity and self-worth formulated or manipulated by opportunist leaders. For example, constructivists suggest that the existence of contrasting security *cultures* hamper EU efforts to design an effective security and defence policy, without referring to the contrasting security *interests* European states often have. The conceptual error lies in the failure to understand that interests can and do often shape ideological attitudes, and strategic cultures often evolve according to changes in the pursuit of interests, or even in the interests themselves.

Strategic Rebellion: A Theoretical Framework

The theory of relative deprivation offers a solid basis for investigating a sufficient number of variables relating to the emergence of conflict. However, the theory itself does not elucidate the exact conditions influencing the decision to use violence. Although we believe that the intensification of mobilization increases proportionally to the severity of deprivation, we are sceptical as to whether the existence of deprivation alone can actually produce violence. The mere existence of social and economic grievances does not presuppose a certain pattern of political reaction, let alone a violent one. Obviously, the existence of grievances is a common denominator in risk prone countries, and therefore we must assume that the largest factor preventing civil war is the constraints on the ability to mobilize. As a rule, some degree of social and economic deprivation exists among ethnically conscious and politically active groups in most cases where violent conflict erupts (Gurr and Moore, 1997). Yet deprivation alone does not necessarily trigger a violent reaction by politically active ethnic groups.

Strategies of competing ethnic groups may vary depending on the opportunities available at every stage of the conflict. Numerous regional ethnic populations have claimed to suffer under social and political oppression, and many ethnic groups have publicly manifested their demands for further autonomy as a safeguard against such oppression. However, there is a remarkable diversity of practices adopted by different ethnic groups. Some groups choose constitutional participation and political integration while others choose to resist the existing state mechanism through extra-constitutional action. These heterogeneous practices adopted by politicized ethnic groups, conscious of their deprivations, indicate that ethnic mobilization and the strategies employed depend upon other variables. Such variables determine the decision of ethnic groups to take up arms and their influence varies from one region to another. These variations and inconsistencies in the levels and types of violent and peaceful mobilization pose a significant problem for conflict analysts. We are therefore presented with a genuine puzzle about the exact influences (opportunities and constrains) that motivate or trigger violent behaviour. Hence, we shall explore the stimulants of violence, and seek to explain how grievances combine with environmental variables outside the immediate control of the group and the government. Thus, we shall assess geographical conditions (rough terrain thesis), resources and incentives relating to regional conflict spillovers that appear to influence the decision to use violence. Prior to the presentation of the theoretical model of strategic rebellion, it is essential to sum up the basic hypotheses underlying this model:

(a) The motivation for conflict relates more to the existence and improvement of socio-economic and political structures (rights and opportunities), and less to the desire for mere economic gains (Regan and Norton, 2002).
(b) Grievances stemming from deprivation (the pre-conditional factor) form the backbone of conflict, but opportunities determine the decision of rebel groups to use violence.
(c) Rebel groups seek opportunities to enable them to challenge a given social status or a perceived injustice, and bring about changes of a more general scope in government, the political system or society.
(d) Opportunities do not necessarily relate to the maximization of elite resources, although wealth-seeking practices appear throughout the course of conflict.

Starting with the assumption that deprivation creates and sustains conflict, the theoretical design goes on to suggest some significant factors (opportunities/conditions) that hypothetically determine the use of violence. The analysis acknowledges that relative deprivation is a necessary but not sufficient condition for violent conflict to erupt. We are convinced that permissive conditions facilitate the decision to use violence; remove or repress these conditions, and violent conflict may never emerge regardless of the severity of deprivations (Fearon and Laitin, 2003). As a result, we assume that the final decision of aggrieved ethnic groups to resort to violence depends on the existence of conditions conducive to the emergence of violence (i.e. opportunities) and not so much on the levels of deprivation.

For this purpose, we demonstrate that resentment and protest translate into organized armed violence through the rational calculation of opportunities available in the wider geo-strategic environment (ibid., 2003; Mahnken and Maiolo, 2007; Buhaug, 2002, 2004). We question the favourite idea that spontaneity characterizes most or even all ethnic insurgencies in the Cold War era, and instead put forward an elaborate analysis of ethno-strategic positioning. Although we emphasize the seminal role of opportunities in violent conflict, the strategic framework is different from typical greed-based assumptions. Profits, looting and natural resource rents are not deemed major motives for conflict; rather, the framework generally regards these as collateral and secondary phenomena in the evolution of armed rebellions (conflict degeneration). Instead, we prefer to treat opportunities as conditions that favour the decision to use violent means for the reversal of a disagreeable social status or threat to one's identity or survival. The analysis puts forward an interest-based formula that supersedes the assumption of greed and finds the original motivation of violent conflict in ethno-strategic advancement and the maximization of well-being.

In their work *Ethnicity, Insurgency and Civil War*, Fearon and Laitin suggest that cultural diversity and grievances fail to predict civil war onset, while measures of conditions that favour insurgency do fairly well. The two analysts admit that ethnic antagonisms, nationalist sentiments and grievances can often motivate rebels and their supporters, but such broad factors are too common to distinguish the cases where civil war breaks out (ibid., 2003:76). For this reason, Fearon and Laitin concluded that the right environmental conditions and opportunities better explain violent transformation of conflict than deprivation. More precisely, the conditions that favour the outbreak of organized violence seem to be state weakness, population size and political instability rather than deprivations directly, such as lack of civil liberties and democracy and outright oppression (ibid., 2003:88).

Although we partially disagree with the generalizing greed-based assumptions as explanations of the emergence and motivation of violent conflict, our analysis recognizes the explanatory significance of parameters other than the usual deprivation variables in measuring the likelihood of violent eruptions, without dismissing the essential role played by deprivation in the emergence of conflict. The present theoretical framework does not associate the motivation of conflict with elite efforts to maximize wealth through criminal and predatory practices. Rather, opportunities for rebellion are principally linked to favourable environmental conditions that facilitate the expression of grievances through violent means. The strategic motivation of rebellion and conflict, according to the present theoretical construct, is all about feasible rectifications of intense grievances of one's society or group, rather than the immediate wealth maximizing and predatory goals of militants.

Without a doubt, the involvement of actors seeking private gain and influence in rebellions is a regular part of war. Warmongers, bandits and common criminals are all too common in disorderly situations of conflict. Criminal behaviour is more endemic during political insecurity, social injustice, fear and economic decline – partially or simply because such behaviour gets more room to flourish in these conditions. The conditions of insurgency bolster criminal activities of the sort created by the war itself. The motives prompting such actors to behave in purely criminal ways is a mixture of destitution, capacity, and an endless array of war-related opportunities such as looting, extortion, arms-trade, smuggling, racketing and protection. In long-term conflicts, criminal activities may even extend to other forms of organized crime related to the trafficking of humans, drugs and organs. Moreover, the belief that ethnic rebel groups act under the orders of a vanguard elite seeking to exploit natural resources such as oil and diamonds, is only true to the extent these natural resources are exclusively used for multiplying personal gain rather than sustaining the rebellion itself. Although ethnic elites and ethnic elite groups seem to benefit disproportionally compared to ordinary combatants, just like political and business elites in peaceful societies enjoy privileges that ordinary citizens are denied, the drastic changes brought about by conflict settlements have generally elevated the social status of marginalized ethnic groups. Hence, predatory behaviour seems to be a by-product of violent conflict, part of the generalized pathologies created by war, such as societal erosion, moral degeneration, brutalization and opportunism.

Having clarified this important distinction between authentic motivation and symptomatic behaviour, we will explore the environmental conditions and rationale in the decision to use violence. In an effort to emphasize the influence of (a) oppression, (b) resources, and (c) territory, analysts reinvented and remodelled the idea of geopolitics in a way that suited current ethno-geographic concerns (Johnsen, 1994; Paquette, 2002; Duffy, 2003). These analysts underscored the role of strategy as "a plan of action designed in order to achieve some end; a purpose together with a system of measures for its accomplishment" (Baylis et al., 2007:5). Murray and Grimslay provide a very relevant and useful extension of this definition: "strategy is a process, a constant adaptation to the shifting conditions and circumstances" (Dannreuther, 2007:77). Strategic analysis relies on the calculation of objectives, capabilities and resources within acceptable bounds of risk to create outcomes that are more favourable to the fulfilment of an objective (Yarger, 2006:1).

The strategic rationale of oppressive policies in ethno-political conflict stems from the fundamental perception of insecurity (Lake and Rothchild, 1998; Roe, 1999; Kirwin, 2006; Kaufman, 1996, 1998, 2001). This observation relates to the existing Realist tradition in the study of International Relations. Political Realists propose that rational actors function in a disorderly environment in the search for security (Dannreuther, 2007:37). In a condition of anarchy, security is what actors look for (Posen, 1993). Barry Posen explains that rival ethnic groups function in an anarchic setting, thereby triggering intense fears and temptations within each group to use force so as to improve its relative position (ibid.). In an effort to improve their positions and maximize their safety, ethnic groups often try to oppress or exterminate their antagonists, thus spawning a multitude of grievances. Although security is not always seen as a zero-sum game, the multitude of frozen conflicts and rejected settlements, as well as the numerous fruitless wars suggest that actors are often unwilling to reduce the level and intensity of their perceived security interests (Walter, 1999).

Therefore, conflict participants, governments and rebels, make strategic calculations, and aim for the optimum security outcome. Every strategy is directed towards the fulfilment of a politically desired objective and incorporates the calculation of external and internal environmental factors in relation to subjective interests (Duffy, 2003). Paquette explains that ethnic conflict involves a strategic calculation of values and interests, and emphasizes the role of national priorities in the formulation of interests. Members of a community define, with specific reference to their own society, what to them is good for society, and hence put forward a communal set of interests to increase security (Paquette, 2002).

However, the struggle to increase security leads to competition because the perceived security interests of different groups usually collide. What one ethnic group does to enhance and protect its own security triggers a counter-reaction by another group (Posen, 1993). In conflict-prone multi-ethnic societies, ethnic groups tend to be either subservient or dominant, a result of a series of violent or non-violent power-struggles. Groups that are more powerful naturally tend to supervise and suppress less powerful groups, aiming to control the latter's activities and reduce their potential to react forcefully, (re)gain power or exact revenge.

Therefore, the desire of a dominant ethnic group to acquire the largest share of resources and wealth in order to increase its power and security tends to marginalize other competitors. The instinct of collective survival and repulsion of alien competitors require the accumulation of territories and resources, protectionist governmental structures, and control over every aspect of public life. Consequently, the unfavourable position in which subordinate ethnic groups find themselves can obfuscate the original source of frustration. Just as Thucydides stated in the *History of the Peloponnesian War*, "Of great danger are the subjected when they rise up and win over those who ruled them". Deliberate suppression of subordinated groups provides the basis for resistance and conflict, and the desire for revenge.

Therefore, one could ask why a dominant group should introduce such oppressive measures, since these obviously create an explosive mix of frustration-aggression in the subordinated ethnic group. In short, repressive domination ultimately becomes counter-productive. The dominant group would argue that the granting of extended freedoms to subjugated groups would endanger their own security and well-being. The elevation of subjugated groups would only bolster potentially vindictive competitors. This can directly affect the distribution of wealth, create pressures for new forms of governance, and lead to loss of territories. Thus the emancipation of dissident groups, with diametrically different territorial, political and cultural designs, would endanger the vital interests of the dominant ethnicity (Olzak, 1994). This clash of security interests prompts dominant or regime-holder ethnic groups to resist concessions, defy meritocracy and devise ways of manipulation and control. Consequently, this "zero-sum" rationale creates actual or perceived deprivation(s) among the "losers" (ibid.). The efforts of dominant groups to retain control over resources and territory is evident in many cases of conflict, like the Protestants in Northern Ireland, the Greek-Cypriot community in Cyprus, the Albanian community in present-day Kosovo, the Sunnis in Iraq and the whites of South Africa. The fear of economic dependency, political subordination, or territorial annexation is a major driving force of competition, and usually results in some type of conflict. A good example of this link between security and oppression is the case of the Albanian minority in the Former Yugoslav Republic (FYR) of Macedonia. For many years, the Albanians in FYR Macedonia constituted a subordinate group that desired to maximize political power, improve its socio-economic status and provoke significant institutional changes in the status quo to the detriment of the Slav Macedonians. By contrast, the Slavic majority aimed to preserve the status quo, one in which political, military and administrative power remained in the hands of the Christian Orthodox Slavs. The majority group, feeling insecure despite its dominance, insisted that the political and territorial interests of the minority group do not match with the interests of the majority, and sustained a policy of oppression, characterized by systematic ethnic engineering and institutional discrimination. In many cases of conflict, ethnic groups adopt far-reaching, often radical ideologies and aspirations. For example, the ethnic identity of groups such as the Irish Catholics, the Kosovo Albanians, the Basques, or the Kurds incorporates political ideas that go beyond the cultural characteristics of the ethnic group. Competing groups are inclined to interpret their respective ethno-cultural identities as symbols of conflicting ethno-political designs, and therefore treat them as security threats to their own well-being. In an attempt to prevent or contain the other's ethno-nationalist projects, rival ethnic groups exercise oppressive policies and justify these policies on the basis of the security threat argument. Ethnic groups pursue policies inspired by their own actual or perceived insecurities and opposing interests. In weak multi-ethnic societies where groups have different ethno-political designs and aspirations, as well as different alliances and loyalties, certain identities are further reinforced by images and historical events in which one ethnicity has benefited at the expense of another. Hence, ethnic groups will naturally seek for solutions that will enable political and territorial control at the expense of others.

Therefore, ethnic groups clash over territory and resources. This conflict of interests can turn violent exactly when the appropriate environmental conditions and circumstances allow it to erupt (Fearon and Laitin, 2003). Most ethnic groups resorting to insurgency or terrorism are sufficiently rational to evaluate conditions and calculate the costs and benefits of these radical, violent means. In the decision to use violence against an oppressive regime, the politico-military leadership of a rebel group takes into account the repressive capacity of the state (state-strength), the geographical terrain, the availability of resources, and the impact of regional conflict spillover effects. These factors may either permit or prohibit the use of violence against an oppressive regime. Even so, rebel movements tend to underestimate long-term detrimental effects of, for instance, their resort to terrorist violence against civilians, as the Chechen separatists found to their cost. So their strategic analysis is often far from perfect, even if based on rational yet utilitarian short-term calculations.

Finally, an independent factor, which may critically influence the decision to use arms against the state relates to a tradition of violence. Strategic analysts understand that the majority of conflicts today are ethnically driven, and therefore identity based. For this reason, it is imperative to have some basic knowledge of the culture of each country and ethnicity we study (Manheim and Rich, 1986:225; Ten Dam, 2009, 2010, 2011). Thus, political culture has a critical bearing on the relationship between deprivation and violence. Some particular cultural values and traditional morals favour decisions to use violence and determine the norms and practices of violence (Ten Dam, 2010). The process of identity formation, no matter if primordial or constructed, depends upon a series of environmental and socio-cultural conditions. These conditions relate to the availability of resources, the type of geographical terrain, the tradition of politico-economic autonomy, the capacity for self-defence, the degree of interaction with other ethnicities. Additionally, socio-cultural elements such as vendettas, local codes of honour, banditry, notions of masculinity and rituals relating to the development of ethnic bonds, can generally influence the formation of identity. The acceptance and integration of such conditions into the in-group rules and norms determine the group's internal outlook, societal functioning and its violent tendencies.

In purely empirical terms, the degree of rebelliousness seems to relate well with the acceptance, consolidation and reproduction of social conditions that facilitate the use of violence. For example, population groups with a strong tradition of rebellion, anti-state activity and violent resistance, such as the Chechens, the Albanians, the Cretans, the Sicilians, numerous African tribes and the Mexicans, all have a lenient attitude towards the everyday use of arms "in peacetime", for activities like vendettas, honour killings, self-defence, robberies, theft and so on. In other words, often subservient, discriminated ethnic groups become, for historical and cultural reasons, permissive to the use of arms and tolerant to certain types of violence. This constitutes a serious risk factor in weak or tense multi-ethnic states or societies, and increases the likelihood of violent conflict to erupt.

Strategic Coercion

The following section concentrates on the use of coercive diplomacy by governments and international organizations in the management of violent ethnic conflicts across the world. Here we present the key points in the debate between advocates of military coercion and those who propose diplomatic coercion i.e. a repertoire of measures through mainly diplomatic means. Further, we underline the dangers of military coercion and peace enforcement as opposed to the effects of coercive diplomacy in our case study. The theory of coercion and the negotiating strategies used in coercive diplomacy are extensively discussed in many theoretical works. For this reason, the present analysis does not reiterate all the theoretical concepts, strategic approaches and methodologies, but rather provides and empirical account of coercive settlements on intrastate conflicts.

Notably, the decision to concentrate on the use of coercive diplomacy (strategic coercion) stems from the accumulated experience of the North Atlantic Treaty Organization (NATO) and the United Nations (UN) in the Balkans (Bosnia-Herzegovina, Serbia-Kosovo). The case of the armed conflict in the Former Yugoslav Republic (FYR) of Macedonia exemplifies the superiority of coercive diplomacy over military force, and defines the precise conditions allowing for a diplomatic resolution of such a crisis.

What is Coercion?

Coercion is a prevalent mechanism for reaching desirable political outcomes or averting undesirable ones, with the use or the threat of use, of a wide range of measures ranging from diplomatic censure and economic sanctions to military intervention. The aim of strategic coercion is to alter the decision-making calculus of one or more a political entities and halt the progress of ongoing or intended hostilities. As Michael A. Berger points out, "coercion aims to either dissuade an opponent from taking an undesirable course of action, or to stop and undo an undesirable course of action already taken, by making the costs of intended action exceed the benefits of possible rewards associated with pursuing it" (Berger, 2009:5). More precisely, coercion is about manipulating the recipient actor's cost-benefit calculus through a limited but adequate scale of force and/or sanctions for doing so. In short, coercion is based on the ability to force someone to do something he or she would not otherwise do by using, preferably, the least intensive methods (Ury, Brett and Goldberg, 1988:7). In his book *Arms and Influence*, Thomas Schelling was the first to coin the threat of force with the term "compellance" (Shelling, 1966). According to Shelling, the theory of coercion incorporates two broadly defined subsets, deterrence and compellance. Deterrence is concerned with preventing a political entity acting in a certain way, forcing a target to behave in desirable ways before acting, whereas compellance describes a uniform response based on threats against a target that has already initiated hostile or undesirable action (Levy, 2008:539). The analysis is exclusively concerned with responsive coercion, and the consequences of such actions in intrastate conflicts, particularly the differences between and the effects of military, non-military and mixed types of coercion.

Military Coercion and Coercive Diplomacy

In recent times, the traditional aggressive-military forms of coercion have come under criticism of policymakers and scholars advocating a more moderate, less drastic approach in the settlement of disputes. They emphasize the benefits of non-military coercion over the humanly, politically and financially costly methods of military force. Crucially, a military attack destroys the enemy's capabilities to act, while coercive diplomacy leaves the target state (or other actor) with the ability to choose whether to comply or not (Licklider, 1994:38). In fact, strategic coercion can be conceptualized as a process with a potential or available scale of increasing severity. Coercive diplomacy exists in the lower, more moderate end of the scale, whereas military intervention, occupation and (nuclear) war represent the extremes (Berger, 2009:4). Coercive diplomacy does not require an exemplary use of force. The diplomatic toolkit provides the coercer with "soft methods", such as positive inducements, rewards, reasoning and persuasion, as alternatives to military force. However, Robert Art (2003:7) explains that the possible use of limited military force as part of coercive diplomacy is confined within the larger frame of other essentially non-military means of persuasion, yet paradoxically the use of force remains an important aspect of coercive diplomacy. Indeed, the threat of employing military force constitutes a key factor in such diplomacy. When a political entity such as a state (or a rebel movement) moves past latent or very limited applications of force and begins to use more drastic military means, that actor has moved along the spectrum of coercive diplomacy into that of military coercion. The latter form of coercion involves the application of force on a massive or at least highly violent scale in order to achieve political and military objectives (Berger, 2009:6). In that sense, coercive diplomacy is a limited, moderate variant of military coercion, placing the initial emphasis on non-military measures over military responses in order to avoid or delay the costly deployment of soldiers, which brings human costs (deaths, injuries, etc.) and financial burdens.

The Prussian military theorist Carl Von Clausewitz observed that "every age had its own kind of war, its own limiting conditions, and its own peculiar preconceptions". In the early 1990s, the limited success of military operations in the Gulf War prompted military and political analysts to adopt a more critical attitude towards the financial and human costs and effectiveness of large-scale military interventions. Analysts were forced to reassess the security threats and accordingly adjust their policies to fit the requirements of a new dogma in military intervention characterized by (a) limited, non-protracted war, (b) political restraint, and (c) the importance of a better state of peace (Ellwood, 2002:4–5).

Inspired by Schelling's work, the renowned foreign policy analyst Alexander George brought in a fresh and more nuanced approach to coercive power, beyond the use of mere threats and brute force. Alexander George grasped the changing conditions, and insisted on developing more flexible approaches as alternatives to military coercion. His major objective was to show that coercive policies could include methods of persuasion and accommodation, as well as coercive threats in an effort to avoid escalation and resolve the so-called politico-military dilemma in the most effectual way (George, 1991). Alexander George integrated a number of essential policy elements such as pressure, threats, persuasion, positive inducements and accommodation into a crisis bargaining strategy that provides political leaders with an alternative to outright or immediate war or military intervention (Levy, 2008:539). George admits that a fundamental tension exists between political-diplomatic and military-strategic considerations in efforts to manage certain kinds of crises and in efforts to keep limited conflicts from escalating (George, 1991:15). Being aware of the risks contained in military responses, George believed that "we should not stick to the dogmatic use of threat and military force in coercion, but we must develop a political-military strategy appropriate for the situation at hand ..." (ibid.:15). A coercive strategy should generally rely on a mix and sequencing of persuasion, threat, accommodative offers and concessions.

In his conceptual framework, George emphasizes two variables: threat of punishment for noncompliance, and the possible use of incentives (ibid.). Moreover, he put emphasis on the role of negotiations, and underscored the use of coercion as part of an overall strategy to persuade an opponent to act in desirable ways (ibid., 1991).

Contrary to threat-driven approaches (Art, 2003), George concentrated more on the role of non-military pressures, such as economic sanctions or the withdrawal of foreign aid, in which the use of force even in a demonstrative fashion is one of many options. He suggested that coercive strategies should combine the use of threats with credible and attractive positive incentives, and pointed to the role and importance of a negotiations system. Thus, he set the basis for what we currently know as modern *strategic coercion*, which arguably constitutes the fullest and most applicable description of coercive diplomacy. The theory of strategic coercion is an alternative approach that seeks to manipulate an agent's behaviour through political and military means, i.e. induce or compel that agent to do something against its will (Sullivan, 1995). In short, coercive diplomacy is largely based on strategic coercion, and it is best viewed as a flexible strategy based on the recognition that by itself the "stick" cannot or will not achieve much without the "carrot". The aim of strategic coercion is to persuade the leaders of an adversary state (or non-state entity) that the costs and risks of a contemplated or initiated action will outweigh its expected benefits through principally diplomatic means (George, 1991). Strategic Coercion is generally dependent on three primary principles: Time, Flexibility and Coordination.

Time

The tempo and momentum of coercion determines the chances of its success. The success of coercive diplomacy depends on choosing the right timing in relation to existing conditions. The selection of an appropriate strategy should normally take into consideration the existing global and regional security conditions, assess possible counterweights and potential alliances, and determine the exact state the conflict is in (emergence-escalation-diffusion). Choosing the right moment can drastically increase the likelihood of a successful outcome of a coercive policy. Moreover, *time* allows for the engaged sides to exchange diplomatic signals, assess the situation, make decisions and respond to proposals. Finally, coercive responses are most effective and appropriate at the early stage of a dispute, conflict or insurgency.

Flexibility

Diplomatic-military actions should be chosen to signal a desire to negotiate a way out of the crisis rather than to seek a military solution. The coercing party should promise and grant rewards and exercise credible threats (i.e. if necessary carry them out) with the same vigour and commitment. The success of strategic coercion relies on the thin balance between the appropriate amount of pressure and the considerate use of incentives. One should not threaten the target-party with immediate economic collapse or deprive its population of access to basic goods. Although this type of pressure has yielded some positive results in the case of the international embargo against Serbia, it has failed in the case of Iraq. Intense pressures, which can be felt at the grassroots level, can possibly stimulate popular reactions against the government of the coerced state, but also run the risk of intensifying, popularizing and spreading the conflict or stimulating popular support for that government in a national solidarity reflex. Pressures should alternatively focus on military embargos, blockage of prospective development funds, boycotts and other symbolic gestures rather than restricting the free flow of food and medical equipment.

Apart from granting political and economic incentives, the inclusion of rogue elements into the bargaining process is a frequently used strategy for resolving violent disputes and reducing the probability and costs of warfare. The strategic aim of inclusion is to weaken extremists by incorporating parts of them into mainstream decision-making (Capoccia, 2001:12). The elimination of extremism through force is a costly venture, marked by high risks and ambivalent results as to the final settlement of grievances held by the conflicting parties. For this reason, intermediary policies are generally preferable to confrontation. Direct engagement strategies, either covert or overt, exist at the end of the elimination-inclusion spectrum. Inclusion involves the establishment of contacts with either extremist or moderate representatives (Wanis, 2008).

In coercive methodologies, inclusion is the result of persuasion through incentives or pressures. With the inclusion of extremists into mainstream political processes, the coercing body attempts to entice dissident and often violent actors with political access and resources. Together with the granting of financial aid, this probably constitutes the other major incentive in strategic coercion for the termination of conflict.

Coordination

A carefully designed *coordination* of different interested parties is crucial. Given the nature and complexity of intractable conflicts, successful mediation requires a co-ordinated approach between different mediating actors and coercers with resources to nudge the parties towards a settlement, and an acute psychological understanding of the parties' feelings and grievances. The effective coordination of military and diplomatic actions is essential in terminating a crisis or preventing an escalation to higher levels of violence like war. Vertical and horizontal forms of coordination are essential parts of a coercive strategy. Vertical coordination refers to unimpeded, multilevel communication between the coercer and the coerced. Such communication drastically minimizes the risk of confusion, misunderstanding and errors. This helps policymakers to draw a precise sketch of the target party's intensions and needs, and helps them to devise appropriate policy responses to a given situation. Horizontal coordination refers to the establishment of an integral and interdependent security mechanism by interested, involved parties, international organizations and governments. Involving relevant international actors like the UN strengthens the legitimacy and effectiveness of (strategic) coercion, especially if the competence and expertise of the actors reinforce each other.

Coercive diplomacy should concentrate on the weakening of the opponent's military confidence and political resolve (Pape, 1992:423–475). Robert Pape advocates an indirect, non-military strategy of "thwarting an adversary's military strategy as a means of denying him the opportunity to achieve any substantial benefit" (ibid.:2). For Pape, a coercer should attempt to raise the expected costs for the opponent and thereby lower the latter's confidence in his military strategy, and hence reduce the latter's expected probability of success. This manipulation of the opponent's military vulnerability was exactly what international mediators did in the case of FYR Macedonia. Pape's proposal requires the coercer to hold power on all diplomatic and military levels in order to break the opponent's will and resolve, but offers the means to force a party to terminate a conflict without the costs of military intervention.

Yet, while strategic coercion aims to avoid the use of military power, Pape's version of coercive diplomacy suggests doing so by denying potential benefits and elevating the costs of continuing conflict rather than offering positive incentives. However, multiple factors such as strength of resolve, interest and risk should not be neglected. In the case of FYR Macedonia, the success of coercion relied not only on the ability of the coercing party to raise the expected costs in the recipient's decision-making calculus, but also in the ability to offer incentives to help the recipient take difficult decisions.

By contrast, critics of George's theoretical framework suggest that the use of positive inducements can be interpreted as signifying less than "steely resolve on the part of the coercer and their presence may actually backfire and strengthen the target's resolve" (ibid., 2003:23). Thus, even when positive inducements are offered, the ultimate recourse in coercion is always the threat of force (ibid.). Analysts who regard non-military coercion as a potentially dangerous and often ineffective strategy have questioned the overall effectiveness of strategic coercion in its moderate and offensive forms (Brown, 2003). For example, Robert Art conducted a set of tests based on multiple crises, which showed the limits of coercion, although he remained hesitant to call the entire concept of strategic coercion a failure. In contrast, Peter Jakobsen found that in most cases strategic coercion had negative results. In his words, "the strategy's potential for peaceful conflict resolution has only been realized in two of the 37 coercive diplomacy exchanges ... five lasting successes in 37 attempts is hardly an encouraging success rate, and it underlines the principal conclusion drawn in the literature: that coercion is a high-risk, hard to use strategy" (Jakobsen, 2003:27–40). Yet, he attributed this failure to the inability and unwillingness of policymakers to exercise coercion effectively (ibid.). The success of strategic coercion depends upon a number of interrelating, mutually reinforcing conditions, such as the extent of the demanded changes, the type of force used (limited or exemplary) and the granting of appropriate positive inducements through a negotiation process (Carlson, 2005). Hence, in the exercise of strategic coercion, the coercer must appropriately select those coercive methods that maximize the chances of a durable settlement.

Ethnic Conflict, Strategic Coercion and the Backlash Effect

Although there is no systematic, validated theory to suggest that coercion may actually perpetuate socio-economic and political grievances, a number of theoretical contributions emphasize the shortfalls of coercion as a conflict management tool, and relate it explicitly to the aggravation of previous resentments (Dugan; 2003 Burgess, 2004). A good peace settlement avoids the creation of bitterness among the parties, and refrains from exercising excessive pressure. Outside coercion, however, may function as a grievance-maximizer and precipitate a new round of conflict. The risk of counter-productive effects is probably the major shortfall of strategic coercion.

Ironically, coercion may foster or perpetuate inter-ethnic hatred and even a conflict relapse. This so-called backlash effect is a major prohibiting factor against the use of coercive approaches, and it is one reason why seemingly resolved conflicts tend to re-ignite (Dugan and Burgess, 2004). Once the original losers (re)gain enough power, they seek revenge against the earlier victors. As noted, ethnic groups and their armed organizations, just like ordinary people, do not like to be forced to do things against their will (ibid.). Even when one ethnic group succumbs to the threat or use of force, it is likely to become resentful and revengeful at a later stage. More precisely, resentment is likely to increase when the force used is seen as illegitimate, immoral, or excessive.

Thus, if the victims of aggression, in this case outside intervention, do not feel that justice has been done, they are likely to try to regain their power so as to get even at the first opportunity. This backlash effect reflects the tendency of the disadvantaged group to lash out against the advantaged party. In this way, many imposed settlements freeze into a negative peace, whereby a so-called peace process becomes protracted and produces a new set of grievances (McGinty, 2002:5). In contrast, a genuine, durable peace, wherein grievances are addressed and conflict-generating sources resolved or neutralized, a negative, "frozen" peace still harbours conflict-generating sources that continue to fester (Harris, Fisk and Rank, 1998). Thus, Galtung defines negative peace as the absence of direct violence, while positive peace refers to the absence of indirect and structural violence (Galtung and Jacobsen, 2000).

Hence, we assert that coercive tools are often too cumbersome, drastic, risk-prone and counterproductive for reliable and durable conflict resolution. This book demonstrates that coercive diplomacy is a risky strategy that should only be employed as a last resort, given the likelihood that outside interference could backfire i.e. create new discontent, deprivation and a fresh desire for revenge among those parties who deem themselves disadvantaged by the peace settlement. Even so, strategic coercion is frequently used to manage crises and settle violent disputes. Despite the disagreement among analysts on the effectiveness of force versus inducements, coercive approaches are largely based on power, and the ability to use it effectively. The principal risk, however, is found in the possibility of generating resentment among the conflict participants. Hence, it is very likely that the receptor of pressures feels disappointment and dissatisfaction with an enforced settlement. This resentment could take the shape of active resistance to the negotiated settlement. Consequently, the policy of coercion seems capable of creating new confrontations and new sources of grievance. This gives rise to a state of negative peace Thus, we regard the coercive method as a high-risk approach for settling disputes, one capable of preserving or even creating multilevel deprivations through the perpetuation of grievances. In the methodology section, we present a model for examining the evolution and effects of coercive diplomacy in the continuation of grievances through a consistent pattern of negotiations.

The armed insurgency of ethnic Albanians in FYR of Macedonia made the use of externally applied strategic coercion a feasible alternative to direct military intervention (Hagmann, 2004). Given that neither side was willing to back off or accept its losses damage, NATO and EU mediators devised a strategy of persuasion based on a mixture of threats, force and positive inducements. The conflict evolved between a weak government overseeing a poor economy and a weak national army, and a well-positioned but small rebel force. Mainstream accounts regard the so-called Ohrid peace settlement as one that accommodates the most vital Slavic Macedonian concerns while addressing the rebels' main demands. EU and NATO mediators present the case as a successful paradigm of conflict resolution through diplomatic coercion. Coercive policies, however, were tailored to influence the leaders of a weak state whose freedom of action and decision-making options were limited. Emphasis was placed on the fact that international mediators resolved the crisis solely through diplomatic means, albeit indirect military threats or pressures were frequently exercised. Soon after the termination of the hostilities and the reaching of the Ohrid peace settlement in 2001, the Slavic Macedonian side was evidently disappointed due to the pressures exercised by NATO and the EU, and most Slavs were quick to engage in severe victimology. International coercion was followed by the enforcement of a peace settlement that was based on the hasty introduction, or rather imposition, of civic-liberal principles, ignoring the incapacity of the state to effectively apply them.

Despite the widespread enthusiasm among Albanians, many of them have become disillusioned with the feasibility of implementing a settlement that has never been fully endorsed by the Slavic Macedonian side. Most Slav Macedonians believe that external actors have forced their government into a humiliating, painful compromise with the Albanians, and many of them feel their rights and securities have been dramatically reduced as a result of the Ohrid Agreement. Consequently, a significant part of the Slav Macedonian community attempted to block the implementation of the agreed reforms, triggering angry reactions from the Albanian community. The backlash effect was equally evident in many aspects of social and political life in the country. After a short-lived honeymoon period, Slavic Macedonian ethno-nationalism re-emerged as a refuge of protection and resistance against change. Nationalist parties regained their political eminence, inter-ethnic relations reached rock bottom and ethnic polarization increased.

CHAPTER 2

The Collapse of Socialist Yugoslavia

This chapter examines the sources of minority discontent in the Former Yugoslav Republic (FYR) of Macedonia, and underlines the strategic factors that influence the violent transformation of ethno-political conflict. We analyse the impact of socio-economic decline on the attitudes of the Albanian community in the Socialist Federal Yugoslav Republic of Yugoslavia (SFRY) and assess the grievances expressed by the Albanian community in FYR Macedonia throughout the first ten years of the post-Yugoslav era. Using the analytical framework of "strategic rebellion", we demonstrate how socio-political oppression and economic marginalization impacted on the Albanian community in FYR Macedonia, causing an intense feeling of aggressive frustration among them. However, the systematic political and socio-economic deprivation of the minority Albanians in FYR Macedonia cannot sufficiently account for, or justify, the organized violent rebellion, unless other factors of vital strategic importance are taken into consideration. Hence, in Chapter 5 we examine three major pre-conditions allowing for the decision of politically active minority groups, in this case the Albanians in FYR Macedonia, to use violence: (a) state strength and denial of external state legitimacy, (b) rebel resources and (c) regional conflict spillovers.

Political Oppression and Economic Decline

On 31 January 1946, the Yugoslav Communist Party of the Socialist Federal Republic of Yugoslavia officially declared the new Constitution of the Socialist (People's) Yugoslav Republic (SYR) of Macedonia. The

Constitution provisioned for the protection of ethnic minority rights, and the regional branch of the Communist Party promoted the incorporation of the Albanian community into the economic and social life of the new socialist state through education, professional training and other social opportunities (Miloslavlevski and Tomovski, 1997:49–105). Yet the inter-ethnic distrust between the Slavic and Albanian populations of Yugoslavia proved far more durable. The collaboration of Albanians with the Axis forces during the Second World War, and the inter-ethnic violence committed during the war between Albanian nationalists and Slav Partisans, intensified a climate of distrust towards the Albanians.[1] Consequently, the Yugoslav authorities were unwilling to provide full autonomy and equality to Albanians; they pushed the Albanians to the margins of politics and society and only a few Albanians ever got to occupy influential political and economic positions (Shoup, 1963:64–81 and 75–76). Albanians were thus not trusted to uphold the Socialist-Yugoslav project.

In fact, the political marginalization of Albanians and other minorities relied on an elaborate system of discrimination, one in which everything seemed to be politically correct on a legal and public level. Despite the political correctness evident in Socialist rhetoric, the architects of Yugoslavia introduced a political-administrative system structured along ethnic lines, one in which ethnicities got political access according to previous allegiances. As a result, an ethno-political ranking system grew within the federal and republican structures of Yugoslavia, with the Serbs at the top. The Communist authorities generally mistrusted the Albanians, along with the Croats and the Slovenes. Thus the Serbs, who constituted approximately 40 per cent of the Yugoslav population, made up 78.9 per cent of the personnel in the federal administration, while Croats made up only 8 per cent (Norman, 1995:212 and Veselica, 1980:12). Additionally, Serbs

1 In the Second World War, many Albanians sided with the Axis forces in order to promote the unification of territories inhabited by Albanian populations under Italian and German patronage. The Albanian leadership functioned as a proxy occupying force on behalf of the Italian and German forces in the regions of Kosovo, Western Yugoslav Macedonia and Albania proper. This legacy of conflict was destined to haunt post-war interethnic relations in Yugoslavia.

made up around 70 per cent of the military officialdom of the Yugoslav People's Army (Jugoslovenska Narodna Armija, JNA); Croats made up only 15 per cent, while the remaining 15–20 per cent was left for Slovenes, Bosnians, Albanians, Macedonian Slavs and smaller groups (Hashi, 1992:73; Karadjis, 1999).

Following the Tito-Stalin split in 1948, Albania sided with the Soviet camp, breaking the Yugo-Albanian Treaty of Friendship, which allowed the Yugoslav authorities to press for a solution of the "internal Albanian question" (Kola, 2003). The Yugoslav Minister of the Interior Alexandar Rankovic, a devout Serb centralist, installed an elaborate system of state surveillance in order to monitor Albanian nationalist activity within and outside Yugoslavia. The leadership of the local Macedonian Slav Communist Party, influenced by anti-Albanian attitudes in Belgrade, implemented a policy of soft discrimination by accusing those Albanians who demanded a greater role in society to be irredentist puppets of Enver Hoxha's Stalinist regime in Albania (Blumi, 2002). Thus in 1959 the Communist Party of SYR Macedonia had only 5 per cent Albanian members, while no Albanian had ever become a member of the party's executive committee until 1965 (Palmer and King, 1971:81). Furthermore, in an attempt to explain the small numbers of skilled workers coming from the Albanian minority, Lazar-Penev Kolishevski, the first communist leader of the SYR Macedonian state, argued that "all minorities must learn the language of the Republic in which they reside on the basis that the language barrier makes training of minority labour more costly and less efficient" (ibid.:79). Thus, as a rule, Albanians had little access to state jobs, while Slav Macedonians occupied almost all state posts. (Lynn, Ackerman, Janev, 2000:7).

Therefore, the Albanians in SYR Macedonia became increasingly frustrated by the perceived – and arguably factual – injustices of discrimination. In November 1968, the Macedonian Albanians, influenced by a disorderly pro-republic demonstration in Pristina, rioted and clashed with the security forces in Tetovo and Skopje; many hundreds were arrested and imprisoned (Palmer and King, 1971:181). The Yugoslav People's Army (JNA) was sent in to suppress the revolt, as concerns grew that Albanians in SYR Macedonia were collaborating with Albania's intelligence service against the integrity of Yugoslavia in order to annex the western part of Macedonia to Albania (Kola, 2003:181). Criminal proceedings began against twenty of the most prominent Albanians, scholarships were denied to any Albanian student proved to have participated in the riots, and numerous Albanians involved in the demonstrations were dismissed from their jobs while hundreds were imprisoned (Palmer and King, 1971:181–182). These developments confirmed the Albanian perception of political oppression and persecution by the Yugoslav state.

Albanian discontent with the political system in SYR Macedonia was partly rooted in the oppressive structures of Yugoslavia, put in place by the dominant Serb majority. A generalized sense of socio-economic deprivation, generated by the slow economic development and the constant underperformance of the country within Yugoslavia, was another source of grievance and frustration. On the one hand, the rural, introvert and conservative nature of Albanian society placed severe limitations on the progress of Albanian communities. Educational restrictions on women, large numbers of unskilled labour, and a strong reliance on family-oriented agricultural practices meant that Albanians could hardly work for the developing industry or the wider public sector. This self-inflicted marginalization contributed to the socio-economic backwardness of many Albanians in Yugoslavia. On the other hand, SYR Macedonia was never a prosperous republic and its underdevelopment was reflected in all economic indicators. Arguably, deliberate state discrimination intensified the effect of economic underdevelopment. While the three northern republics, Slovenia, Croatia and most of Serbia, were able to increase production through new technology and foreign investment, the less developed southern regions, especially Kosovo, SYR Macedonia, Montenegro and southern Serbia, kept relying on traditional forms of labour intensive, low-paying economic activity such as textile manufacture, agriculture and handicrafts. This contrast produced sharp differences in employment, investment, income potential and social services among the eight political units of the federation (Goodrich, 1990). In SYR Macedonia, the deficient energy resources (despite investments in hydro-electric power-plants), the mountainous terrain, a primitive transport system, a high illiteracy rate among the Albanians, the lack of skilled labour and the absence of special bonds with more developed nations outside Yugoslavia, resulted in a generalized failure to attract or successfully sustain investments. As a result, SYR Macedonia presented the lowest GDP per capita, well below the Yugoslav average, followed only by Kosovo, and constituted the most unattractive destination for investment in the whole of Yugoslavia (Chichok, 1985:211–288). Instead, the republic's economy relied on its tobacco industry, which approximated 60 per cent of the total Yugoslav produce, as well as sesame oil from poppy seeds, textiles and furniture. However, the tobacco industry steadily decreased because of taxation on tobacco products and competition from much bigger tobacco producers abroad (Wilkinson, 1952:309–405). By 1990, SYR Macedonia continued to present the second lowest GDP per capita average after Kosovo. The country's agricultural output exceeded only that of Montenegro's and Kosovo's, at a mere 7.3 per cent. The volume of exports was also significantly lower to those of Slovenia and Vojvodina, two regions with approximately the same population size. Slovenia alone had an exports contribution seven times larger, and Vojvodina – which, like Kosovo, lacked Republic status – had twice the percentage of exports of that of SYR Macedonia.

Clearly, Yugoslavia was a country of multiple economic and development speeds. Slovenia and Croatia belonged to the prosperous industrialized north with a higher than the average GDP per capita and the highest export and import index, Serbia and Vojvodina were found somewhere in the middle presenting an average GDP per capita and large levels of agricultural product and import-exports. Finally, Montenegro, SYR Bosnia-Herzegovina and SYR Macedonia belonged to the lagging south. Generally, SYR Macedonia was, along with the autonomous province of Kosovo, the poorest region in the Yugoslav Federation and this disparity impacted heavily on the Albanian populations residing in these Yugoslav areas by increasing inter-ethnic competition over scarce resources.

Yugoslavia's Economic Recession and Political Collapse

The Yugoslav economy was based on a mixed system of "market socialism" composed by two major pillars.[2] The Yugoslav market relied on extensive decentralization of decision-making and the coordination of localized procedures. This model made Yugoslavia a unique type of economy with equally strong ties to the capitalist West and the communist East. The first major pillar of Yugoslavia's economic development was self-management, by which industrial and commercial work organizations were divided into smaller units managed by workers. Agriculture, tourism and small businesses remained in private hands, albeit under heavy taxation. These work organizations enjoyed freedoms over decisions on administration, borrowing and investing. However, the capital equipment of these socially owned organizations belonged to the state, and workers were given no incentive to invest and acquire shares in the ownership of the self-managed organizations. Hence, workers were given a nominal right to control the management of the organization they worked for, but were unable to claim collective ownership. For at least two decades since its inception in 1951, the self-management system delivered an impressive performance; from 1965 to 1979 Yugoslavia enjoyed a 6 per cent annual growth and the per capita consumption rate increased by 4.5 per cent per annum (Estrin, 1991:190).

In the mid 1970s, most work organizations started to decline and the local executive members and directors were becoming significantly more powerful in decision-making procedures. In 1976, Edward Kardelj laid the ground for the Law on Associated Labour, according to which industries and companies were further compartmentalized into independent enterprises as a means of decreasing the power of directors and boosting competition between departments within a single organization while strengthening self-management. The new law created an inter-regional

2 A mixture of social ownership coupled with access to foreign markets and limited private initiative.

nexus of bargaining among the enterprise managers, the local governments and the bankers for the allocation of funds. The political impetus behind this regulation was to control the increasingly diverging developmental tendencies among the republics and contain the emerging nationalisms. Yet ironically, the developing nationalist movement in Croatia pressed hard for the 1974 constitutional revision and for the adoption of the associated labour law.

In 1971, a movement of Croatian nationalists, intellectuals and students backed by Croatian politicians protested against the existing re-distribution of profits within Yugoslavia, and demanded further decentralization. At the same time, Croatian nationalists rallied for increased civil rights, historical rectification of the Croatian image and the defence of the Croatian language (Ramet, 1992:98). The Croatian nationalist movement publicized their national and economic grievances, and encouraged the Slovenes and the Albanians to do the same. Consequently, Albanians started to organize and react against a system that excluded them from any substantial say in the decision-making process, a system that kept them in the margins of social development and industrial employment. This time Albanians demanded recognition of republican status and unification of Albanian territories into a single Yugoslav Republic. Protests escalated into violent riots in several cities of Kosovo.

In order to prevent a dangerous backlash of Albanian discontent, Tito ordered the elevation of Kosovo's status into that of a Socialist Autonomous Province. However, Albanians were convinced that Kosovo's problems could be substantially reduced only if Kosovo was granted full republic status. Ultimately, in 1974 the revised Yugoslav constitution gave Kosovo a significant degree of autonomy within Serbia, granting the province virtual republic status. Ironically, the increased competencies granted to Kosovo, including the transfer of economic responsibilities from Belgrade to Pristina, were aimed at mitigating Albanian nationalist sentiment. However, instead of doing so, these changes boosted a sense of self-reliance among the Albanians in Kosovo. Albanian nationalist organizations started operating in Kosovo with the tolerance of local authorities and with few counter-reactions from Belgrade. The Albanians occupied the administrative and party positions of Kosovo at the expense of the Serbs, and the numbers of Serbs living in Kosovo decreased from 27.5 per cent in 1968 to 13.2 per cent in 1981.

Contrary to expectations, the decentralizing elements of the 1976 labour law, emphasizing bargaining among directors, local political elites and bankers, empowered the regional business and industrial elite. The antagonism between the republics increased, and funds were allocated to companies not according to Socialist or proportional principles but according to profit-generating prospects. Federal subsidies had also become a matter of bargaining. The negotiating procedure effectively created losers and winners. The wealthier republics, namely SYR Slovenia and Croatia, were reacting to the generous re-distributions from the federal budget, and the weaker republics, namely SYR Macedonia and Montenegro, were pressing for more. SYR Macedonia was marginalized, and lacked the necessary competitiveness to keep up with the other republics. At the same time, Albanians in SYR Macedonia, lacking the capacity to secure the same political demands as their counterparts in Kosovo, were becoming increasingly frustrated while Slavic Macedonian protectionism intensified.

The other pillar of Yugoslavia's economic growth was its openness to international financial transactions with the capitalist West, leading to considerable foreign investments and Joint Ventures. Crucially, Yugoslavia remained open to Western influences as a counterweight to the USSR, as a means to remain self-sufficient. In order to sustain the high rates of growth, Yugoslavia systematically borrowed from Western states. Its non-aligned status gave Yugoslavia the opportunity to attract financial assistance from Western countries for investments in its export products. For the Western states, assisting Yugoslavia was a worthwhile venture, as it secured the latter's role as a buffer zone against the Soviet Union and the Eastern Bloc. Foreign investments helped Yugoslavia to gain the technological expertise to increase the production of export goods. From 1965 to 1979, the ratio of investment to GDP was higher than that of any other OECD country except Japan (Estrin, 1991:70).

Nonetheless, the diverging growth potentials of the regional units prevented the equal and uniform development of all regions. Foreign investments in SYR Slovenia and Croatia amounted to 39 per cent and

31 per cent of all Joint Ventures respectively, whereas in the SAP Kosovo and SYR Macedonia these amounted to only 2 per cent and 8 per cent of Joint Ventures respectively (Artisien and Buckley, 1985:111–135). Investment productivity varied among the regions, with some regions utilizing their investments in more productive ways than others do due to their technological advancement, better infrastructure, and more efficient management. Despite the benefits, the long-term effects of Western involvement had a detrimental impact on Yugoslavia's economic survival. Firstly, international competition in export production was antithetical to the socialist self-management model, which was largely protectionist and responsive to workers rights. Secondly, some regions were better equipped to respond to the required levels for producing goods capable to be marketed in the West while other regions could not respond equally well to the renewed demands.

Therefore, in the early 1980s, due to excessive hyper-borrowing and mismanagement, Yugoslavia stagnated and loans poured into the country from the International Monetary Fund (IMF) only to increase pressures towards further liberalization. The sources of Yugoslavia's indebtedness were multiple. The endogenous macro-economic mistakes emanating from political rather than economic decisions, disproportionately higher consumption rates to the growth of the national domestic product (due to generous wage increases), politically targeted investments, borrowing instead of liquidation of fragile or failed enterprises, and the need to further boost investments to ensure fast growth. The desire to grow fast prompted heavy investments and "when the domestic savings were insufficient to finance heavy investment expenditures, savings from abroad had to be brought in" (Matic and Primorak, 1986:66–88). The oil crises of 1973 and 1979 increased consumption prices and industrial costs, exposing this irrational pursuit of fast growth. Moreover, Yugoslavia's expectation to repay its debt through its exports failed to materialize because of Western trade barriers, which slowed down the influx of Yugoslav products. The self-management system also had a serious inflationary effect, as it had little resistance against demands for wage increases by workers. Wage concessions (increases) inevitably led to drastic increases in market prices, resulting in the decline of purchase potential (Estrin, 1991:191). Although the Yugoslav administration designed a policy for accelerating productivity, its politicians and economists aimed neither at the creation of a free market economy nor at the consolidation of a strictly interventionist system. The Yugoslavs increasingly viewed market liberalization as a set of internal deals between enterprise directors and local government elites. Again, these procedures increased the power of regional governments at the expense of the centre, as it solidified the bargaining position of the former. The uneven development and polarization among the republics eventually created a framework of political behaviour in which the weaker regions allied with Belgrade for as much as the redistributionist policies were concerned, and with the wealthy north on issues of political rights and decentralization.

In 1982, the so-called Krajgher Commission released the "Long-Term Economic Stabilization Programme for Economic Stabilization", which formulated a revised strategy for the 1980s. Self-management would remain at the centre of the system, but substantial reorientation would occur (Serbia and Montenegro Economy Index). Coordinating and redistributing investment between industrial and agricultural sectors, diversifying energy resources, investing more in technical development and improving incentives for the private sector, recognized as the most efficient part of the national economy. Unemployment reached 16 per cent in 1982 and inflation peaked at 40 per cent in 1983. At the end of 1983 the Yugoslav debt reached 20,000 billion dollars and annual rates of growth were decreased from an average of 6 per cent (1966–74) to 1.5 per cent in 1982; Yugoslavia turned to the IMF for borrowing in return for further liberalization of the economy (Matic and Primorak, 1986).

The IMF insisted that funds would be transferred only if Yugoslavia entered a strict liberalization scheme known as "Shock Therapy" (1988–1989). Decisions over the implementation of IMF's requirements spawned a serious political breach in relations between the centralists and the republicans. The preceding economic decline had already laid the ground for a reactionary ethno-localism, and local politicians used it as a vehicle of increasing popular support for national self-determination and thus Yugoslavia's dissolution. In 1988, *The Economist* wrote:

> The country has Europe's highest inflation (zooming beyond 200 per cent), communism's highest unemployment (15 per cent and likely to rise), many angry workers (800 strikes in the first half of this year) and a foreign debt of about $ 1,000 for every Yugoslav. Since Tito's death in 1980, the country has muddled on with the disastrous constitution Tito left behind. Designed to prevent any bit getting too powerful for any other bit's comfort, it has created paralysis in politics and fragmentation in the economy. The other main force, which used to hold Yugoslavia together – fear of a Soviet invasion – has all but vanished since unmenacing Mr. Gorbachev took over the Kremlin. ("Yugo minus Slavia", *The Economist*, 15 October 1988)

The economic stabilization programme set by the IMF required strong central decision-making and coordination, inter-regional synchronization and strong political will in order to impose painful though necessary measures in all republics. Belgrade would have had to regain a total politico-economic control in order to secure Yugoslavia's survival. The IMF's main demands included a further opening to foreign investment, full foreign ownership rights, wage freezes, freeze of transfer payments to the republics, deregulation of the banking system, equality of public and private ownership, and greater flexibility for enterprise managers in the self-managed enterprises (Beams, 1999).

The Financial Operations Act required that:

> If an enterprise was insolvent for 30 days running, or for 30 days within a 45 day period, it had to settle with its creditors either by giving them ownership or by being liquidated, in which case workers would be sacked, normally without severance payments. In 1989, according to official sources, 248 firms were declared bankrupt or were liquidated and 89,400 workers were laid off. During the first nine months of 1990 directly following the adoption of the IMF programme, another 889 enterprises with a combined work force of 525,000 workers suffered the same fate. In other words, in less than two years the trigger mechanism (under the Financial Operations Act) had led to the lay off more than 600,000 workers out of a total industrial workforce of the order of 2.7 million. A further 20% of the work force, or half a million people, were not paid wages during the early months of 1990 as enterprises sought to avoid bankruptcy. The largest concentrations of bankrupt firms and lay-offs were in Serbia, Bosnia-Herzegovina, Macedonia and Kosovo. Real earnings were in a free fall, social programmes had collapsed creating within the population an atmosphere of social despair and hopelessness. This was a critical turning point in the Yugoslav tragedy. (Beams, 1999)

This process was initiated in 1988–1989, coordinated by the federal government under Prime Minister Branco Mikulic and later President Ante Markovic (both of them Bosnian Croats). In 1989, a bankruptcy law was enacted in order to liquidate failing social enterprises. Michael Karadjic argued that while "much of the western left continues to insist that imperialism broke up Yugoslavia, this only reflects continued illusions in bourgeois – not socialist – Yugoslavia. In reality, western powers continued to insist not only on the maintenance of Yugoslav unity to the bitter end, but in fact on the strengthening of the central apparatus" (Choddusovsky, 1997:375–383). Today we are in a position to understand that the Yugoslav government was forced to operate under IMF instructions in order to promote economic liberalization, while knowing that this process would fuel ethno-political turmoil (centralism vs. republicanism) given the economically incongruous forces in Yugoslavia. The IMF, fixated on a rather simplistic free market model, similarly imposed on Albania, Bosnia and Kosovo macro-economic reforms with devastating economic and social consequences (Choddusovsky, 1997).

In many other non-European states, similar IMF policies such as extensive borrowing, forced privatization, monetary devaluation, trade union and labour reduction, have intentionally led to increased inflation and a lowering of purchase power, and a fall in the standard of living. This usually aggravated the social tensions, impoverished and effectively eliminated the urban middle classes, and widened the gap between rich and poor. Examples of such consequences can be found in Somalia and Rwanda, two cases where ethnic conflict resurfaced due to shrinking resources, widening inequalities and increasing regional disparities. The IMF's involvement in Iraq – where the IMF, in exchange for giving a loan of $685 million to the Iraqi government, insisted that the Iraqis lift subsidies on the price of oil and open the economy to more private investment – shocked Iraqis, accustomed to and relying on hefty subsidies of gasoline, kerosene, cooking gas and other fuels (Rothschild, "IMF Occupies Iraq, Riots Follow", *The Progressive*, 3 January 2006). The IMF underestimated or wilfully ignored the difficulty of restructuring formerly centralized economies through strict and speedy market-economy liberalization, thereby unnecessarily contributing to social unrest and ethnic tension. Rothschild concludes that the IMF has failed, and is still failing, to balance the need for economic reform with political realities (ibid.).

Deprivation and Grievances in SYR Macedonia and Elsewhere in Yugoslavia

The economic liberalization scheme, which took place throughout the 1980s, dramatically worsened the existing disparities among Yugoslavia's regions. The increased emphasis placed on a free market, and the drastic reduction in public spending, severely weakened economy of SYR Macedonia. Ironically, the liberalization programme's monetary devaluation scheme and the rise of interest rates gave the final blow to SYR Macedonia's economy. Patrick Blum describes that "the imposed wage controls, resulting from reductions in public spending, had a different effect in Serbia where the average wage was roughly 150,000 Dinars, 200,000 Dinars in Slovenia, and 90,000 Dinars in Macedonia" (Blum, 1987). In the more prosperous and developed republic of Slovenia an effective devaluation of the Dinar was welcome, since it could help Slovenian industries to export, while for the less developed, poorer and more indebted regions devaluation made life much harder (ibid., 1987). The raise of interest rates posed a more serious danger to the enterprises in the less developed regions because of their lower efficiency and greater dependence on financial assistance. Measures to strengthen the market economy threatened the poorest regions, which already had the highest rates of unemployment with yet more job losses. The economic crisis was clearly exacerbating disparities between the regions, thereby fostering new political and social tensions, which could ultimately threaten the cohesion of the country (ibid.).

As far as the Albanians were concerned, it has been observed by Musliu and Ademi that poverty in SYR Macedonia affected all communities in different ways (Musliu and Ademi, 2002:1–2). On the one hand, at the end of the 1980s and early 1990s the closure of state industries in SYR Macedonia affected the Albanians less, as fewer of them were employed in those. On the other hand, the Albanian community had long been dependent on remittances sent back from those who had migrated to Germany in the 1960s and 1970s. Figures estimate that of the 150,000 citizens of SYR Macedonia registered in Germany, 120,000 were Albanians (ibid.). In the late 1970s and 1980s, their modest individual remittances funded many small and medium-sized enterprises (SMEs) in the local economy. This income benefited the whole community, and brought a degree of self-sufficiency independent of the state and its economy (ibid.).

Increasing unemployment brought many Slavs, whose fortunes were closely tied to failing state businesses, to resent the wealth of members of the ethnic Albanian minority, which became more entrepreneurial after being shut out of state jobs while receiving income from relatives abroad (Smith, 2001). From 1990 to the present, the unemployment rates have steadily increased, reaching socially unsustainable levels ("Document of The World Bank Report No. 13867-MK: Report Former Yugoslav Republic of Macedonia", 21 March 1995).[3] SYR Macedonia suffered a much higher unemployment rate compared to the Yugoslav average. In 1952, SYR Macedonia ranked top in unemployment; by 1965 and again in 1975 unemployment rates in SYR Macedonia, along with Kosovo, were the highest in Yugoslavia. Again, in 1989 the region demonstrated an even higher level of unemployment, reflecting the impact of economic liberalization. Although all republics suffered from an increase in unemployment, the poorest ones had reached alarming levels with almost one-third of their populations out of work.

The rates of unemployment were exacerbated by the numbers of people, mostly of Slav origin, who had previously been employed in state

3 The unemployment rate rose from 23 per cent in 1990 to 29 per cent in 1993 at the same time as various subsidies were cut and prices soared. Annual inflation averaged 407 per cent during 1990–1993. For more details see: Document of The World Bank, Report No. 13867 – MK, Report, Former Yugoslav Republic of Macedonia, 21 March 1995, Infrastructure Operations Division, Country Department I, Europe and Central Asia Region.

enterprises (SOEs). In 1988, at the meeting of the League of Communists of SYR Macedonia, it was maintained that unemployment was the biggest economic, social and political problem in the republic; over 70 per cent of the unemployed were young people under the age of thirty (LC of Macedonia Conference, 1988). The unemployment rate fell temporarily in 1990 to approximately 23.5 per cent (according to the World Bank), which meant approximately 156,000 unemployed, while the inflation rate reached a staggering 608.4 per cent (Micevska et al, 2002; Saveska et al, 2002).

Despite the absence of any data or indicators depicting and distinguishing the severity of unemployment according to each ethnicity, it was generally believed that rates of unemployment were highest among Albanians and lowest among Slovenes, because Slovenes were geographically concentrated in the industrially developed parts of Yugoslavia with the lowest overall rate of unemployment, while Albanians were concentrated mostly in Kosovo and SYR Macedonia, the least developed regions of Yugoslavia. The rising unemployment among the Albanians in SYR Macedonia was officially attributed to their higher fertility rates, which made local Slavs fear for the potential Albanization of areas within the republic (LC of Macedonia Conference, 1988).

By and large, Yugoslavia's economic "shock therapy" accelerated the radical macro-economic restructuring of the socialist economy and ironically empowered of reactionary forces. This process came to a halt in 1990, when George Bush senior stipulated free democratic elections as a precondition for continuing US financial aid to Yugoslavia. By that time, the democratic forces in Yugoslavia were synonymous with the non-communist nationalist formations, which had sprung up in all republics as a reaction to the centralization required for the macro-economic reforms. Local bureaucrats, enterprise directors, local party officials, and previously purged nationalists preferred explanations of ethnic dominance rather than economic mismanagement. Otherwise, they would have had to admit some responsibility for being complacent about a system that bred regional inequity and socio-economic fluidity. Rather conveniently for the local ethnonationalists, the centralization of decision-making automatically meant that the Serbs – who dominated the federal government structure – could be singled out as the culprit, the oppressor of "rightful" self-determination.

The Serb socialists were viewed as the guards and guarantors of Yugoslavia and the ones with the most centralist tendencies.

In this period, a significant conservative-nationalist backlash emerged among the Serbs and Montenegrins of Kosovo. SYR Macedonia effectively imported this anti-Albanian syndrome from Serbia. As tensions between Serbs and Albanians mounted in Kosovo, the government of SYR Macedonia rushed to take measures to forestall an Albanian insurgency in the country (Blumi, 2002). The increasing birth rates of Albanians in SYR Macedonia alarmed the authorities. Approximately 400,000 ethnic Albanians lived in SYR Macedonia amidst 1,341,420 Slav Macedonians, Turks, Vlachs, Serbs, Roma and others (Dempsey, 1998); with their higher birth rate, the proportion of Albanians in the republic was bound to increase. As a result of widespread reductions in public spending, many Albanians sustaining large families were deprived from state welfare benefits (which increased their economic grievances, and decreased the incentive to maintain small families). Notably, the Slav Macedonians perceived the high fertility rates among Albanians were as a deliberate nationalist expression, which threatened the state. The dominant Slav Macedonians, consumed by their own insecurities (i.e. fear of disintegration), passed in the early 1980s a series of laws curtailing Albanian rights. Borjan Tanevski asserted that decisions on education angered the Albanians in SYR Macedonia. Tanevksi pointed at the revision of a law on secondary school education in 1985, which stated that:

> Classes with Albanian as the language of instruction could only be created if over 30 Albanian pupils enroll for the class and decided to withdraw the right of the Albanians to be taught in their language at the Pedagogical Academy at Skopje University while in Pristina Albanians could freely attend University in Albanian. (Blumi, 2002)

According to another source, special legal measures banned the use of the Albanian language in all state institutions and social organizations ("Macedonia's Anti-Albanian Policies", *Drita*, 10 January 1988, Tirana). Albanians became convinced that their ethnicity was the sole target of the government. The rights of the Albanians in Kosovo were increasing – to the level of *de facto* independence – whereas the rights of the Albanians in SYR Macedonia were being curtailed.

In the period of economic depression, ethnic majorities throughout Yugoslavia took measures to limit the political access and resources of already marginalized ethnic minorities. The scarce resources and the rising fear of an imminent disintegration generated a backlash effect that ironically helped to destroy Yugoslavia. Centralization and the deterioration of living standards brought disillusionment with Yugoslavia and fostered an upsurge of ethno-nationalism. Consequently, Albanian nationalism intensified, and anti-Albanian attitudes and measures increased in response. Thus, the tensions throughout the 1980s in Kosovo encouraged the SYR Macedonian government to pass legislation targeted against a much-feared homegrown insurgency in order to minimize the prospects of potential disintegration. There is little doubt that Milosevic's tough policies against the Albanians echoed positively in the leadership of SYR Macedonia. Undoubtedly, Milosevic capitalized on the frustration felt by Serb and Montenegrin émigrés from Kosovo following the elevation of Kosovo's status and the subsequent taking over of Kosovo's public administration by Kosovar Albanians. Because of Kosovo's Albanian ascend, the Slav Macedonian authorities amended the republic's constitution to redefine the Socialist Yugoslav Republic of Macedonia as a nation-state of the "Macedonian people", replacing the previous formulation that defined it as a collective state of the "Macedonian people" and the Albanian and Turkish minorities. This fateful decision radicalized Albanian demands for equal rights, autonomy and even independence from the Slav Macedonians.

The government of SYR Macedonia revised the educational curriculum at schools, withdrawing any textbooks thought to contain nationalist references. It even enacted a law on "the personal use of names", prohibiting the use of names with a nationalist connotation. In 1988, the government suspended child support for the fourth child of a family ("Kosovo Albanian complains of names being Slavified", *Albanian Telegraph Agency*, 8 June 1985). This law, despite its seeming impartiality, was expected to curb the tendency among Albanians to sustain large families, as "the Albanian population was more than twice as likely as the Macedonian population to have more than three children" ("Albanian Denunciation of Neo-Malthusian policies in Yugoslavia", *ATA*, 28 January 1988). In a Kosovar Albanian newspaper of the time, a commentary suggested that:

> The natural growth of the Albanian population has assumed another meaning; it has been turned into a political problem. The great natality of the Albanians of Macedonia, Kosovo, and Yugoslavia in general, as compared with other nations is described by the top state forums and political and social organizations as the cause of the aggravated political situation in Kosovo, as a deed of Albanian nationalism that allegedly aims to create ethnically pure territories in Kosovo and Macedonia. ("Albanian Denunciation of 'Neo-Malthusian' Policies in Yugoslavia", *ATA*, 28 January 1988)

The government in Skopje also sought to punish, restrict or close Albanophone radios and newspapers for their nationalist content. The Albanian press claimed that:

> 3,000 Albanians were punished for taking part in weddings where Albanian songs were sung and Kosovo's newspaper *"Flaka e Vellazerimit"* accused the Republican Secretariat for People's Defence for taking measures against 34 Albanian officers who were discharged from the army for attending weddings at which Albanian songs were sung, which in Macedonia were considered nationalist. ("Macedonia's Anti-Albanian Policies", *Drita*, 10 January 1988, Tirana)

Finally, in 1989 the politico-economic anomaly in Yugoslavia was epitomized by Slobodan Milosevic's order to amend the Serbian Constitution as part of an anti-bureaucratic revolution. In March 1989, the police and army blocked Kosovo's Parliament and practically abolished the autonomy of the province. The security forces arrested Azem Villasi, the President of the League of Communists of Kosovo. Subsequently, with the help of many Kosovar Serbs, Slobodan Milosevic forcibly replaced the local governments in Vojvodina and Montenegro with pro-Milosevic leaders. With the ascendancy of Milosevic as President of the League of Communists of Serbia in February 1988, a wave of Albanian migration from Kosovo to SYR Macedonia followed, burdening the fragile inter-ethnic relations there.

In sum, the existence of oppressive socio-political structures, as described by Daniel Horowitz, and the political effects of economic recession, as described by Susan Woodward, corroborate the proposition that relative deprivation, as reflected in the oppressive and declining economic conditions of Yugoslavia, is a necessary condition for the emergence of ethnic conflict (Gurr, 1970; Horowitz, 2000; Woodward, 2003). Although frustration existed among the Albanians, there was no organized form of armed rebellion at any clearly defined point in the history of socialist Yugoslavia. The Yugoslav authorities fiercely repressed any attempts by any ethnicity or other (sub-)group to organize underground rebel movements at the grassroots level. Yugoslavia deprived the Albanians from their actual and perceived rights, while its authoritarian structures reduced the likelihood of an armed Albanian rebellion in SYR Macedonia or Kosovo.

Fundamentally, the Slav-dominated SYR Macedonia failed to integrate the local Albanians. The introduction of oppressive and marginalizing socio-political measures infuriated the Albanians. The Albanians of SYR Macedonia were deliberately excluded from the industrial labour force and the public administration. The marginalization of the Albanians was evident in the sphere of political participation, as well as in state administration and education. Yet the Albanians also proved resistant to integration due to their own cultural protectionism and social conservatism. SYR Macedonia's comparative economic disadvantage in Yugoslavia prompted the intensification of oppressive measures as a result of antagonisms over resource-scarcity. SYR Macedonia suffered from severe socio-economic retardation and dependency, and it was the poorest of all the republics. Therefore, the Albanians of SYR Macedonia constituted a comparatively unprivileged group located in the second poorest region of Yugoslavia. The scant resources intensified the internal economic competition along ethnic lines. Interestingly, developments in Kosovo after 1974 seem to corroborate Collier's greed and grievance theory. Despite the reduction of oppression in Kosovo, and the granting of extensive political rights, Kosovo Albanian nationalism intensified and demands increased. Nevertheless, Kosovo's economy faced similar structural problems with those of SYR Macedonia. Therefore, the elimination or amelioration of oppression cannot constitute an adequate explanation without regarding the influence of economic development. Furthermore, it is not a coincidence that inter-ethnic relations deteriorated in the 1980s, a period of serious economic decline for Yugoslavia. The recession had severely affected SYR Macedonia and gradually resulted in further social decay and restrictive measures. Given the evolution of Albanian nationalist activity, and observing the type of demands and the course of mobilization, we can safely assume that oppressive policymaking provided a solid basis for violent conflict. Cultural and educational rights for the Albanians were restricted, job-cuts increased, cultural associations were prohibited while wages fell and inflation rose. Many Albanians viewed this as a deliberate state policy against them.

Hence, we can safely conclude that restrictions create perceptions of deprivation and lead to confrontations between subordinated and dominant ethnicities. Therefore, the proposition that systematic socio-economic deprivation of minority groups within states accounts for violent conflict between majority and minority groups is valid only to the extent that deprivation forms the major source of frustration. The changing international environment and the gradual collapse of Yugoslavia were favourable conditions for the organization of internal rebellion. The following chapter will demonstrate how after the disintegration of Yugoslavia perceptions of relative deprivation among the Albanians in the new Former Yugoslav Republic (FYR) of Macedonia continued to exist and intensify, within a changing regional environment that allowed for the violent expression of deprivation-cum-frustration grievances.

The Final Collapse of Yugoslavia

In January 1990, the Slovenian and Croat delegations decided to withdraw from the 14th Congress of the League of Yugoslav Communists after a disagreement on Yugoslavia's constitutional reshaping. The Slovenian constitutional proposals were outvoted by the 4,000 delegates of the Communist League, despite an effort by the Slovenian delegation to convince the Congress to accept a limited set of constitutional amendments.

The Slovenian proposals failed to materialize due to the heavy influence exercised by the Serbian block on the voting procedure.

The first free elections took place in Croatia and Slovenia in May and April 1990. Shortly afterwards, President Franjo Tudjman changed the Croatian Constitution, provoking angry reactions from the local Serbian population of Kraijna, who declared a referendum on Serbian "sovereignty and autonomy" within Croatia. After the ratification of the new Croatian Constitution in December 1990, thousands of Serbs were forcibly removed from their jobs in the public service and the first signs of an imminent clash became visible within Croatia. In August 1990, the Serbs of Kraijna, which at the time numbered about 600,000 people, stepped up their protests under the guidance of Milan Babic, the mayor of the provincial capital Knin, with the help of the Yugoslav State Council.[4]

In May 1991, amidst violent incidents between Serbs and Croats, Croatia held a referendum on independence with a vote of approximately 94 per cent in favour. As tensions escalated, the US Secretary of State James Baker visited Belgrade to warn of the dangers of violent secession while suggesting that only peaceful and democratic means of dissociation were acceptable. Despite the international warnings, Milan Kucane, the Slovenian President and former head of the League of Communists of Slovenia, and Franjo Tudjman, the Croatian nationalist leader – and later Croatian President – declared independence from Yugoslavia, triggering a military response by the Yugoslav Army (JNA). As early as November 1990, the Slovenes transformed their Territorial Defence Unit into a republican military body so as to resist a potential assault by federal forces in the event of secession. The JNA entered Slovenia on 26 June 1991. Fighting between the JNA and the Slovenian militias lasted for ten days. However, the absence of sizable ethnic minorities in Slovenia and the more urgent situation in Croatia forced the JNA to withdraw after agreeing on a bilateral cease-fire with the Slovene leadership. Unlike the Serbo-Croatian war, which lasted until 1995, the Slovenian conflict was short and far less deadly. On 23 December 1991, before the completion of the European Community's

4 Borislav Jovic, a Serb, held the chairmanship of the Yugoslav State Council.

Badinter Commission's mission in Yugoslavia, Germany and Austria rushed to recognize the two breakaway republics in what was seen as an act of political solidarity, violating the earlier international and European consensus on preserving the unity of Yugoslavia.

On 15 January 1992, the European Union (formed as a successor to the European Economic Community (EEC) in February 1992) recognized Croatia and Slovenia as independent states.[5] Parallel to the developments in Croatia and Slovenia, Bosnia-Herzegovina was facing the possibility of secession with tremendous agony as to the consequences such an act of defiance would have for the Bosnian Muslims ("Bosniaks"), Croats and Serbs given the multi-ethnic makeup of the country. The three major ethnic groups of Bosnia-Herzegovina came under pressure for siding with either the secessionists, namely Croatia and Slovenia, or the Serbian unionists. Inter-ethnic relations polarized, and the fragile tri-ethnic governmental alliance collapsed. In October 1991 the Bosnian Serbs formed their own assembly as a reaction to the Croat-Muslim secessionist movement. In April 1992, the EU recognized Bosnia-Herzegovina as an independent state. The recognition of the country as an independent republic intensified the ethno-territorial insecurities and intensified the inter-ethnic strife among the Serbs, the Croats and the Bosnian Muslims.

The first free elections in the Yugoslav republics unleashed long-suppressed ethno-nationalist forces. Franjo Tudjman's nationalist party, the Croatian Democratic Union (*Hrvatska Demokratska Zajednica*, HDZ), topped the polls in Croatia with two-thirds of the vote (40.79 per cent); the smaller nationalist but strongly anti-communist alliance DEMOS won 54 per cent of the Slovenian vote. The votes in Bosnia were principally divided among the purely ethnocentric parties, the Party of Democratic Action (*Stranka Demokratske Akcije*, SDA; Bosniaks, 29.6 per cent), the Serbian Democratic Party (*Srpska Demokratska Stranka*, SDS; Serbian nationalists, 23.5 per cent) and the Croatian Democratic Union in Bosnia-Herzegovina

5 Government of the Republic of Slovenia: Public Relations and Media Office, Path to Slovene State, 2001. Available at: <http://www.ukom.gov.si/10years/path/>.

(*HDZ-Bosna i Hercegovina*, HDZ-BiH; Croat nationalists (14.4 per cent).[6] In Montenegro, following a premeditated coup by Slobodan Milosevic's local allies, the League of Communists transformed into the Democratic Party of Socialists of Montenegro (*Demokratska Partija Socijalista Crne Gore*, DPS) and gained almost 50 per cent of the vote.

SYR Macedonia swiftly jumped into the nationalist bandwagon. By 1990, economic conditions touched rock bottom; federal subsidies froze, failed state enterprises multiplied, unemployment rose, and insecurity peaked. The secessionist course of Slovenia and Croatia added to the perception that socialist Yugoslavia was nearing its end. The collapse of Soviet communism in 1989–90 also meant that the West no longer needed a Yugoslav buffer state, which in turn implied to the Slav Macedonians that the time had come to settle old scores with the Greeks and Bulgarians. Finally, years of systematic efforts to curtail Albanian rights aggravated fears for an Albanian backlash. Nationalism, a notion so hypocritically despised by the Yugoslav communists, justified the implementation of measures that were thought to protect the socialist state from "reactionary" ethno-nationalism.

In November 1990, the citizens of SYR Macedonia voted for a new parliament in the first free multiparty elections. The ultra-nationalist party VMRO-DPMNE (*Vnatrešno-Makedonska Revolucionerna Organizacija Demoktratska Partija za Makedonsko Nacionalno*: Internal Macedonian Revolutionary Organization-Democratic Party for Macedonian National Unity) ranked first, with thirty-eight seats and 31.7 per cent of the vote. The reformed communists of the Social Democratic Alliance of Macedonia (*Socijaldemokratski sojuz na Makedonija*, SDSM or SDAM) received thirty-one seats and 25.8 per cent of the vote; the Liberal Democrats gained 18 per cent. Finally, the only Albanian party, the PDP, received a total of twenty-three seats, scoring 23.3 per cent of the vote (almost equivalent to

6 Parties and Elections in Europe, Croatia, 1990–2003, available at: <http://www.parties-and-elections.de/croatia2.html>; Parties and Elections in Europe, Slovenia, 1990 –2004, available at: <http://www.parties-and-elections.de/slovenia2.html>; Parties and Elections in Europe, 1990–2002, available at: <http://www.parties-and-elections.de/montenegro2.html>.

the official percentage of the Albanians in Macedonia at the time). The overtly ultra-nationalist VMRO-DPNME absorbed many of the fears and insecurities of the Slav Macedonian electorate. VMRO-DPMNE entered the political stage in the early 1990s as an anti-communist right-wing party with an explicitly irredentist agenda. Under the leadership of Lujbco Georgievski, a young poet and self-confessed Bulgarophile, the party helped Slav Macedonians to break away from the pretentiously anti-nationalist taboos created by the socialist regime. In an effort to establish a connection with Slavic Macedonia's nationalist past, the party's coat of arms portrayed a crowned lion (identical to Bulgaria's national symbol) with the inscription: "1893–1990", a clear symbol of the legacy with which VMRO identified.

Although the party succeeded in winning the elections, it was nevertheless unable to form a majority government, largely because it opted not to cooperate with the Albanian Party for Democratic Prosperity (*Partia e Prosperiteti Demokratike*, PDP). As a result, a coalition government emerged consisting of the reformed socialists of SDSM, the Liberal Party, the Socialist Party and the PDP. The PDP was at the time the sole Albanian political force contesting for the elections, and inevitably attracted a multifarious membership ranging from moderates to radicals opting for secession. Based in Tetovo, and under the leadership of Nevzat Halili, who was arrested in September 1991 for refusing to give information to the census commission, the party attracted almost the entire registered Albanian vote (23.3 per cent), and with twenty-three parliamentary delegates the party became a significant political force in the Socialist Yugoslav Republic (SYR) of Macedonia.

On 25 January 1991, the Assembly of SYR Macedonia set the preconditions for the right to "self-determination and secession" in the Declaration of Sovereignty. Two days later Kiro Gligorov, a leading (former) communist figure, ascended to the Presidency of the republic. Gligorov's major aim was to "secure a parliamentary democracy and a new constitution" (Daskalovski, 2004:55). At the same time Gligorov, recognizing the threat posed by Yugoslavia's disintegration, took the initiative – together with Bosnian Muslim leader Alia Izetbegovic – to mediate for a reconciliatory solution. Gligorov proposed the re-establishment of a loose Yugoslav Federation with a common army, currency and foreign policy. But as tensions mounted in Slovenia in the summer of 1991, support for the initiative faded and efforts focused back to preserving the territorial and political integrity of Yugoslav Macedonia. On 8 September 1991, SYR Macedonia held a referendum with a voter turnout of 72.16 per cent, resulting in a 95 per cent (96.44 per cent) support for "a sovereign and independent state of Macedonia, with the right to participate in a future union of Yugoslav states", and the parliament ratified the results of the referendum on 17 September 1991.[7] In November 1991 the *Sobranie* (FYR Macedonian Parliament) officially declared its disassociation from rump Yugoslavia, and announced the new Constitution of the "Republic Of Macedonia".

In the same month, the last chapter of FYR Macedonia's Yugoslav history ended with the withdrawal of the Yugoslav Army. The JNA literally dismantled the entire military infrastructure, and even confiscated the arms assigned to the Territorial Defence Unit, virtually adopting a scorched earth policy.[8] Border posts were abandoned by defecting JNA soldiers; the Serbs took down the military hospital. Although the JNA withdrawal occurred under an agreement with Gligorov, it took all of the army equipment stored in FYR Macedonia. The JNA withdrawal from FYR Macedonia was done with the strategic purpose of transferring more troops and equipment to areas outside Serbia proper, where the Serbs were more numerous. Consequently, the newly independent state of FYR Macedonia was left without an effective military force to protect the country from internal rebellion or external aggression.

7 On the name dispute in the former Yugoslav Republic of Macedonia after the signing of the interim Accord, see Aristotle Tziampiris (2001), *European Political Cooperation and the Macedonian Question*, Ashgate, p. 226.

8 John Philips (2003), *Macedonia: Warlords and Rebels in the Balkans*, Yale University Press, p. 51.

CHAPTER 3

Relative Deprivation

Socio-political oppression and economic decline produced a shared feeling of deprivation among the Albanians in socialist Yugoslavia, which ultimately caused intense frustration with the political system. The existence of real or perceived deprivation may indeed constitute a rational basis for the emergence of conflict; however, the levels of real or perceived deprivation have not created the conditions for the outbreak of organized armed forms of confrontation, other than recurrent public riots and protests. In other words, relative deprivation may constitute a primal source of conflict but does not necessarily produce organized forms of domestic warfare. Hence, this chapter examines the degree of relative deprivation in combination with those strategic factors thought to affect the eruption of violence.

The analysis establishes a correlation between deprivation and violence in the Former Yugoslav Republic (FYR) of Macedonia, based on the measuring of indices of political oppression and fluctuating levels of reported violence. Following this, we will examine in Chapter 5 the influence of three preconditions, which we believe facilitate the decision of deprived groups to use organized forms of violence: (a) state strength and denial of external state legitimacy, (b) rebel resources and (c) regional conflict spillover. We argue that relative deprivation does adequately explain violent conflict, when enabled by such preconditions. The combination of relative deprivation and strategic preconditions is the most appropriate and convincing explanation for the appearance and increase of violent intra-state conflict.

The Constitution of FYR Macedonia

The 1991 Constitution established a clear link between the new state of FYR Macedonia and the Slavic Macedonian nation in an attempt to solidify the link between the state and the Slavic Macedonian ethnic group. The new national constitution overtly proclaimed that "Macedonia is established as a national state for the Macedonian people, in which full equality as citizens and permanent coexistence with the Macedonian people is provided for Albanians, Turks, Vlachs, Roma and other nationalities living in the Republic of Macedonia."[1] The Constitution established a national state for the Slavic Macedonian people, one in which the Albanian people were perceived as a nationality with equal rights, rather than a constituent nation. The Albanians claimed that equal rights guaranteed by the republic's new constitution were only rhetorical, and that it should have stated that the new republic is a state for all Macedonian citizens irrespective of ethnic origin. In short, Albanians believed that the designated constitutional status of the Albanians in FYR Macedonia paved the way for more discrimination against them.

By contrast, most Albanians wished to see a constitutional amendment that would elevate their political status into a constituent nation rather than a host-nationality provided with equal rights by the "state-owning" Slavic Macedonian people. From a Slavic Macedonian perspective, a separate Macedonian ethnic group, with a unique and non-negotiable identity, was entitled to its own nation-state, home of the ethnic Macedonians that is non-Greek, non-Bulgarian, non-Serb, and naturally non-Albanian. By regarding other ethnicities as non-Macedonian or less-Macedonian, the Slavic Macedonian political elite recycled the ideas of Yugoslav nation-building in the most parochial and unrealistic manner.

1 See the 1991 Constitution with its amendments (PE Official Gazette of the Republic of Macedonia, Constitution of the Republic of Macedonia: With the amendments to the Constitution I–XXX, Skopje 2006).

The Slavic Macedonian constitutionalist logic derived from the classical notion that "membership in a state is viewed as the natural consequence of membership in a nation" (Roudometof, 1996:253–301). The *de facto* existence of Macedonians as an ethnically separate entity provided the Slav Macedonians with the justification to claim prime ownership of the state. The Constitution clearly stipulated that ethnic Macedonians of Slavic origin are entitled to their own national state, while the Albanians, who are not regarded as Macedonians by origin, would coexist together with the Slavic Macedonian people in a state belonging to the latter. Yet the very presence of so many Albanians disturbed this mono-dimensional formula of nation-state building. In reality, very few Albanians in FYR Macedonia pretend they are Macedonian, given that the term "Macedonian" is used by the Slavic majority to describe a Slav-speaking Christian inhabitant, rather than the entire national collective.[2] Most Albanians accept the term Macedonia as a designation of a territorial entity, one in which multiple ethnic groups reside. By contrast, Macedonian Slavs regard FYR Macedonia to be the national state to which they are entitled. What is at stake therefore is the very distinctiveness of the Macedonians as separate people. This in turn is closely associated with their claim of forming a separate Macedonian nation, for if there is no single and unified Macedonian nation, how can there be a Macedonian nation-state? (Engstrom, 2002:15). As a result of this perceived constitutional injustice, the Albanians in FYR Macedonia adopted a dual strategy of subversion and protest. The spearhead of their campaign was the conduct of a national census that would reflect the large numbers of Albanians in FYR Macedonia, and would therefore justify the elevation of the Albanian's status to a constituent nation in an amended Constitution.

Ethnic headcount is a usual practice employed by ethnic groups in an effort to gain a more privileged position within a given state: "censuses are not neutral events in divided societies. They are generally hot-button issues because they establish rough parameters for the division of state resources and power" (Carter, Ackermann and Janev, 2000:11). This ethnic

2 A small minority of Slav-speaking Macedonian Muslims also exists.

headcount can be achieved in two different ways: through ethnocentric voting, or through the conduct of a national census. The rationale behind the ethnic headcount is simple: the more populous an ethnic group is, the more recognized, powerful or privileged it becomes. Large ethnic groups enjoy larger legitimacy and governments cannot easily dismiss their grievances. In the Balkan states, being a small minority usually means having fewer rights. Therefore, having a strong population basis is a prerequisite to be respected by those in power, and be granted equal status and equal rights.

Moreover, the census affects the degree of an ethnicity's proportional representation in public services, institutions and the state administration. The Albanians have always been a large minority in Yugoslav Macedonia, and later in FYR Macedonia. The first census in FYR Macedonia was conducted in 1991, but the two Albanian parties, the Party for Democratic Prosperity (PDP) and the smaller National Democratic Party (in Slavo-Macedonian: *Narodna Demokratska Partija*, NDP), called for a pan-Albanian boycott. Under these conditions, the 1991 census gave an estimation of the Albanian population at around 21.7 per cent (441,987 people) of the total population of 2,033,964 people (Gaber and Joveska, 2004). According to the census, a quarter of the country's total population were ethnic Albanians. Albanians were unsatisfied and pressured for a renewed census. Disputed estimates about the size of minorities, forced the government to accept EU assistance and supervision for the conduct of a new census in 1994.

The new census revealed a slight increase of 1.2 per cent, raising the estimated number of Albanians to 22.9 per cent (442,914 people). Once again, Albanian politicians were frustrated about the authorities counting only those Albanians with FYR Macedonian citizenship, and claiming that they constituted at least 30 per cent of the total population (Human Rights Helsinki Watch (HRHW), 1996:7). The Slav Macedonians disputed this number. Be this as it may, the Albanians argued that the 1992 Citizenship Law Act excluded those Albanians who had entered FYR Macedonia from other Yugoslav regions before the dissolution of the federation. The Citizenship Law only permitted citizenship based on origin, birth on the territory of FYR Macedonia, naturalization or by international agreements. The law required that a person who applied for citizenship must have resided continuously, for at least fifteen years, on the territory of Macedonia, have living facilities and a permanent source of funds, and speak the Slavic Macedonian language. The law intentionally ignored the fact that many people from other parts of former Yugoslavia lived in FYR Macedonia, who do not necessarily speak Macedonian or have a Macedonian origin ("A threat to stability? Human Rights violations in Macedonia", ICG, 1996). Worse still, the new law denied these people the rights they previously enjoyed. The law was finally amended in 2004, reducing the years of residence to eight, requiring the applicant to be proficient in the Slavic Macedonian language, and easing naturalization so that spouses of Macedonian citizens would be granted citizenship (Law for Amending and Supplementing the Law on Citizenship, 2004, FYROM, Legislation Online). The 1994 census, however, failed to resolve the issue of ethnicity numbers. The Slav Macedonians above all feared the fast-growing birth rate of the Albanians, which was gradually changing the demographic balance in parts of the country. In combination with other factors, such as migration and internal relocation, several areas within the country have become ethnically homogeneous.

Deprivation in Education and Language

The limited provisions for third level education in the Albanian language, and the limited use of the Albanian language in public institutions and parliament were major sources of Albanian discontent. For many years, the Albanian University of Pristina served as an educational centre for the Albanians of Yugoslav Macedonia. However, after SYR Macedonia's secession from the Yugoslav Federation, the Albanians were no longer provided with access to third level education in the Albanian language ("A threat to stability, Human Rights violations in Macedonia", Human Rights Helsinki Watch (HRHW), June 1996).

Although the constitution of FYR Macedonia provided primary and secondary education in the Albanian language, third level education was carried out exclusively in the Slavic Macedonian language (Engstrom, 2002:3–17). Of the 27,000 students enrolled in higher education in 1991, only 1.5 per cent were Albanian (ibid.:16). Albanian accusations of discrimination in registering with schools were frequent. According to the Ministry of Interior, only 30.75 per cent of the Albanian pupils who completed their eight years of elementary education in 1994 went on to an Albanian secondary school. The percentage rose to 40.12 per cent in 1995. The government rejected claims that the low rates of Albanian attendance in high schools are due to deliberate discrimination. Instead, government spokespersons argued that ethnic Albanians were consciously choosing not to continue their education on the secondary level (ibid.).

Today, the Slav Macedonian Ministry of Education suggests that the low rate of school attendance and the high rate of dropouts among the Albanians are not an issue of deliberate under-representation but a matter of choice. As far as the Slav Macedonians are concerned, there is no real need for education figures to correspond proportionally to the population numbers of the different ethnicities, Albanians included, especially given the conservative views rural Albanians hold against women pursuing higher education. Many believe that the Albanians are involved in business or rural activities, in Macedonia or abroad, and derive fewer financial benefits from a university degree ("A threat to stability, Human Rights violations in Macedonia", HRHW, June 1996). The Helsinki Human Rights Report asserted that the Albanians' lower educational performance is in part a reflection of their demographics and socioeconomic status (ibid.).

The Albanians in Macedonia are in fact more rural and traditional, and do place less emphasis on obtaining higher education (ibid.:20). However, many Albanians do face serious difficulties with the Slavic Macedonian language: it was the only official language in third level education until 2001, and Albanian students coming from segregated Albanophone schools could hardly ever pass the university exams. The Albanians argued that they would be more interested in obtaining higher education if they could study in their mother tongue at an institution that did not discriminate against them (ibid.:23). After the inauguration of the two Albanophone universities in Tetovo and Gostivar, many hundreds of Albanians did continue with higher education. Therefore, the elaborate system of exclusion and lack of opportunity rather than a voluntary Albanian abstention from third level education explain the disparity in the educational development of the two communities.

According to Helsinki Watch's human rights reports, "in 1996 Albanians comprised only 12.4 per cent of all high school students in FYR Macedonia, and 6.5 per cent of university students … these numbers were marked by an increase since 1992" (ibid.:9). The report acknowledged that the increase in numbers was due to efforts by the FYR Macedonian government to expand instruction for Albanian teachers, introduce a 10 per cent quota for minority groups, and open up new elementary and secondary schools. However, "Albanians believe changes were slow and inadequate" (ibid.:23). Their limited access to higher education inhibited their socio-economic development in FYR Macedonia. Hence, due to the language and education barriers, the Albanians had considerably fewer opportunities to occupy the higher-ranked state professions.

In 1994, the Party for Democratic Prosperity of Albanians (*Partia për Prosperitet Demokratik të Shqiptarëve*, PPDSh or PDPA) actively supported the newly founded "Albanian Free University of Tetovo". The central state authorities refused to grant the university legal status, because it saw it as an academic hub for "Greater Albania" enthusiasts, and a vehicle for Kosovo Albanian extremists to interfere in the internal affairs of the Republic of Macedonia (Chiclet Christopher, "Victim of a new Balkan crisis? Macedonia risks falling apart", *Le Monde Diplomatique*, 1999). Moreover, the Slav authorities regarded the creation of a separate Albanian university as a move towards segregation and not as a solution to the educational grievances of the Albanians. In 1995, at the inauguration of the unrecognized Albanian university in Tetovo, Rector Fadil Sulejmani and Miljaim Fejziu, president of the university's senate, were arrested by the police and given a one-year sentence for incitement of hatred after demonstrations in 1995 (HRHW, Human Rights Developments in Macedonia Report, 1998). The Albanian representatives raised their concerns over the educational situation of Albanians in FYR Macedonia to Max Van Der Stoel, High Representative for Human Rights and Minorities from the Organization for Security and Cooperation in Europe (OSCE). They complained that since the Serbian authorities closed the University of Pristina in Kosovo, the Albanians in FYR Macedonia were left with virtually no opportunity to study. In protest, deputies from the PDPA party began to boycott parliamentary sessions until March 1995. On 4 July 1996, more than 10,000 ethnic Albanians rallied in Tetovo against the jailing of Fadil Sulejmani. The demonstrators demanded the university's recognition and its integration into the Macedonian education system (Chihlect, 1999). B.J.,[3] a Skopje-based journalist, believes that the lack of higher education lies at the roots of the Albanian's socio-economic backwardness and higher fertility rates, and suggests that:

> One argument is that Albanians should be able to do their education; they should be included in the administration, not because they are Albanians, but because that is a way to integrate them in the system. If we integrate them into the system, we will share the same destiny, and we will have a decline of fertility rates … This natality of the Albanians is because of their slower social development, they live in the mountains and they are less motivated … the Albanians don't have the opportunity to visit a doctor, or receive information on contraception. Another argument is that they should have a good education because today the Albanians who are educated are well-situated and they have no more than one or two children, like all Macedonians. If we keep them out of the educational system, what could we expect? (Interview with the author, 15 December 2006, Skopje)

The eventual legalization of the State Tetovo University in 2004 and the opening of the multilingual South-Eastern European University or "Max Van Der Stoel University"[4] have helped to overcome the educational deadlock. Yet the University of Tetovo lacks the resources and infrastructure, and since its recognition its educational quality and standards have been fiercely criticized. Generally, the Tetovo University affair has come to symbolize the Albanian struggle for the free and official use of the Albanian language, not only in higher education but also in the parliament as well

3 Names of selected interview participants are encrypted and remain confidential.
4 Named after the OSCE High Representative of Minorities Max Van Der Stoel.

as in the local constituencies in which Albanians have a strong presence or are in the majority (Myhrvold, 2005).

The Constitution provides for Albanian to be used as a working language in local municipalities with substantial Albanian populations, but Albanians were allowed only to use Slavic in parliament. The events in Tetovo indicate that radicalism was growing among the Albanians, as the Party for Democratic Prosperity of Albanians grasped this opportunity to mobilize its supporters and expose the PDP's passivity in government. Consequently, the Slavic Macedonian community viewed all these equal-language-and-education demands with suspicion. Even if ethnic Albanians wish to create a genuinely bilingual society, the Macedonian Slavs are adamantly opposed to learning Albanian (a minority language), fearful that a multitude of Albanian-language institutions will create the kind of parallel society that emerged in Kosovo during the 1990s (USAID Macedonia Report, 2000:13–14).

Decentralization and Self-Government

The issue of local self-government system has been another source of frustration and dispute for the Albanians. For the Albanians, an increase in local self-government reflects their right to regulate their affairs in their own ways, free from the political intervention of central authority. The empowerment of local self-administration, although compatible with the European subsidiarity principle, has raised reservations among the Slav Macedonians, especially among those who reside in ethnically mixed areas. The Albanians persistently favoured local self-governance with more powers on financing, healthcare and education, but the Slav Macedonians practised the exact opposite by recentralizing the state. The Slav Macedonians were afraid that reforming the municipal system would eventually encourage Albanian secessionism. Ackerman et al argue that there "does not appear to be a single case of decentralization in a multi-ethnic environment leading to independence. Largely, decentralization appears to satisfy minority demands for self-governance. Waiting too long to offer it can, by contrast, have negative consequences for stability" (USAID Macedonia Report, 2000:13–14).

However, Ackerman et al ignore the fact that nation-based decentralization (1974 Yugoslav Constitution) helped to solidify 'Croatian' and Albanian nationalism in the Socialist Federal Republic of Yugoslavia (SFRY) and weaken the integrity of Yugoslavia as a whole. Moreover, most secessionist movements come from areas that already enjoy a degree of decentralization and rights, which by itself works towards secession or disassociation with the state. The Former Yugoslav Republic (FYR) of Macedonia inherited from its predecessor thirty-four municipalities. Local government was divided between two levels: local units of the Ministries, and local self-government bodies. Deconcentration of power is achieved through the local ministerial branches, while decentralization of power is achieved through the local self-government structures. Municipalities in FYR Macedonia are first-order administrative divisions and constitute the sole level of local self-government. Therefore, strengthening local municipalities is the only existing way to transfer decision-making powers from the centre to the periphery. The self-government question has evolved around two major issues; increasing local decision-making powers and redrawing municipal boundaries. The one-tier decentralized municipal system in FYR Macedonia was extremely weak and provided no real competencies to any municipalities. During the 1990s, Slav Macedonians reduced the competencies of municipalities in an attempt to minimize the threat of disintegration of the new state during the Yugoslav wars of secession. In their view, the more centralized the state, the more control it could exert over its minorities and local affairs.

An argument could be made that in a small country with an accommodating central political elite, tensions may be better managed by a centralized system. Decentralization may embolden mid-level political elites in the municipalities to use ethnic rhetoric and issue radical demands in order to mobilize local popular support. Be this as it may, many of the new municipalities are so small that they are likely to remain dependent on the central government, no matter how much fiscal decentralization is achieved

(USAID Macedonia Report, 2000:13–14). More importantly, with the preservation of a highly centralized system, the central state authorities could maintain control over developments on the local level. This policy deprived the local bodies from their ability to make decisions that could go against the perceived national interest in sensitive fields such as education, culture and security. The anti-decentralization position held among the majority of the Slavs could be summarized as follows:

> After the disintegration of the Yugoslav federation, the Republic of Macedonia enacted the reduction of responsibilities of the municipal authorities and centralized the system to counter internal and external threats and separatist tendencies. A centralized coordination and decision making was much more needed in order to guarantee the survival of the state and its non-infiltration by disloyal elements or the taking up of unfriendly and threatening initiatives by local administrations. (Todorovski, 1999:106)

Hence, the country's state authorities, through their local ministerial branches, virtually dictated all spheres of local interest. Local administrations held few and minor competencies on issues not affecting the social, cultural and economic development of the communities. While the Slav Macedonians passively accepted this state of affairs, the Albanians saw this arrangement as another attempt to infringe their socio-economic and cultural development. A purely organizational affair like local self-government was transformed into an inter-ethnic issue of state domination versus minority emancipation. Admittedly, early calls for autonomy in the north-west of the country, where many Albanians lived, did not help to reassure the country's Slavs over the real nature of the self-government demand, which they increasingly viewed as a "Trojan Horse" i.e. a sure yet stealthy step towards Albanian secession.

The 1996 Law on Territorial Division reduced the territorial and population size of municipalities in order to decrease bureaucracy and create rural municipalities so as to preserve their budgets for rural projects instead of diverting them to urban needs (*Macedonian Official Gazette*, Skopje, 49/1996). The number of municipalities increased from thirty-four to 123 and eventually 129, including the six municipal units comprising the capital city of Skopje. The rationale of the re-arrangement was to grant the municipal bodies flexibility and enhance their problem solving capabilities by focusing on local-specific issues.

The 1995 Law on Local Self-Government brought significant changes in the structures and decision-making process of local bodies. Thus, twenty-five-member local councils replaced the multi-member municipal bodies, and proportional voting was introduced as a means to increase ethnic participation. The law also recognized "the right to use in public administration both a minority language and Macedonian when the population in a given municipality is over 50% minority" (Todorovski, 1999:50). Given the economic disparities among municipalities, the new law provided the Ministry of Finance with financial control over the municipal projects, establishing a monitoring mechanism over local initiatives.

Furthermore, sensitive areas such as security and policing remained exclusive prerogatives of the state. Despite the proclaimed modernization of the local self-government system, the increase in the number of municipalities from thirty-four to 124 generated angry reactions from Albanians. Throughout the 1990s, the Albanians accused the Slav Macedonians of redrawing municipal borders to their electoral advantage in local elections. With the new law, out of the 129 municipalities, approximately twenty-six would fall under Albanian mayorship. The fact that some of the resulting municipalities became very small, with perhaps as few as 1,600 persons living in them, raised concerns (USAID Macedonia Report, 2000:13–14), while urban municipalities with majority Slav populations had become even larger, with several thousands of people or more. Hence, it appeared to many Albanians that:

> The boundaries were created to line up with ethnic divisions, so that a small Macedonian enclave in the middle of a much larger Albanian population might end up as a new municipality, in order to give its people some sense of control over their own destiny. Of course, political explanations also underpin the choice of 124 units. (USAID Macedonia Report, 2000:15)

Albanian parties participated in all parliaments, but their numbers were generally lower than their population shares, due to gerrymandering and the unequal distribution of single-member constituencies. Thus in 1996, thirty-five of the 120 parliamentary members were chosen based on proportionality, while the other eighty-five members were elected in single-member districts. Some ethnic Albanians complained that the Albanian-majority districts had more voters than districts with predominantly ethnic Macedonian populations, thus violating the one-person-one-vote principle (US Department of State, Country Report on Human Rights, 26 February 1998). Even before the passing of the 1996 Law on Territorial Division, Etim Aziri claimed that "We have cases where 15,000–16,000 people have voted for an ethnic Albanian deputy, while 3,000–4,000 people voted for one ethnic Macedonian deputy. This is unprecedented. As you can see, the vote of three Albanians is equal to the vote of one Macedonian" (USAID Macedonia Report, 2000:18). The PDPA head Arben Xhaferi compared the voting districts in Bitola and Tetovo: "Bitola, with an 85 per cent ethnic Macedonian population has 96,000 registered voters, while Tetovo with an 85 per cent Albanians has 136,000 registered voters. Both cities elect 9 deputies to the national parliament. He also said that the western city of Debar elects one deputy even though they were 16,000 registered voters, 90 per cent of whom are ethnic Albanians" (ibid.:18).

Therefore, districts with small numbers of Slav Macedonians elected the same number of deputies as districts having larger numbers of Albanian voters. According to Arben Xhaferi, "the ways in which the Slav Macedonian power structure misuses the forms of democracy to subjugate the Albanian population, which it tragically misconstrues as a dangerous competitor, can correctly be termed ethnic engineering" (ibid.:18). Normative and civic arguments against the local self-administration reforms failed to convince the Slav Macedonian ruling parties to restructure the reforms towards a truly self-governing system. The underlying fear of disintegration ruled out any option other than preserving and strengthening a centralized system. Although local competencies existed on paper, the state, through the ministries of Finance and Interior, controlled the content, direction and implementation of local projects.

Hence, the Albanians expressed their disapproval of the centralized system by refusing to pay income taxes. Sam Vaknin, an economic and political analyst who has worked for the FYR Macedonian Ministry of Finance, observed that "tax evasion among Albanians is much higher than among Macedonians. Albanians contribute much less than their share in the population to tax intake. Tax inspectors are reluctant to enter Albanian villages for audit, collection, *or* enforcement work" (Deliso, "How to take a government down", *Antiwar*, 26 August 2002). Thus the "tax receipts from the western part of Macedonia, – are now virtually non-existent –, and they were never sizable" (Vaknin, "Surviving the Uprising, A conversation with the Macedonian Finance Minister", *Central European Review*, 2002). According to Albanians, they have little incentive to pay taxes to a government that ignores their needs and fails to redistribute a fair share of the wealth to Albanian regions. However, according to the Slav Macedonians, this is because the Albanians do not wish to pay taxes for a state they feel they do not belong to. In addition, Albanians have constructed a parallel economic system (grey economy) that is largely disengaged from the state.

Tensions escalated in 1996 when the PDPA, after winning the two large municipalities of Tetovo and Gostivar in the municipal elections, immediately demanded financial autonomy for the two towns (Chiclet, 1999). In July 1997 the PDPA swallowed up the smaller radical National Democratic Party (NDP), resulting in the creation of the Democratic Party of Albanians (Democratic Party of Albanians – *Partia Demokratike Shqiptare*, PDSh or DPA), led by Arben Xhaferi and Bedredin Ibrahimi. By 1997, the Albanian political scene was simplified: the PDP represented the moderate faction, while the DPA had clearly taken up the role of the radical. In July 1997, the mayors of Gostivar and Tetovo established the practice of hoisting the Albanian flag next to the flag of FYR Macedonia in front of their town halls (Report of the High Commissioner on national minorities to the chairman in office of the OSCE of the OSCE Mission in FYROM, 1997).[5]

5 The Democratic Party of Albanians or DPA is a political party of the ethnic Albanians in the Republic of Macedonia. The DPA results from the merger of the Party for Democratic Prosperity of Albanians (PDPA) and the People's Democratic Party (NDP), which took place in June 1997.

The new party Democratic Party of Albanians called for the Constitution to be changed to create a federation, a "State of the Macedonian and Albanian peoples" (Chiclet, 1999). The parliament swiftly amended laws concerning ethnic flags, allowing these only to be raised alongside the official state flag on national holidays. On 9 July 1997, the police forcefully removed the flags in front of the town halls of Tetovo and Gostivar and shot two Albanians during clashes with demonstrators, provoking a wave of protests. The Albanian mayor of Gostivar, Rufi Osmani, was subsequently charged with inciting ethnic hatred, organizing anti-state activities, and refusing to implement a court order. He was sentenced to thirteen years and eight months imprisonment, which the Appeal Court later halved. The sociologist and mayor of Tetovo, Alajdin Demiri, received two and a half years in prison. Two months later, the DPA's nine mayors, eight MPs and 240 town councillors resigned, hoping to provoke early legislative elections (ibid.). In this way, the DPA successfully stirred up Albanian passions against the judicial amendments that only allowed the display of ethnic symbols on national holidays. Hence the Albanians viewed the police operation as an assault against their symbols. As a result, many Albanians became convinced of the need to replace PDP's cautious policies with DPA's decisive actions.

Discrimination and Unemployment

The inequitable representation of Albanians in the public services has been a source of constant frustration. According to the 1994 census, Albanians make up 22.7 per cent of the population but by 2000, they accounted for only 10.2 per cent of the overall state administration ("The Other Macedonian Conflict", German Foreign Ministry, 2002:5). In 1993, Albanians made up approximately 3 per cent of the overall state administration. Most Albanians believed they were marginalized deliberately by the state. Discriminatory practices and poor education prevented Albanians from holding key positions in the state. This resulted in the proportional under-representation of Albanians in all public and security services.

Today, the two major communities agree that the Albanians were grossly under-represented in the public sector ("A Threat to Stability? Human Rights Violations in Macedonia", Human Rights Watch Helsinki, 1996:17). H.I., a journalist working for Skopje-based daily newspaper *Dnevnik*, commented that "by 2001, in some institutions, representation of ethnic Albanians was no more than 2 per cent" (interview with the author, 12 December 2006, Skopje). Albanians were denied access, in particular, to the most critical areas of security. Before 2003, the percentage of Albanians employed in the Ministry of Interior, for instance, was less than 6 per cent (Matveeva, 2003:9).[6] In the Ministry of Defence, Albanians made up 2.9 per cent of the total personnel, even though they constituted between 16 per cent and 26 per cent of army recruits ("The Other Macedonian Conflict", German Foreign Ministry, 2002:5). Finally, only 5 per cent of Albanians worked for the police. Prior to 2001, in the predominantly Albanian cities of Tetovo and Gostivar, Albanians constituted only 17 per cent and 12 per cent of police respectively (ibid.:5).

Slav Macedonians emphasized the Albanians' poor education and the language barrier. They attributed under-representation to the Albanian's lagging socio-economic development; a result of conservative perceptions on women and work, high rates of school dropouts and unwillingness to blend into the mainstream social domain. Despite these perceived hindrances, legal restrictions undermined Albanian efforts to integrate in society. For example, a diploma from the Tetovo University (with 74.4 per cent Albanian students) was not recognized in other parts of FYR Macedonia. The Constitution provided for the education of the Albanians in their language from primary to secondary level. However, linguistic

6 According to the Ministry of Foreign Affairs, Albanians constituted 8.7 per cent of the total employees in the Ministry of Interior prior to 2000. See: Ministry of Foreign Affairs, "Facts about National Minorities in the Republic of Macedonia", Skopje, April 1997:28.

restrictions introduced an educational threshold for those Albanians who desired to compete for higher posts.

Actually, the problem of equitable representation exposed the state's complacency with the system inherited from the former Yugoslavia. The Slavic Macedonian state authorities proved unwilling to speed up the pace of reform. Although the state never directly institutionalized discrimination, it did little to improve employment prospects for the Albanian citizens. DPA supporters believe that there has been a systematic effort to minimize the Albanian presence in all institutional sections with the use of legal restrictions and the pretext of national security. Arben Xhaferi explained that:

> the Slav Macedonian power structure misuses the forms of democracy to subjugate the Albanian population. This 'ethnic engineering' leads to a permanent reductionism in public life. The Constitution is narrower than reality; because that which is allowed under the Constitution is prohibited by law. The institution in turn, limits what law permits, and what the institution allows is not realized by the individual. This phenomenon is manifest at all levels of society, down to the desk of the petty bureaucrat. (Xhaferi, 1998)

The media and publishing sector provides a notable example of what can be termed as lawful discrimination. *Nova Makedonija*, the then largest national newspaper with close ties to the socialist government of the Social Democratic Alliance of Macedonia (SDAM), constituted until 1998 an absolute monopoly. The "*Nova Makedonija* Media Company" published a number of state sponsored papers and magazines including the Albanian weekly newspaper *Flaka*. The state company owned all the means for printing papers and charged prohibitively high prices for printing and distribution. Due to the high printing costs, independent publishers were discouraged from publishing. In this way, the state prevented the publishing of dissident or incompliant Albanian opinions. Another example of lawful discrimination was the May 1995 closure of many private radio and television stations, allegedly for technical reasons ("A Threat to Stability? Human Rights Violations in Macedonia", Human Rights Helsinki Watch (HRHW), 1996:29). On this matter, the Helsinki Human Rights Watch Report suggested that:

> Ethnic Albanians complained that the government used the pretext of technical reasons to launch an attack against Albanian owned media. As the Director of Radio Vox and President of the association of commercial radio and television stations in Macedonia Dragan Pavlovic stated at HRWH, 55 per cent of the closed stations were run by ethnic Albanians, all of the closures were against the constitution. (ibid.:29)

By 1997, the numbers of Albanians increased in several government ministries from less than 2 per cent in 1990 to levels between 7 and 12 per cent (US Department of State, Macedonia Country Report on Human Rights Practices, 1997). In May 2000, the parliamentary commission on Inter-Ethnic Relations released a report on the ethnic composition of the workforce. The report revealed that 84.5 per cent of the entire workforce was Slav Macedonian and 9.4 per cent ethnic Albanian. In the police service, Albanians had a share of 3.1 per cent of the total force, with the rest being almost entirely covered by Slav Macedonians (ICG Balkans Report No. 98, "Macedonia's Ethnic Albanians: Bridging the Gulf", 2000:17). In 1998, quotas and special competitions were introduced in order to improve the representation of the Albanians in the police. Unfortunately, the pace of reform was slow and the new measures did not have the envisaged results. Even today, 25.9 per cent of the population firmly opposes the idea of the equitable representation of all nationalities in the public institutions, while only 28.3 per cent is clearly in favour of it (Popovski et al., UNDP EWR June 2006). We shall examine the post-crisis developments more closely in a following chapter.

One of the major arguments expressed by the Albanian rebels in 2001 related to the deterioration of socio-economic conditions in the Albanian community (Perry, 1997; Strauss, 2004). There is little doubt that the Albanians of FYR Macedonia were severely affected by the economic hardship since the country achieved independence. However, deprivation and poverty in FYR Macedonia was, and still is, a cross-ethnic phenomenon. Throughout the 1990s, widespread tax evasion and the absence of economic resources posed a major barrier to the even redistribution of wealth and benefits. The lack of resources caused the collapse of the rudimentary state welfare system, leading thousands of unemployed to further destitution. At the same time, a tiny minority accumulated a large part of the national wealth, while a growing portion of the population existed on the verge of poverty (Government of the Republic of Macedonia, Ministry of Finance, Committee for Preparation of the National Strategy for Poverty Reduction in the Republic of Macedonia, August 2002:1–152). Table 1 depicts the rates of unemployment from 1990 to 2000.

Table 1: Registered Unemployment
("Macedonian National Poverty Reduction Strategy", Macroeconomic Review, 2007:5–16. Source: Ministry of Finance of FYR Macedonia.)*

Year	1990	1991	1992	1993	1994	1995
Registered (%)	–	24.5	26.2	27.7	30	36.6
Overall (%)	–	–	–	–	–	–

Year	1996	1997	1998	1999	2000
Registered (%)	38.8	41.7	41.4	43.8	44.9
Overall (%)	31.9	36	34.5	32.4	32.2

* See <http://www.finance.gov.mk/gb/download/poverty_reduction.pdf>.

Two important observations can be made: first, registered unemployment (unemployment among those who previously worked and lost their jobs) steadily increased, and more people turned to social welfare benefits; second, overall unemployment estimates (unemployment including those who have not previously worked) oscillated in equally high levels, with a little less than one-third of the population defined as formally unemployed. The proportional share of a minority in unemployment closely follows the proportional share of a minority's population according to the 2002 census ("Report on the labour market in Macedonia", Centre for Economic Analyses, Skopje, 2005:1–26). For example, in 1999 Albanians made up 20.2 per cent (50,782) of the total registered unemployed. Slav Macedonians represented some 67.4 per cent (176,278) of the total registered unemployed. Therefore, the unemployment figure for all other ethnic groups is proportional to their population size. However, many Albanians who are officially unemployed (unregistered and uninsured) receive seasonal work in the black market. The numbers would surely increase with the inclusion of uninsured workers, part-time workers, conscripted soldiers and other unspecified contract-based workers. Be this as it may, high unemployment gradually produced high levels of poverty.[7] In the 1998 "Poor Households Survey in Macedonia", 48.5 per cent of those polled said that they were neither rich nor poor – but 39.9 per cent considered themselves poor. Only 5.6 per cent declared they were averagely rich and just 0.3 per cent considered themselves very rich, while the rest remained undecided (Dimitrevska, 1998:81). As Table 2 indicates, the monthly wage indicator is an accurate sign of wealth and economic development, and therefore constitutes a useful tool for estimating poverty.

Table 2: Average Monthly Wage (Source: US State Department Human Rights Reports on FYR Macedonia 1995–2004 – Average Wage Indicator.)

Year	1995	1996	1997	1998	1999
Average Monthly Wage	–	134 Euros	163 Euros	125 Euros	132 Euros

Year	2000	2001	2002	2003	2004
Average Monthly Wage	121 Euros	117 Euros	114 Euros	137 Euros	180 Euros

7 In measuring poverty in FYR Macedonia, the definition provided by the statistical service of the European Union, EUROSTAT, is used: individuals, families and groups of people are considered poor when their resources (material, cultural, and social) are on such a level as to be below the minimum acceptable way of living in the country where they live. See: "National Strategy for the Reduction of Poverty in the Republic Macedonia", Government of the Republic of Macedonia, Ministry of Finance, August 2002, Skopje. Generally, poverty is the condition in which the person or the family lacks the essential means for a minimum degree of well-being that goes beyond basic human needs (food, housing, health and hygiene).

According to the US State Department Human Rights Reports, throughout the 1990s the average monthly wage did not surpass 132 Euros. Naturally, the lowest income per month is evident in 2001, the year of the armed crisis; an indication that armed inter-ethnic violence can significantly affect the income of ordinary salary-based workers and professionals. However, there is no steady drop in income. Average monthly wage increased from 1998 (election of VMRO-DPMNE and DPA government) and dropped by 2000, the year following the military intervention in Kosovo and the refugee crisis. The decrease of trade with Serbia, the closure of factories, and the blockade of major trading channels may account for much of this drop. Be this as it may, the positive prospects created by the alliance of VMRO-DPMNE (Internal Macedonian Revolutionary Organization-Democratic Party for Macedonian National Unity) with the DPA quickly diminished by 2000.

As Table 3 shows, Slav Macedonian households were the most affected by the increased levels of poverty. That was due to their significant reliance on state employment. By contrast, the Albanians were primarily engaged in private ventures, farming and trade. Many of them had previously emigrated to Western countries. Nevertheless, according to data produced by the Ministry of Labour and Social Policy, 31.8 per cent of Albanian households relied on social benefits. This means that approximately one in three Albanian households relied on social benefits.

Table 3: Welfare Beneficiaries by Ethnicity in 1996
("National Strategy for the Reduction of Poverty in the Republic Macedonia", Government of the Republic of Macedonia, Ministry of Finance, August 2002, Skopje. Source: Ministry of Finance of FYR Macedonia.)

Nationality	Percentage of Population	Percentage of Households on Welfare
Slav Macedonians	66.6	43
Albanians	22.7	31.8

Table 4 demonstrates the number of registered unemployed in a number of selected cities. However, there has been no precise data depicting the actual percentages of unemployed Albanians per city/town. As a result, we can only speculate about the actual percentages of unemployed Albanians in the following cities. The following table shows the total numbers and percentages of unemployed by city, including the percentage of Albanians residing in those cities.

Table 4: Registered Unemployed Persons by City, December 2001
(Source: State Employment Bureau, FYR Macedonia.)

Town/City	Unemployed		Population in 1994 Census	Percentage of Albanians in 1994 Census
	Number	Percentage		
Skopje	86,026	15.7	545,228	20.4
Veles	15,280	23.1	65,945	4.2
Kumanovo	31,985	25	127,814	37.5
Prilep	26,470	26	94,183	29
Tetovo	23,530	13.6	172,171	75

Skopje, a city with the largest number of Albanians, is heavily affected by unemployment, with almost one out of six declared unemployed. In the municipality of Tetovo, a predominantly Albanian area, the number of unemployed was also high. All communities in FYR Macedonia suffer from varying degrees of deprivation; and the welfare disparity between the Slav Macedonians and the Albanians becomes narrower and less diverging.[8] State employment, probably the most notable advantage enjoyed by the Slav

8 While income divisions do not line up with ethnic ones, economic competition is increasingly seen as something of a zero-sum game. One community is viewed as having profited at the expense of the other, and this increases the risk of conflict. However, Albanians have apparently been quicker to spot opportunities and develop

Macedonian community, quickly diminished. The closure of many state-owned enterprises in the early 1990s left thousands of Slav Macedonians unemployed. Even after the 2001 crisis, a State Statistical Office report of April 2002 estimated that 25 per cent of the population lived below the official poverty line, while unemployment peaked at an incredible 35 per cent (Sandrin, 2007:1–8, European Agency for Reconstruction). In 2006, according to the data of the Employment Agency, the number of registered unemployed was approximately 33.6 per cent. By ethnicity, 33.2 per cent were Slav Macedonians and 27.4 per cent were ethnic Albanians (Popovski et al., UNDP EWR, June 2006).

Structured Content Analysis

In this section, we examine levels of deprivation as reflected across a set of socio-political indicators. The US State Department Human Rights Reports (USSD HRR) illustrate the human rights compliance of each investigated UN member state with a set of fixed indicators, reflecting the type of direct and indirect misconduct by the state and its institutions. These indicators determine the severity of governmental oppression and, by extension, the degree of political deprivation felt among Albanians in the case of FYR Macedonia. The USSD HR reports help us to determine the intensity of governmental oppression, and the deprivation this oppression generated in relation to the levels of violence. The analysis of the USSD HR reports allows us to identify the degree to which institutional misconduct and maltreatment intensify ethno-political conflict, understand how this oppression generates perceptions of deprivation, and determine the ways in which deprivation transforms into violence. A careful analysis

businesses when the economy was liberalized, due to a history of being forced to rely on their own initiative (see USAID Macedonia Report, 2000:8).

of the trends in violence can possibly reveal interesting linkages between political deprivation and decisions to engage in violence.

The US State Department Human Rights Reports contain qualitative data reflecting a wide range of indicators of potential deprivation. Although there is a notable lack of focus on ethnically targeted misconduct, the reports demonstrate an overall level of state and institutional misconduct and maltreatment that affect all portions of society. However, evidence of a systematic institutional misconduct in relation to ethnic minorities does exist. This may have constituted an enhancer of anti-systemic action. Crucially, we attempt to assess the impact of misconduct (and oppression) as a determinant of deprivation and conflict.

Misconduct refers to wrongful, improper, or unlawful conduct motivated by a premeditated or intentional purpose or by obstinate indifference to the consequences of one's acts. Misconduct and maltreatment have different meanings in different places. For the purpose of this study, the terms wrongful, improper and unlawful indicate i) deviation from established – and commonly accepted – rules of conduct, ii) practices that lie outside the legal or constitutional framework and iii) excessive or disproportionate use of force, abuse of official office, and biased treatment. Maltreatment refers to cruel or inhumane treatment, which may often result in physical injury, psychological abuse, or even death. Perceptions of maltreatment are often the result of bad conduct. Maltreatment is often a manifestation or by-product of misconduct.

Crucially, the notion of "state and institutional misconduct and maltreatment" is relative to the regional or national context. Fixed western notions of freedom and justice usually judge what constitutes a violation of human, political and civil rights. These notions fail to take into consideration the regional ethics and past experiences in certain countries. In addition, they fail to take into account the resources available for establishing monitoring mechanisms. Generally, when assessing good governance we should refrain from absolutisms. "Good enough" could be a more appropriate characterization for describing the state of affairs in a given environment, always taking into consideration the socio-economic hardships, the political antagonisms and the segmented ethnic structures.

Method of Analysis

The USSD HR Reports cover the time period from 1994 to 2004, with the following themes: i) respect for the integrity and freedom of the individual, and ii) respect for civil liberties and political rights. These themes illustrate numerous cases of misconduct and maltreatment by the state authorities (e.g. police) or institutions (e.g. justice). The aim is to present the evolution of "state and institutional misconduct and maltreatment" in a systematic fashion. For this reason, timeframes and measurements are introduced to help the reader examine the evolution and degree of misconduct and maltreatment. For doing so, three selected sets of indicators, as set by the USSD HR Reports, are used to define i) respect for the integrity and freedom of the person (six indicators) and ii) respect for civil liberties (four indicators).

Set A: Respect for the Integrity and Freedom of the Person Indicators:

1. Political and Other Extrajudicial Killing
2. Disappearance
3. Torture and Other Cruel, Inhuman, or Degrading Treatment or Punishment
4. Arbitrary Arrest
5. Detention, or Exile, Denial of Fair Public Trial
6. Arbitrary Interference with Privacy, Family, Home or Correspondence

Set B: Respect for Civil Liberties Indicators:

1. Freedom of Speech
2. Freedom of Assembly and Association
3. Freedom of Religion
4. Freedom of Movement, Emigration

The third "set" is a single-indicator set which defines respect for political rights. This will be examined separately through one single indicator, namely, "the right of citizens to change their government". The above two multivariate sets and the additional single indicator will be used to assess "state and institutional misconduct and maltreatment". A measurement system based on content analysis has also been developed. Coded signs are used in order to describe the degree (significance) of "state and institutional misconduct and maltreatment" in every indicator: NR= No Reports, A= Allegations, I = Indications, and E = Evidence. This codification helps explain the type and severity of "state and institutional misconduct and maltreatment". The "No Reports" sign refers to the absence of reported incidents in the USSD HR Reports; "Allegations" refers to unverified claims; "Indications" refers to well-founded suggestions; and "Evidence" refers to the factual, well-founded and publicized cases in which "state and institutional misconduct and maltreatment" have existed.

For example:

SET X	Years		
Indicators ↓	1996	1997	1998
Arbitrary Arrest	Allegations (A)	Evidence (E)	Indications(I)

One can detect "Allegations", "Evidence" and "Indications" in the content of the USSD HR Reports as follows: "No Reports" are easily traced due to the absence of reported or recorded incidents per year. "Allegations" are usually unfounded or unconfirmed claims by citizens, in cases where no further NGO or police investigation has occurred, or where little cross-verification has taken place. Below is an example of what would be categorized as "Allegations":

> There were no confirmed reports of arbitrary arrest ... Some ethnic Albanians continued to report instances of unprovoked harassment such as the June 25 detention of a number of Albanians for approximately 4 hours ... (USSD HRR, 1994)

The above and all other similar reports are treated as "Allegations" because there was no formal verification or any other confirmation. "Indications" are concrete hints of misconduct or maltreatment by the state and the institutions, for example:

> Early in the year, a number of ethnic Albanian prisoners claimed mistreatment was occurring at the Idrizovo prison near Skopje. Government sources stated that 37 cases brought against police officers for exceeding their authority ... (USSD HRR, 1994)

The "Evidence" sign is used only when incidents are adequately confirmed and verified by state authorities, NGOs or the media.

In order to make it easier for the reader to conceptualize the significance of each coded sign, and allow for practical comparisons to be made, fixed values have been assigned to each codified sign: NR = 0, A = 10, I = 20, and E = 30. This should enable the reader to compare and examine trends from 1994–2004 and gather overall scores per year and between years. The reader will be able to calculate the total-sum per indicator – throughout the time period – as well as the total-sum of each indicator per year (horizontal and vertical calculation).

In the first set-table, the scale is 0 to 180, with 0 depicting the total absence of "state and institutional misconduct and maltreatment" and 180 depicting the peak. The specific fixed values have been selected because SET A has six indicators and SET B has four. The total maximum sums in the case that all codified signs show "Evidence" are 180 and 120 respectively.[9] There is no real measurement or any sample that determines the actual value assigned to the codified signs. By selecting E = 30, we have a 10-point distance between every sign: E = 30, A = 20, I = 10, NR = 0. Hence, the fixed values have been determined according to the perceived severity of each sign. The method works by multiplying the fixed numerical weight by the number of codified signs, producing

9 The scales 0–180 and 0–120 have been inserted for depicting the highest and lowest scores: 30 × 6 (indicators) or 30 × 4 (indicators).

a scale on which we can visualize both the degree and the type of "state and institutional misconduct and maltreatment" (codified sign E = 30 multiplied by number of indicators). For the second table, the same logic applies on a scale from 0–120 (codified sign E =30 multiplied by number of indicators). The scale comes to a top score of 120 because the second table has fewer indicators.

Structured Analysis

The types of "state and institutional misconduct and maltreatment" (measured by "respect for the integrity and freedom of the person") are depicted in Table 5. There appears to have been no gradual evolution (i.e. increase or worsening) of "state and institutional misconduct and maltreatment" against civilians. Firstly, the year 1995 was marked by widespread riots, mass arrests and imprisonments of hundreds Albanians. Albanian protestors were confirmed to have been killed in shootings. It could be argued that state oppression increased due to tensions over the education affair and the inauguration of Tetovo University. Scores fluctuate until 1997 and then take an upward trend, peaking in 2001. Secondly, by 1998, inter-ethnic tensions were almost entirely (if temporarily) diffused, and for this reason, we observe a relative drop in "state and institutional misconduct and maltreatment". With the election of VMRO-DPMNE in 1998, and its decision to invite the radical DPA to form a coalition government, "state and institutional misconduct, and maltreatment" reached an unprecedented low. The incorporation of the radicals in the power sharing structures was thought to be crucial in constraining and even preventing further extremism among Albanians. The two major ethnic Albanian parties received 214,360 votes – 19.26 per cent of the vote and consequently won fourteen and ten seats respectively (ICG Balkans Report No. 51, "Macedonia: New Faces in Skopje", Skopje – Brussels, 9 January 1999:2). The more reserved PDP won the majority of seats.

Table 5: SET A: US State Department Human Rights Reports on FYR Macedonia 1994–2004 – Respect for the Integrity and Freedom of the Person.

	Indicators ↓						
Year	a. Political and Other Extrajudicial Killing	b. Disappearance	c. Torture and Other Cruel, Inhuman, or Degrading Treatment or Punishment	d. Arbitrary Arrest, Detention, or Exile	e. Denial of Fair Public Trial	f. Arbitrary Interference with Privacy, Family, Home, or Correspondence	Total Sum
1994	NR	NR	I	A	NR	NR	30
1995	NR	NR	I	A	I	I	60
1996	NR	NR	NR	I	A	A	40
1997	E	NR	I	NR	NR	NR	50
1998	NR	I	NR	NR	NR	NR	20
1999	NR	NR	I	I	NR	NR	40
2000	I	NR	E	I	NR	A	80
2001	E	E	E	E	NR	E	150
2002	E	NR	E	I	NR	I	100
2003	NR	NR	I	I	I	I	80
2004	NR	I	E	I	I	I	80

Yet the new government of Georgievski's conservative right-wing VMRO-DPMNE and Vasil Tupurkovski's Democratic Alternative selected the DPA as their coalition partner. Georgievski argued that by incorporating the radicals he showed the international community that FYR Macedonia is a "real democratic state".[10] Finally, the radical DPA became a government coalition partner with the nominally ultra-nationalist VMRO-DPMNE. A government decision to grant amnesty to local Albanian politicians arrested in July 1997 reinforced a climate of trust and cooperation and the government's willingness to initiate institutional reforms had an overall positive short-term impact on inter-ethnic cooperation. Moreover, in mid-1999 thousands of Kosovo Albanian refugees entered FYR Macedonia. This event increased dramatically the numbers of Albanians in the country and temporarily affected the state's ethno-demographic balance. Slav Macedonian fears and suspicions mounted and anti-Albanianism increased. Naturally, the highest score occurred in 2001. Worryingly enough, the levels of "state and institutional misconduct and maltreatment" after the 2001 crisis remain at comparatively high levels. A horizontal analysis reveals that most cases involving bad conduct are found in the areas of "Torture and Other Cruel, Inhuman, or Degrading Treatment or Punishment" and "Arbitrary Arrest, Detention, or Exile". "Disappearance" ranks bottom with "No Reported" events in eight years. Nevertheless, the problem of kidnappings and disappearances in the country is considered important. Table 6 offers a general picture concerning civilian rights.

The basic democratic/civilian freedoms have been generally respected, at least until 1999. In 1994, a year of parliamentary elections, the USS HR Reports mentioned no serious obstructions to civilian rights. In 1995, despite the turbulent events in Tetovo, no impingement of democratic/civilian freedoms occurred. The next two years followed an equally stable pattern despite the continued levels of violence in Albanian inhabited areas. In 1998, there is an almost total compliance with norms regarding democratic/civilian freedoms, the only exception being evidence, which suggests barriers in the free expression of media and press.

10 The reasons for doing so remain disputed. Others argued that Georgievski and some of his political followers wanted to accelerate the process of political disintegration among the Albanians. A third argument claims that VMRO-DPMNE and Xhaferi's DPA formed a secret pact or a gentlemen's agreement over splitting the market into ethnically controlled sectors of jurisdiction. None of these allegations have been verified so far.

Table 6: SET B: US State Department Human Rights Reports on FYR Macedonia 1994–2004 – Respect for Civil Liberties.

Indicators ↓					
Year	a. Freedom of Speech and Press	b. Freedom of Peaceful Assembly and Association	c. Freedom of Religion	d. Freedom of Movement, Emigration and Repatriation	Total Sum
1994	I	NR	NR	NR	20
1995	NR	NR	I	A	30
1996	NR	NR	A	A	20
1997	NR	NR	A	A	20
1998	E	NR	NR	NR	30
1999	NR	NR	I	I	40
2000	A	NR	A	E	50
2001	E	I	A	E	90
2002	E	NR	NR	I	50
2003	E	I	E	NR	80

From 1998 to 2000, with the worsening of regional conditions in Kosovo and Presevo (a southern region in Serbia where many Albanians live), and due to the influx of Kosovo refugees, the state adopted a harder line. Again, the high total violation score for 2001 suggests a natural correlation between the eruption of armed violence and the dramatic restriction of democratic/civilian freedoms, a result of armed violence rather than its aetiology. However, a worsening of the security environment, regional and internal, seems to have a negative impact on the quality of democracy. Additional information is shown in Table 7.

Table 7: Single-Indicator SET C: US State Department Human Rights Reports on FYR Macedonia 1994–2004 – Respect for Political Rights: The Right of Citizens to Change Their Government.

1994	1995	1996	1997	1998	1999	2000	2001	2002	2003	2004
NR	A	A	NR	NR	I	E	E	I	NR	I

Generally, evidence and allegations of electoral violence and voting irregularities are common in the least developed of the post-socialist states (e.g. Albania). FYR Macedonia is no exception. Tensions rise to alarming levels during election periods. Force, blackmail and threats, as well as other illegitimate practices have been recorded by analysts and observers of the OSCE. FYR Macedonia's highly segmented political environment runs across ethnic lines. Political parties exhibit a culture of mutual antagonism, which clearly produces winners and losers. Ethnic coalitions are interest-based formations, and in some cases the coalition forming parties ignore the electoral percentages of the ethnic parties they chose to cooperate with. This has resulted in two instances (1998–2006) in the formation of coalitions with secondary Albanian parties. The basic civil liberties indicators (Table 6) functioned well, regardless of perceived threats and frequent occurrence of violent incidents. Democratic/civilian rights have been respected to a high degree considering the economic hardships (caused by high unemployment, and the Greek embargo imposed to punish the adoption of the country's name) and the increasing assertiveness of the Albanian community. It could be argued that the (more or less) functioning democracy in FYR Macedonia could not justify the triggering of violent responses against the state. However, as mentioned earlier, the functioning, efficiency and overall quality of democracy is relative to the regional context. In an attempt to ensure a higher degree of accuracy, we have incorporated a modified version of the Helsinki Human Rights Reports on the same subject of democratic/civilian liberties and democratic governance. This additional qualitative dataset provides a control mechanism for assuring objectivity in the analysis. The Helsinki Human Rights Watch (HRHW) offers qualitative descriptions on the conduct of large institutional bodies based on empirical evidence as well as allegations. Other researchers already have analysed HRHW reports on FYR Macedonia (Sokalski, 2003). For this reason, we will only explore the HRHW assessments within the crucial period between 1998 and 2002, i.e. from the outbreak of serious hostilities in Kosovo to the end of violent crisis in FYR Macedonia. The reports assess six institutional categories where misconduct, discrimination and bad governance have been observed: i) the free and democratic conduct of election, ii) the freedom of media, iii) the proper functioning of the judicial system, iv) police conduct, v) freedom of religion, and vi) minority rights. The HRHW reports cannot offer explanations on the origins and logic of discrimination, or suggest realistic accommodations of minority grievances. It offers an insight on discrimination itself however, which seems to have constituted one of the main grievances that propelled some Albanians into violent activity. According to the following table, the judicial system and the police generate the most violations. From 1998 to 2002, Helsinki Watch – by then known as Human Rights Watch – described the judicial system as eroded, inefficient and often corrupt. The conduct of the police service is described as inefficient, abusive and excessive.

Human Rights Watch offers descriptions for the quality of "Minority Rights and Inter-Ethnic Relations". From 1998 to 2002, the Helsinki Human Rights reports suggest the existence of intolerance, violations and polarization in FYR Macedonia. The 1999 report explains that intolerance is due to the absence of education towards the respect of differences, and due to restrictions over the usage of minority languages in the administrative and legal authorities (Helsinki Committee for Human Rights, Annual HHR Report: Former Yugoslav Republic of Macedonia, Report, 1999). Moreover, police misconduct includes arresting people without a previously issued warrant, holding people more than the legal maximum of twenty-four hours (prescribed by the Constitution Act), not reading rights to suspects, impeding access to counsel, applying force or pressure to sign a statement or a confession, and not stating a reason for arrest at the time of arrest (ibid.).

Table 8: Helsinki Human Rights Watch – Former Yugoslav Republic of Macedonia Report, 1998–2002.

	1998	1999	2000	2001	2002
Parliamentary Elections	Fair and democratic	N/E	N/E	N/E	Pressures, violations, widespread irregularities
Freedom of Media	Generally good	Generally good but strictly partisan	Pressures, limited access to information, non transparent	Prejudice, misinformation, nationalistic	Pressures and violence, hate speech and biased information
Judicial System	Inefficient	Inefficient and corrupt	Weak	Inefficient, unequal treatment	Inexpertness, erosion
Police Conduct	Occasional misconduct	Irregularities and misconduct	Inadequate and unnecessarily coercive	Abuses, intolerance misconduct	Excessive use of force, irregularities. erosion
Religious Rights	Intolerance and restrictions	Legal restrictions	Discrimination and intolerance	Institutional amendments	Stagnation
Minority Rights and Inter-Ethnic Relations	Intolerance and discrimination	Violations	Discrepancies	Polarization, aggression, intolerance	Lack of confidence, polarization, slow progress, displacements

In 2000, HRW stressed that: "Although the state has declared the principle of independence of courts, in practice the state implements this principle according to the needs of its politics. The desire to use courts as political instrument, and the reduction of the level of their independence seems to be unavoidable feature of the government" (ibid.). Judging from individual cases, incompetence of the judiciary and police misconduct are practices affecting not just Albanians, but all citizens of the state, especially those who belong to the most vulnerable minorities i.e. the Roma and the Vlachs.

We have established that "state and institutional misconduct and maltreatment" (SIMM) are consistent with the growth of violent incidents. A structured analysis of the US State Department Human Rights Reports and the Helsinki Watch Human Rights data shows that SIMM patterns follow trends of increased violent mobilization. Therefore, we can safely argue that political oppression generates or at least helps to generate deprivation and grievances, and has a proportionate effect on the lower levels of violence in non-authoritarian states. In 2001, we have the highest score for SIMM. The evolution of violent radicalism is marked by a rise in SIMM, and then stabilizes at somewhat higher levels than those prior to the crisis. Additionally, the rising frequency in violations of individual integrity and civil liberties is proportionate to increases in the number of violent events. Yet we should bear in mind that any sudden restriction of democratic/civilian freedoms is a result of an already looming crisis.

CHAPTER 4

The Strategic Environment

State Strength and External Legitimacy

Without the existence of certain preconditions, or enabling factors, the emergence of organized forms of violence would be less likely, regardless of any existing forms of deprivation. From 1991, state-building efforts in FYR Macedonia were almost entirely swamped by economic difficulties, social hardship and political corruption. Most importantly, the new post-Yugoslav republic lacked a functioning economy, while state and democratic institutions existed only at a rudimentary level. Furthermore, the political system in FYR Macedonia lacked the consensual culture and democratic tradition that would allow for the different ethnic communities to progress in democratic ways. At the very outset of the new country's independence, there was an evident lack of social cohesion and consensus over what organizing principles should determine the contest for state power and how that power should be executed (Biljana Vankovska, 2004). The state demonstrated a remarkably low capacity to provide for all citizens, and there was a significant democratic deficit in the state institutions, reflected in the perceived and real levels of public corruption and institutional weakness. Notably, ethnic minorities, and in particular the Albanians, interpreted the lack of capacity to address popular expectations as a failure of political will. On top of these structural deficiencies, the turbulent relations in the area put pressure on a still immature culture of consensus at home. From 1991 onwards, external economic and political pressures influenced greatly the internal political agenda, thereby influencing the course of inter-ethnic relations in the new state. At the same time, social injustices, persistent poverty and ethno-political stratification transformed these existing social problems into ethno-political ones.

The ethnically fragmented political system aggravated the problems in FYR Macedonia's transitional economy. In fact, it could be argued that the political and economic spheres were both in parallel transition from Socialism to a distorted form of liberal-civic democracy. According to Biljana Vankovska, the absence of an "implicit contract" between state and society made an efficient realization of internal sovereignty impossible (Vankovska, 2004). The inherent identity disputes and the contrasting ethno-political affiliations held by the different communities posed a major threat to the state's integrity and legitimacy. Throughout the 1990s, politically active members of the Albanian minority pressed for accommodation of minority demands and modification of the new state's constitutional foundations, while the Slavic majority remained unwilling to make these changes. These issues relating to the socio-political rights of the Albanian minority remained unresolved, intensified existing ethnic dichotomies, and helped to ignite a low intensity rebellion among frustrated Albanians. Naturally, the conflict in Kosovo presented a time-bomb that was pending to explode for over a decade, providing the human and material resources and the logistical support for a local insurgency in FYR Macedonia. Prior to the conclusion of the war in Kosovo, paramilitary groups had already started to operate and control areas within FYR Macedonia. By the same time, the state had gradually lost the capacity to exercise control in areas that only nominally came under the state's jurisdiction. As Biljana Vankovska accurately observed, violent conflict was predestined by both internal and regional developments, and in early 2001 the state introduced a new chapter to the *circulus vitiosus* of the state strength dilemma (Biljana Vankovsa, 2004).

This transitional status has been prolonged due to the long-term non-participation of the country in international organizations, such as NATO and the EU. On the one hand, the Slavic majority controlled and abused those sections of public life directly dependent on appointments by the centre, and reduced the power of regional centres of decision-making that could benefit the Albanian minority. On the other hand, the state of FYR Macedonia lacked the political, institutional and operational capability to maintain the oppressive policies against the Albanians (Vankovska, 1998; Rakipi, 2002). Unlike socialist Yugoslavia, FYR Macedonia could not afford the imposition of repressive measures, and the sustaining of discriminatory and centralized structures. The protectionist orientation of the nationalist Slavic Macedonian political elite existed within a political system whose legitimacy was fiercely disputed by the Albanians. The state mechanism was incapable to either sustain policies of discrimination against the Albanians, or integrate Albanian demands into the political curriculum. Consequently, the state had no control over the western Albanian dominated areas of the country. State laws, policing regulations and fiscal arrangements were rarely implemented in areas where Albanians were the majority (Deliso, 2002).

Moreover, the country lacked an effective military to support the political objectives of its dominant Slavic Macedonian political elite. As it withdrew, the JNA literally took down the entire military infrastructure of SYR Macedonia, and confiscated the weapons assigned to the Territorial Defence Units (Philips, 2003:52). The developing war fronts in Croatia and later in Bosnia meant that JNA forces had to be transferred from SYR Macedonia to the conflict hotspots of Kraijna and Slavonia in order to restore order and counter the Croatian secessionist moves. The bloodless withdrawal of the JNA from FYR Macedonia in 1991 manifested clearly the absence of an intense Serbian interest in the country. The Serb minority in the country was tiny, and in spite of some early tensions between the Serbs and the Slav Macedonians, relations remained relatively stable.

As a result, the newly independent state was left without an effective military force to protect the country from internal rebellion or external aggression. The Slavic leadership of the Former Yugoslav Republic of Macedonia was confronted with a serious security vacuum and economic collapse. The country's arsenal included a few Soviet T-55 tanks and the army and police were equipped with antiquated firearms. Military expenditure never exceeded 2.5 per cent of GDP (Zoran Kusovac, "Macedonian army lacking strength", *Janes Intelligence Review*, 23 March 2001). Yet the most serious problem came from within the structures of the military. Approximately half of the army's soldiers were ethnic Albanians. This rendered a large part of army highly unreliable. Generally, the state did not possess the capacity to sustain the oppressive policies, and consequently made the possibility of rebellion increasingly attractive.

Other than the state's operational weakness, the aggravating impact of external non-recognition points to the link between the denial of external legitimacy and internal oppression. From an empirical point of view, it seems that states lacking regional or international approval seem to be more vulnerable to internal dissent. Typical examples are Georgia, Israel, Turkey, China, Albania, South Africa and Mexico. In cases where states enjoy widespread public and political approval, it is harder for dissenting groups to make political demands, or initiate a widespread and sustainable violent campaign even in the presence of severe deprivation. For example, the Hungarians in Slovakia and Romania have in several instances mobilized against the state, but their protests did not give rise to any serious form of organized armed violence. Russians in Estonia and Lithuania have similarly made explicit complains regarding their perceived inferior status. The Catalans in Spain have considerable grievances, though political violence has never been an appealing option for them. Some Corsicans in France engaged in sporadic violence. The case of the Basques in Spain is probably one of the rare cases of sustained organized violence in a state enjoying undisputed external legitimacy.

Therefore, the denial of external legitimacy triggered a reactionary backlash in the Slavic Macedonian community and prompted national policymakers to preserve policies that deprived the Albanians of their demanded rights, in spite of the state's inability to maintain such polices. Moreover, the denial of state legitimacy by neighbouring states, and the reactionary application of protectionist policies by the state further radicalized the Albanians towards militancy. Particularly the "attitudes of Bulgaria and Greece, and to a lesser extent Serbia and Albania, influence the ongoing conflict between Macedonians and Albanians as to the kind of state the Republic of Macedonia should be" (Engstrom, 2002:15). Indeed, one could argue that external objections and influences were largely responsible for the intensification of Slav Macedonian nationalism, subsequently reflected in internal policies towards the Albanian minority, with the effect of radicalizing many Albanians (ibid., 2002).

Therefore, Macedonia's destiny was shaped by external forces more powerful than those it could generate itself (Zametica, 1992:36). The recognition of a state's external legitimacy is probably the most important political variable in international relations. Recognition of a country's origin, leadership, constitutional name and borders are proven factors in fostering regional stability, thereby ensuring the state's survival and acceptance abroad. These external guarantees are even more important for states with a diverse ethnic make-up, as they help grant legitimacy to a civil authority, which in turn allows it to exercise sovereignty over a territory and its people.

By contrast, non-recognition preserves a status of fluidity and doubt, and the more this status perpetuates the ossified this abnormality becomes. Consequently, political groups may lose their interest in participating in the mechanisms of a country that is internationally isolated and regionally disdained. The additional absence of real economic incentives, coupled with perceptions of discrimination against ethnic populations and violent regional spillovers, may encourage portions of ethnic groups to re-orientate towards a more violent, secessionist route. The mere existence of an independent FYR Macedonian state has constituted a source of dispute in itself. From the very beginning, its contested name, history, and even the originality of the Slavic Macedonian population posed barriers to the country's international recognition, and severely obstructed its relations with other neighbouring states. The internationalization of the country's external non-recognition[1] and the refusal by neighbouring states to accept major constituent components of the FYR Macedonian state, such as its nation and name, was a catalyst in the radicalization of the Albanians.

1 The country cannot participate with its constitutional name in any international organization of which Greece is a member. A mutually acceptable solution to the name issue has been requested based on UN Security Resolution 817/1993. Since the Interim Accord 1995, the governments of FYR Macedonia have acknowledged that the name of the state is a subject of negotiation.

Greece

The declaration of independence by FYR Macedonia on 17 September 1991 triggered a fierce reaction from neighbouring Greece, establishing a feeling of mistrust on the Greek side as to the real intensions and claims of the new state. As Evangelos Kofos points out:

> One should bear in mind that Greek reactions over these issues were a response to nationalist manifestations across the border in the SRM during 1990–1991. As early as October 1989, public demonstrations had been held in Skopje and elsewhere, projecting – for the first time since the 1940s – slogans calling for reunification of Macedonia. Similar leaflets and graffiti covered walls in various towns of the Republic. (Kofos, 1999:3–4)

The ultra-nationalist political party of VMRO-DPMNE, consistent with the nationalist frenzy in Yugoslavia, advocated assertive Slav Macedonian nationalism. The party adopted ancient Greek-Macedonian symbols, and incorporated the Bulgarian lion (national Bulgarian emblem) in the party's coat of arms. Many top-rank party members originated from the province of Greek Macedonia, and their parents left Greece in fear of legal punishment for high treason for collaborating with the communist and fascist forces (depending on their nationalist affiliations) during and immediately after the Second World War. These people have principally led the campaign for a "United Macedonia". Ever since the end of the Greek civil war, Greece had largely ignored the Slav Macedonian nationalist claims, hoping that they would soon be contained in a new, reformed Yugoslav Federation (Kofos, 1999:4). However, as the prospects of a united Yugoslavia diminished Greek policy shifted its attention to "securing international guarantees against changes to the external borders of the Balkan countries" (Kofos, 1999:4).

As a result, SYR Macedonia's declaration of independence revived Greek fears regarding irredentist claims on Greece's northern province of Greek Macedonia. Adding to the Greek fears, Bulgaria and later Turkey – Greece's traditional rival – were the first to recognize the country as "The Republic of Macedonia". Aside from adopting this name, which failed to disassociate the new country and its population from the neighbouring Greek Macedonian province, the new country's name implied that this former Yugoslav republic was the mother state of all "Macedonians". In addition, in the new constitution adopted in 1991, the Slav Macedonian leadership made explicit claims for the existence of a Macedonian ethnic minority in Greece, thus magnifying Greek suspicions (see the Constitution of the Republic of Macedonia, 1991).

A year later, the newly independent country adopted a flag with the "Vergina Star", issued banknotes depicting the Greek city of Thessaloniki, and introduced an educational curriculum that explicitly established connections with ancient Macedonia. As a result, Greece asked for the non-recognition of the Former Yugoslav Republic of Macedonia as the "Republic of Macedonia", and pressed for the exclusion of the term "Macedonia" in its adopted name. Athens objected to the new country's recognition, on the basis that it constituted a threat to the integrity and heritage of the ancient Greek province of Macedonia. For some decades, Greece, in order to preserve good relations with Yugoslavia, swallowed its anger (regarding the name) and kept a low profile (Klok, 1999). The official Greek view at the time was that the Greeks objected to the intended monopolization of the name and heritage of Macedonia, questioned the existence of a distinct Macedonian ethnicity, and resented the utilization of symbols and appropriation of Hellenic history by their Slavic neighbours. However, Greece was more concerned by the geopolitical implications of the emergence of a new state in the north. John Zametica lucidly explains the view Athens adopted in the early 1990s:

> The idea that Greece should find the prospect of an independent Macedonia so worrying was greeted with incredulity both within and outside the EC. The Greeks however were advocating a long-term political view of the situation, including the possibility of an independent Macedonia becoming a Bulgarian satellite [Author's Note: this possibility has indeed become a reality] possibly backed by Turkey [Author's Note: This is also accurate]. A series of unfortunate statements referring to a Macedonian minority in Greece increased the Greek fears. (Zametica, 1992:54)

Amidst Greek suspicions over FYR Macedonia's name and pretensions, on 11 January 1992 the two major ethnic Albanian parties of the time, the

Party for Democratic Prosperity (PDP) and the National Democratic Party (NDP), organized a referendum for the autonomy of the north-western part of the country. The result was well over 90 per cent in favour of autonomy. The Albanian PDP delegation presented the referendum outcome at the Geneva Conference on the Former Yugoslavia and at the London Peace Conference. For the first time, the PDP connected the constitutional status of the Albanian minority in FYR Macedonia to demands over equality, proportional representation in education and public administration. The party insisted also on an internationally monitored census and openly declared that it will respect the will of the Albanians and will do everything in its power to help realize the idea of autonomy for Albanians in FYR Macedonia. On the one hand, PDP Secretary Mithat Emini explained that such autonomy would be constituted necessarily and solely through the state institutions. On the other hand, politicians like Mahi Nesimi, a member of the PDP presidium, explained that "it would prove to be a funny autonomy, which some Albanians would be included, and those living out of it, excluded" (Political Parties, Republic of Macedonia, Balkan Info, PDP). Therefore, autonomy for the north-western part of FYR Macedonia was not a serious option, since as much as half of the Albanian population lived in Skopje. As a result, the Albanian leadership could not instigate, let alone formally propose, full secession, since they were bound by ethnic-geographical realities to accept the existing status quo.

The European Community's Badinter Arbitration Commission finally suggested the recognition of the new country, provoking another fierce Greek response over the adequacy of territorial and constitutional guarantees. The Greek government of Nea Demokratia, headed by Constantine Mitsotakis, initially succeeded in bypassing the Badinter Commission's verdict and attracted international support for the Greek position on the new country's name and its irredentist territorial claims. In line with Greek policy of non-recognition, the Albanians of FYR Macedonia pressed the European Union not to recognize the state unless it took into consideration the objections raised by the ethnic Albanians (Tziambiris, 2002:218–232). On 24 December 1992, a statement signed by the PDP and NDP and sent to all European institutions, the UN, Albanian's President and the President of the self-styled government of the "Republic of Kosovo" pointed out that:

> Macedonia does not meet the criteria for international recognition because the ethnic rights of Albanians are threatened there. With the new Constitution, for which the Albanian deputies in the Assembly did not vote, the Albanians were ghettoised and all their rights were denied. For example, the right to education in their mother tongue at all levels, they were prohibited from using their national symbols, and there is discrimination against the Albanian language and a national hegemony of the Macedonians in the Assembly. All this, the leaders of the PDP and NDP think, is sufficient reason for Macedonia not to be internationally recognised. ("Macedonian Albanians ethnic rights violations should bar Republic's recognition", BBC Summary of World Broadcasts, 4 January 1992)

The head of the PDP visited Albania later in the same year with the request to vote against FYR Macedonia's admission to the Conference for Cooperation and Security in Europe (CSCE; OSCE's predecessor) at the forthcoming CSCE Conference in Prague (Political Parties, Republic of Macedonia, Balkan Info, PDP). The Kosovo-Albanian political analyst Shkelzen Maliqi observed that "in their majority Albanians believe that FYR Macedonia is an artificial state, established to damage Albanians, but they understood that separation could not be easily realized" ("Maliqi: Macedonia", United Nations Interim Administration in Kosovo Press, 2000). He explained that:

> I am not one of those who think that FYROM is a stable and ideal state. On the contrary, it is an unstable and not at all ideal state. It is a danger to itself and it makes trouble for Albanians, and is in trouble with Albanians. However, this paradox of all paradoxes: the reason for the existence of this state, and why it has to be protected, is connected to many regional and continental security interests. Arguments for this have been laid out so many times and have been institutionalized in viewpoints of organized political forces within and out of FYROM. (Political Parties, Republic of Macedonia, Balkan Info, PDP)

At a meeting of the EU Foreign Ministers in Lisbon in February 1992, and following the EU Guimaraes Summit in June 1992, the EU agreed to recognize the former SYR Macedonia "only under a name which could be acceptable to all interested parties" (Kofos, 1999:6). This decision intensified

Slavic nationalism in FYR Macedonia. Denko Malevski, the country's first Minister of Foreign Affairs, associated Greece's insistence on the non-recognition policy with the increased radicalization of Slavic Macedonian political forces as follows:

> The idea that Alexander the Great belongs to us was in the mind of some outsider groups only, these groups were insignificant ... but the big problem is that the old Balkan nations legitimize themselves through their history. In the Balkans, in order to be recognized as a nation, you (a nation) need to have a history of 2,000 to 3,000 years old. Since you made us invent a history ... we invented it. ("Propaganda in FYROM's school books", TV documentary *Erevna*, Mega Channel, 17 March 2007, Greece)

According to Malevski, his country was forced by the Greek position to devise a version of history. The former minister further explained that:

> The pressure we were put under by the Greek political system resulted in the defeat of the moderates and their replacement by hardcore nationalist groups. You (the Greeks) did not allow us to exist with dignity as a nation next to yours and you did not give us the time to sort out historical differences ... hence, you forced us into the arms of the extremist nationalists. (Ibid.)

It is not a coincidence that these very same extreme nationalists were the ones most intransigently opposed to the Albanian demands. Ultimately, the UN endorsed FYR Macedonia's petition, and accepted the country under the provisional name "Former Yugoslav Republic of Macedonia". The country was admitted on the condition to abandon all excessive cultural, historical and territorial pretensions, enter bilateral negotiations with Greece, and for as long as the name issue remained unresolved, the country would be formally and internationally referred to as the Former Yugoslav Republic of Macedonia (UN General Assembly Resolution, A/RES/47/225, April 1993).

However, the country's admission to the UN did not involve any provisions regarding the constitutional status or autonomy of the Albanian population. As a consequence of this perceived international negligence, in 7 April 1992, some municipal officials declared on 7 April 1992 the "Albanian Autonomous Republic of Illyria". At the time, the Albanians were seriously oriented towards increased autonomy within FYR Macedonia, without having a clear picture of the type of autonomy they actually wanted. The autonomy question divided the PDP's top leaders and led to a party schism between the pro-autonomists and the constitutionalists. The PDP was gradually developing a more radical faction within its ranks, although the NDP existed as PDP's radical alternative. In September 1993, "the nationalist radical wing of the PDP confronted the leadership of Nevzat Halili accusing him of failing to obtain autonomy or the equal status of the people in the state" (Political Parties, Republic of Macedonia, Balkan Info, PDP).

In September 1995, both countries' Ministers of Foreign Affairs, Karolos Papoulias and Stevo Crvenkovski, agreed for Greece to recognize FYR Macedonia provided that Skopje would cease all nationalist propaganda, including the use of symbols, irredentist maps and cross-border minority claims. With this "Interim Accord", FYR Macedonia agreed to amend its constitution, and both parties agreed that the name is subject to a mutually acceptable negotiated solution under UN auspices. Despite the decline of support for Slavic Macedonian ultra-nationalism, Albanian political demands remained unaddressed.

For its part, Greece kept objecting to the recognition of a state sharing the same name with Greece's northern province of Macedonia. By contrast, the Albanians objected to the recognition of a state which in their eyes legitimized the most extreme form of Slavic Macedonian nationalism and catered exclusively to the well-being of the Slavic Macedonian majority. Both Greeks and Albanians believe to this day that Slavic Macedonians do not really exist as a separate ethnicity. Moreover, Greece's objections boosted Albanian claims, and both Greeks and Albanians pressed for the revision of the new state's Constitution for different reasons, which happened to work in parallel against the new state's external legitimacy. The Greeks wanted to see a clear terminological differentiation between Greek Macedonia and the new post-Yugoslav state, whereas the Albanians demanded constitutional equalization and an end to the Slav Macedonian exclusive ownership of the state.

The unifying link between the Albanian and Greek claims is the shared view that the state of FYR Macedonia cannot exist as the state of the "ethnic

Macedonians". The Greeks formally claim that such ethnic Macedonians do not exist while the Albanians claim that ethnic Macedonians exist within a multi-ethnic state. The state, therefore, cannot reflect the heritage of one ethnic group over the others. Similar to the Greek position, many Albanians do not wish to reside in a state named after the dominant Slavic Macedonian ethnic group, because it implies exclusive ownership of the state by one ethnic group. Throughout the 1990s, the Slav Macedonians were becoming increasingly insecure, introvert and less co-operative with the Albanians. However, as Ackerman explained, the lack of constitutional recognition of the Albanians as an equal constituent nation, although it safeguarded the development of a Macedonian national identity conflicted with the need of the Albanian minority to preserve its cultural identity. As a result, the more Slavic Macedonians assert their cultural identity, the more ethnic Albanians feel they need to assert theirs, leading to a vicious circle of clashing identity needs and claims (Ackerman, 2000:66). Hence, any delay on the resolution of the name issue intensified nationalism among the Slav Macedonians. This meant that there was even less willingness to consider incorporating the Albanians into a civic rather than ethno-centric state. The continuing name dispute between Greece and the new state became a tool of pressure for the PDP and NDP, and later for the radical Albanian factions, who realized that they can exchange political support on the name dispute (legitimacy) for more institutional, political and socio-economic rights. Simply put, the Albanians bargained their support on the name issue in return for greater rights.

Bulgaria

Bulgaria recognized FYR Macedonia with its constitutional name as being *a de facto* political entity, but denied recognition of the Macedonians as a separate nation while insisting that the Macedonian language was nothing but a Bulgarian dialect. From a geo-political point of view, the dissolution of Yugoslavia, and the subsequent independence of FYR Macedonia, ended Yugoslav control over Yugoslav Macedonia. Bulgaria saw a fresh chance for penetrating FYR Macedonia, this time through culture, trade and citizenship rights. Bulgaria also wished to undertake the role of FYR Macedonia's big brother, by taking an overt interest in its political developments.[2] Given the historical ties between the Slav Macedonians and the Bulgarians, some have labelled Bulgaria's policy towards FYR Macedonia as one of "subtle annexation".

After the initial freezing of inter-state relations during the rule of the socialist-led coalition bilateral relations took off again with the signing of the "language dispute" accord in February 1999. The problem with the language festered for years, marked by many absurdities such as the request by the Slavic Macedonian delegation for translation in formal bilateral meetings with Bulgarians, although they could mutually comprehend each other. In fact, "every time when Macedonian officials visited Bulgaria they were always accompanied by an interpreter – who was redundant – since everyone speaks the same language, almost" ("Macedonians speak the same language, almost", *Agence France Presse* – English Version, 10 February 1999, Bulgaria, Sofia). Bulgarian Prime Minister Ivan Kostov pointed out that "the language accord was a solution to an artificial problem [sic], since Bulgarians and Macedonians understand each other effortlessly" (ibid.). An additional element to the existing controversy is the fact that both Bulgarians and Slav Macedonians have regarded historical figures and events such as Jane Sandanski and Gotse Delcev, or the "Illinden Uprising", to be parts of their own separate national history. The language accord between FYR Macedonia and Bulgaria normalized inter-state relations by putting aside disagreements over history and language, while focusing on economic and trade relations. The influx of Slav Macedonian students to Sofia's universities, the absence of a visa regime (until 2007), and the introduction

2 The non-recognition of the Slavic Macedonian language was the reason for not signing a set of commercial and cultural agreements between the two countries in 1994. See: <http://www.newbalkanpolitics.org.mk/OldSite/Issue_6/todorov.part1.eng.asp>.

of the citizenship law, simplifying the issuing of Bulgarian passports, have all helped to create an atmosphere of fraternity between the two countries ("Bulgaria sent 150 tanks", *Paris Daily*, 23 February 1999).

Therefore, one may wonder how and why Bulgaria affected the decision of Albanians to adopt more radical demands and policies. The impact is less apparent though more substantial than Greece's objections. The trouble lies in the fact that Bulgaria was and is prepared to put the Slav Macedonians and their territories under its sphere of influence. Bulgaria continues to regard the Slav Macedonians as deluded Bulgarians and their lands as part of the Bulgarian national domain. Jenny Engstrom and Kristina Balalovska recognize the long-term negative impact of Bulgaria's external interference on inter-ethnic relations between Albanians and Slav Macedonians. No serious Balkan security and political analyst can bypass Bulgaria's strategic rationale over the "Macedonian Question". The so-called Macedonian Scientific Institute, based in Sofia, in a letter sent to President Gligorov, noted that "the Republic of Bulgaria is the home for over 3 million of Macedonian Bulgarians and their descendants who have been driven away by the Turkish, Serbian and Macedonian authorities. Therefore, we are not indifferent to the fate of the Republic of Macedonia."[3] The official Bulgarian policy of "state yes, nation no" dissatisfied many Slav Macedonians and encouraged Albanians to question the existence of a Macedonian people with the right of exclusivity over the country.

In the late 1990s, Bulgaria's policy approach capitalized on the anxieties of the Slav Macedonians concerning the Albanian's constitutional grievances and their calls for autonomy. Bulgaria openly undermined the state's most fundamental reason for existence: the justification of a separate Macedonian nation. For most Albanians, it could not be acceptable for a national group (nationality), whose actual distinctiveness has been systematically challenged or denied by neighbouring nations, to claim exclusive historic and national ownership of the state. On top of this, the existence

3 Letter of the Macedonian Scientific Institute in Sofia to President Kiro Gligorov, September 1997.

of a separate ethnic Macedonian nation conflicted with the incorporation of the Albanians into an inclusive and civic Macedonian nation. Some would argue that Bulgaria wished to facilitate the Albanian bid to press towards a more civic understanding of nationality and national ownership in FYR Macedonia by denying the existence of a separate Macedonian ethnicity. When relations became increasingly tense with the Albanians, Bulgaria changed its tune by offering an alternative to this "unstable and hybrid" "republic of Macedonia": its partial or complete incorporation into Bulgaria. These continuing challenges led to internally oriented protectionism of the state and thus the nation (Balalovska, 2002). Some believe that Bulgaria's pre-1998 policy had the unintended effect of strengthening Slav Macedonian nationalism (Ivanov, 2006).

Therefore, relations between Bulgaria and FYR Macedonia have complicated inter-ethnic relations within the latter country. Arben Xhaferi, former leader of the DPA, argued that the Slav Macedonian identity is fake and constructed. He explicitly and provocatively accused President Gligorov of usurping the historical and cultural heritage of Greece and Bulgaria, and asserted that there is no real "Macedonism" because it is based on a myth (Greek Helsinki Human Rights Monitor, 13 August 1997).[4] For the Albanians, the collapse of "Macedonism" would ultimately lead to the collapse of the Macedonian ethnicity and its desire and right to have an exclusive national domain. Those Macedonians would eventually have to choose their fate: whether they are Bulgarians, Serbs, or Slavic Macedonians. Of course, in other interviews, and depending on the position his party held, Xhaferi praised Bulgaria's role as the guarantor of FYR Macedonians' well-being ("Macedonian Albanian's Leader Xhaferi: Bulgaria Plays Stabilizing Role for Macedonia and the Whole Region", *B-INFO*, 21 October 2000). Nevertheless, according to Malevska, Albanian political leaders Macedonia have wrongly perceived Bulgaria's intentions with FYR Macedonia:

4 Non-artificial nations or ethnic groups are those presenting a natural historical evolution, heritage and relative uniformity, exhibiting an internally and externally recognized ethno-cultural consciousness.

> The desire for closer ties with Bulgaria was wrongly understood by the political leaders of the Albanian community in Macedonia as a signal towards the partition of Macedonia. That hypothetical partition perfectly overlapped with the interests of some Albanian radicals for closer ties or, even, unification with Kosovo or Albania. Thus was the scene being set up. (Maleska, 2002:12)

However, it is becoming increasingly evident that Albanian perceptions of the Slavic rapprochement with Bulgaria were at least partially accurate. Once a taboo issue, pro-Bulgarianism in FYR Macedonia has become a major trend in recent years. Today, thousands of people have received Bulgarian citizenship (approx. 65,000), and signed documents declaring their Bulgarian origin. Thousand others reside in Bulgaria. The Bulgarian state provides studentships to Slav Macedonian students on the condition that they declare their Bulgarian origin. Thousands of Slav Macedonians have migrated to Bulgaria, and generally, Slav Macedonians have warmly welcomed the Bulgarian rapprochement and overtly expressed their positive attitudes towards it. As noted,

> Bulgaria's self-perceived position as the national homeland is also provoked and justified as the conflict between Albanians and Macedonians intensifies the doctrine that Macedonians are Bulgarians which enables Bulgaria to play the role of guarantor and protector of the Macedonians, as it deems part of her own kin being threatened. (Maleska, 2002:12)

Therefore, the more tense relations become between the Albanians and the Slavs, the more protective Bulgaria becomes, confirming the view among the Albanians that the Slav Macedonians are Bulgarians, and therefore a separate Macedonian state is not needed. By 2001, many Albanians had become convinced that living in a state described as the domain of the "Macedonian people" is both hypocritical and unrealistic, even more so when this controversial state denied constitutional recognition of the Albanians and ignored their demands. This point of view helped to corrode the institutional, political and social links between the Albanians and Slav Macedonians, and ultimately encouraged violent secessionism among the former.

Serbia

Academic circles in Belgrade viewed the Slav Macedonians as being "historically void of any distinct ethnic characteristics that could render them a separate national status" (Engstrom, 2002:10). For the Serbs, as Kyril Drezov explains, the Slav Macedonians have always represented a "*une masse flottante*", something between true Serbs and true Bulgarians (Terzic, 1995). Today, Serbs recognize the Macedonians as nothing but "an officially nationalized mass for the promotion of Titoist geopolitical designs in the same ways the converted Muslim Slavs of Bosnia were characterized as Muslims only" (Engstrom, 2002:10). The Serbian Orthodox Church refused to recognize the schismatic Autocephalous Archbishopric of Ohrid as an independent church body, and continued to appoint Archbishops from Serbia. Moreover, an outstanding legal dispute over Kosovo's border delineation burdened interstate relations until 2001. This problem re-emerged in 2008 after consultations between Pristina and Skopje over a new border arrangement between Kosovo and FYR Macedonia. The Serb Ministry of External Affairs formally accused FYR Macedonia of violating the 1996 bilateral agreement on the mutual respect of territorial integrity and breaking the 2001 border agreement ("Serbs against FYROM", *SKAI TV*, 3 March, 2008, Greece).

During the Yugoslav Wars, the stakes in FYR Macedonia were objectively low, or seemed so to the Serbian leadership and its evolving interests, compared to the costs of any military operation in that country. As early as 1991, President Milosevic proposed to Greece to split up the country's territory between Greece and Serbia. Greece rejected the proposal on the grounds that these acts do not comply with Greece's foreign policy principles (Borowiec, "Greece vetoes Serbia plan to partition Macedonia", *The Washington Times*, 16 June 1993). Until 1994, Belgrade still regarded FYR Macedonia as a weak republic, whose secession led to economic decline and potential disintegration because of internal Albanian and external pressures. The Greek refusal to engage in such a risky act, i.e. dividing FYR Macedonia, convinced Milosevic that although the new state had no reason to exist as national state, geopolitical reasons necessitated its existence. Hence, the notion of the buffer zone emerged. The Serbs swiftly realized that the new state could serve as an ally against Albanian militancy.

Consequently, Serbia recognized FYR Macedonia with its constitutional name in 1996. Serbia also became an important trading partner during the harsh period of the Greek embargo. FYR Macedonia largely owes its economic survival to Serbia's, Albania's and Bulgaria's facilitation of alternative trade routes, ports and commercial transactions. The Serbian leadership consumed by fears of Kosovo's secession, recognized FYR Macedonia with its constitutional name in order to enable the Slav Macedonians to curb Albanian dissent and secessionist tendencies. Of course, some Serbs, especially supporters of Vojislav Seselj's extreme-nationalist Serbian Radical Party (*Srpska Radikalna Stranka*, SRS), opposed the recognition on the grounds that there was no such thing as a Macedonian nation, and that the territory was nothing else but southern Serbia (Engstrom, 2002:10).

The cynicism with which many Serbs refer to the Slav Macedonians as an ethnically unidentified folk has certainly added to the existing climate of doubt and insecurity. Nevertheless, Albanians regard Serbia as an anathema, even if Serbia's non-interference and the relatively small Macedonian-Serb minority in the country have temporarily allayed local Albanian fears. However, the mutual support between Serbia and FYR Macedonia during the height of the Greek trade embargo, the border delineation in Kosovo, and Skopje's hesitation in accepting NATO forces during the 1999 Kosovo war reinforced their perception of a Slav-Macedonian-Serb axis against the Albanians. Even so, Serbia remained a peripheral actor and its impact on inter-ethnic relations between Albanians and Slav Macedonians was relatively minor, at least until the peak of the Kosovo conflict. Nevertheless, the perceived unfair treatment of Kosovo Albanians by the Serb authorities and the influx of Kosovo-Albanian refugees strengthened anti-Serb sentiment among Albanians in FYR Macedonia.

Albania

Generally, the emergence of an independent FYR Macedonia was in the interest of Albania. Belgrade could no longer exert power over issues affecting the Albanians in Yugoslav Macedonia and Tirana viewed that as a positive development. However, the Republic of Albania, "while recognizing the state of FYR Macedonia … does not recognize that the state belongs to the Slavic Macedonian people" (Engstrom, 2002:12). Nevertheless, Albania recognized the state of FYR Macedonia under its chosen name, and urged the latter's Albanian inhabitants to cooperate with its democratic institutions. Aldo Bumci, an Albanian political analyst, asserted that "although relations between Macedonian authorities and the Albanians in Macedonia provided considerable room for intervention, Tirana did not exploit it. The stability of Macedonia, not the ethnic ties, was and still is the main factor that has shaped Albanian-Macedonian relations" (Bumci, 1992:3–5). Even so, relations between the two states were strained during the early 1990s, in part because of recurrent hints of Albanian irredentism:

> Sali Berisha, when he first became President in March 1992 declared that one of his main aims was Albanian unification. By the end of that year, however, Berisha had changed his mind completely, stating publicly that the concept of a greater Albania is not considered in serious Albanian political circles. ("Pan-Albanianism: How big is the threat to Balkan stability?", International Crisis Group, 25 February 2004)

Sali Berisha backed the Albanian bid in FYR Macedonia to delay recognition of the state until the constitutional status and the census problem were resolved. Inter-state relations deteriorated when in early November 1993 Skopje's authorities arrested ten ethnic Albanians for illegal arms trading, establishing an "All Albanian Army" and for preparing an armed rebellion to realize an "Independent Illyrida Republic". Deputy Minister of Defence Hussein Huskaj, one of the PDP representatives in government, and PDP's Secretary-General Midhat Emini were among the arrested. According to Interior Minister Ljubomir Frckovski, the Albanian paramilitary force received 600,000 DM from the Albanian diaspora. The police seized 300 semi-automatic rifles, thousands of rounds of ammunition and a list of 21,000 recruits (Ten Dam, 1997; Koktsidis and Ten Dam, 2008). Prime Minister Crvenkovski announced that these weapons were made in Albania and smuggled across the border. The short prison sentences for Huskaj in June 1994 temporarily de-escalated the situation, though these sentences still contributed to the worsening of inter-ethnic relations (Babuna, 2000:81; Xhudo, 1995:210; Van Moyland, 1995:65; Milivojevic, 1995:68–69).

Slav Macedonian fears mounted with the alleged involvement of Sali Berisha in the split of the Party for Democratic Prosperity (PDP), which was seen as a "hardening of the Albanian stance towards Macedonia" (Bumci, 1992:3–5). Political divisions and realignments among the Albanians in FYR Macedonia benefited those who wished to establish either an independent "Illyrida" or a "Greater Albania". During 1993, a split emerged within the Party for Democratic Prosperity, the then largest Albanian party founded in 1991 and led by Nevzat Halili (replaced by Abdurrahman Aliti in January 1994). Two opposing views dominated the debate. A faction comprised of those in the cabinet and parliament, supported participation in the government as the best way to achieve the Albanians' goals. Another faction, headed by Menduh Thaci and Arben Xhaferi, "maintained that participation in government without any progress towards meeting Albanian grievances had weakened the bargaining position of the Albanians" (Bumci, 1992:3–5).

In December 1993, the PDP leadership resigned. The government of Albania, led by the anti-communist Democratic Party of Albania (*Partia Demokratike e Shqipërisë*, PDSh or DPA – not to be confused with the DPA, formed in FYR Macedonia in 1997) of President Sali Berisha, supported the Menduh Thaci-faction. The picture became more complex when both Thaci and Xhaferi split away from the PDP and jointly founded the Party for Democratic Prosperity of Albanians (PDPA) on 22 April 1994. Berisha continued to support extremist factions within Albanian political parties in FYR Macedonia and Kosovo. He allegedly wanted to ensure a leading role if a "Greater Albania" encompassing Albania, Kosovo and western FYR Macedonia would ever come about (Perry, 1997:43; Van Moyland, 1995:65; Xhudo, 1995:210; Mickey, 1995:40; Babuna, 2000:82).

In March 1992 Berisha disclosed that his Democratic Party "will not stop fighting until her great dream of uniting the Albanian nation comes true" (Vickers, 1998:256). The extreme-nationalist United Liga of Shkoder (ULS) was strong in northern Albania and also dreamed of a Greater Albania (Michielsen, 1997:5).

Tirana had therefore openly supported the radical Xhaferi and Thaci faction, which brought about a strong reaction from Skopje. It seems that the key to understanding and controlling developments concerning Albanians outside Albania resides in Tirana (Bumci, 1992:3–5). Moreover, in 1995 a provocative statement by Sali Berisha on the origin of the Slav minority living in Albania alarmed and angered the Slav Macedonians. The Slav Macedonian press hurried to blast "Berisha's evolution from a well-intended friend of Macedonia and peace-maker in the Balkans into a militant advocate of a Greater-Albania and yet another denier of the Macedonian state and people" ("Berisha's Dilemmas", *Nova Makedonija*, 5 March 1995). As a rule, the more threatened the Slav Macedonians felt by the Albanians, the more aggressive their allegations became with regards to the provenance, size and discrimination against Slavic minorities in neighbouring states, a tactic widely used by all Slav Macedonian governments to divert attention from urgent internal problems. Still, the refusal of neighbouring states to recognize a Slav Macedonian minority deprived the Slav Macedonians of using the Slavic minority elsewhere as a counterweight to internal Albanian claims. Hence, to the Slav Macedonians, it was no accident that Berisha chose to undermine bilateral relations right when there was a pending withdrawal of UN troops from Croatia and probably from Bosnia, thus creating the possibility of a spillover of the Bosnian war ("Berisha's Dillemmas", *Nova Makedonija*, 5 March 1995).

The role of Sali Berisha as an *agent provocateur* played well in the Slavic Macedonian press. The Slav Macedonians believed that Berisha was searching for indirect ways to destabilize FYR Macedonia with an ambition to exert control over the Albanian populated parts of the country. Berisha's interest in FYR Macedonia's internal affairs faded during the economic crisis of 1996, which almost instigated a civil war and ultimately led to the government's collapse (and a near-civil war with its political opponents in 1997). However, Albania's formal and informal interests and interferences in FYR Macedonian affairs never really ceased. Berisha's assertive and often provocative stance did offer a pretext to the Slav Macedonians to delay constitutional changes, – and changes regarding the decentralization of executive power –, by expressing the fear that someday parts of the country may become parts of a "Greater Albanian" state. In reality, despite the naïve interpretation by some of a separate and existing Albanian-Macedonian consciousness, most Slav Macedonians never distinguished the Albanians of their country with those living outside its borders, and therefore believed that Albanians living in neighbouring states could easily manipulate the Albanians in FYR Macedonia.

Albania's position in relation to FYR Macedonia crystallized with the ascendancy of Fatos Nano and the Socialist Party. In 2000, his government sponsored the establishment of an inclusive "All-Albanian political forum" of Albanian leaders and Albanian political parties from Albania, Kosovo, FYR Macedonia and Montenegro:

> Fatos Nano referred to the possible drafting of a common political calendar between Tirana, Pristina, and Tetova that would provide a pan-national integration strategy to integrate all Albanians. According to Nano, he and Hashim Thaci laid out the foundations of this initiative in Tetova, together with the leader of the Macedonian Albanian Democratic Party, Arben Xhaferi. (ICG Balkans Report No 87, "Albania: The State of the Nation", 2002:5)

The Albanian Premier sought to reassure the alarmed neighbours, by stating that it "will be a movement not in support of a Greater Albania but will serve the great European Albanians" (ibid.). In addition, Hasim Thaci, the former leader of the officially disbanded Kosovo Liberation Army (*Ushtria Çlirimtare e Kosovës*, UÇK or "KLA"), said that these "official meetings have been made in the framework of unifying our national political stands towards the international community" (ibid.). Nevertheless, most Slav Macedonians do not believe that the Albanians in FYR Macedonia have a separate identity and separate goals from those held by many Albanians elsewhere (namely, some form of autonomy and territorial unification).

Conflict Spillover

Albanians from Kosovo and Yugoslav Macedonia have always been linked closely with each other (Bieber and Daskalovksi, 2003:286). I.R., a well-known journalist of Albanian origin and President of the Helsinki Human Rights Committee in FYR Macedonia, observes that "especially after the death of Tito, from 1981 until the end of the 1980s, we were always concerned about what was going on in Kosovo" (interview with the author, 15 July 2007, Skopje). Albanians from either side of the internal Yugoslav border could freely travel, work, study, settle and marry their fellow ethnic Albanians. I.R., a Pristina University graduate and now Skopje-based media correspondent for the *Voice of America*, verifies that: "tens of thousands of people from Yugoslav Macedonia have studied in Pristina. As Arben Xhaferi said, when Kosovo gains independence there will be hundreds and thousands of Albanians from Macedonia who would like to go and live in Kosovo" (interview with the author, 15 July 2007, Skopje). I.R. explains that:

> Albanians of Macedonia are literally connected to those of Kosovo. There are so many mixed marriages. Until 1991 when Macedonia proclaimed its independence, closed the borders, and stopped the free circulation of people, intermarriage and communication of the Albanians from both sides of the border was very frequent. (Interview with the author, 15 July 2007, Skopje)

However, it is still debatable whether or to what extent Kosovo contributed to rising tensions in FYR Macedonia during 1997–98. Aldo Bumci, an Albanian scholar, argues against the domino-effect approach; he believes that experience demonstrates that Kosovo does not have – and never had – a radicalizing effect on FYR Macedonia (Bumci, 2003). He argues that in 1981 and 1989 demonstrations in Kosovo left FYR Macedonia largely unaffected. In the early 1990s, Kosovo's Albanians boycotted Serbian rule by establishing a "parallel system", whereas the Albanians in FYR Macedonia decided to participate in the country's political life despite their perceived marginalization (ibid.). Bumci's assertion is questionable; SYR

Macedonia never experienced riots on the scale encountered in Kosovo. The impact of Kosovo on FYR Macedonia has been proportional to the scale and type of deprivation faced by the Albanians in FYR Macedonia. Most Albanians regarded Kosovo as the prime source of Albanianism; Albanian assertiveness and Albanian prosperity in Kosovo was idolized to the point that some believed Kosovo would become the Piedmont of a united Albania. Every time tensions were raised in Kosovo, the rumblings could be felt in FYR Macedonia, though in a much smaller and controllable scale. Many Albanians "in the 1950s rejected the idea of becoming part of the new Yugoslav Macedonian Republic, going so far as to demand autonomy from Tito" (Buck, 1996:5). In the early 1980s, "in SYR Macedonia as in Kosovo, Albanian leaders faced public trials for undermining Yugoslav and Macedonia integrity" (ibid.). In the middle and late 1980s restrictions against Albanian nationalism tightened in Kosovo and rights were reduced, not coincidentally, the same practices were used in SYR Macedonia.

As mentioned before, in January 1992, six months after the "Declaration of the Albanian Republic of Kosova" (following a referendum on Kosovo's independence on September 1991), an Albanian referendum was conducted in FYR Macedonia for the autonomy of the north-western part ("Illyrida"). These separatist manifestations of the early 1990s in Kosovo and FYR Macedonia have not been separate and coincidental events. The grievances felt by Kosovo Albanians after the abolition of Kosovo's autonomy (March 1989) and the radical and often violent reactions can be logically understood. In addition, the Albanians in FYR Macedonia had been denied rights they had enjoyed under Tito until the early 1980s, but they never enjoyed territorial autonomy or any of the privileges cherished by their Kosovo counterparts. Therefore, Kosovo's spillover effect on FYR Macedonia was proportionate to the rights, freedom and authority exercised by the Albanians the latter country.

Although the internal sources of relative deprivation fuelled some of the violent mobilization of Albanians in FYR Macedonia, the obvious attempt to imitate the tactics employed in Kosovo (denial of state legitimacy, referendum, mobilization, calls for independence) require a closer examination. The ease with which the "Illyrida" referendum results were ignored proves the insubstantial character of this political praxis. The emerging violent tensions in Yugoslavia, the threat of generalized war, and the mitigating role of the international community cooled down the Albanian overreactions against the FYR Macedonian authorities. The referendum was a tactical gesture to manifest Albanian intentions in case previous rights were not reinstated. In the same fashion, during 1996–1999 emerging radical Albanian factions in FYR Macedonia capitalized on the suffering of their fellow Kosovo Albanians, and exploited the gradual fading of the pacifist policy initiated and led by self-styled President Ibrahim Rugova and his Democratic League of Kosovo (*Lidhja Demokratike e Kosovës*, LDK). For many, the roots of Kosovo-Albanian extremism in FYR Macedonia can be found in the interaction of Albanians from Yugoslav Macedonia with Kosovo's underground institutions and rebel movements. Most radical leaders among the Macedonian Albanians were educated in Pristina University. As Jankulovski asserted:

> This makes it less surprising that we have such an obvious transfer of the Kosovo crisis to Macedonia. The rights and wrongs of the situation in Macedonia in their polemic do not emerge from the facts of the case, but simply from the prior prejudice and political frustrations. They have not only learned to be vocal, they have also discovered how easy it is to tear the flimsy fabric of Macedonian democracy. They misused the unsolved problems of Kosovo, namely the threat that ethnic conflict erupting there could spill over into Macedonia, to demand more and more. In addition, they believe the more extreme they sound, the more they will get. (Jankulovski, 1999:31)

Under this prism, the Kosovo conflict (1997–99) obfuscated the already burdened ethnic relations in FYR Macedonia. From February 1996, conditions in Kosovo started to deteriorate. Popular support among Albanians for Ibrahim Rugova's pacifist policy was dwindling; the number of armed incidents by the newly formed Kosovo Liberation Army (KLA) or "UCK" increased. Violent incidents multiplied in Kosovo during the first five months of 1997. In 1997, for the first time, the radical DPA challenged PDP's dominance by winning the most important Albanian municipalities (Tetovo and Gostivar) in the 1997 local elections of FYR Macedonia. This signalled increasing popular support for radical Albanian demands and aspirations. In Arben Xhaferi's words:

> The year 1997 was a year of new legitimacy for the DPA, or the former Party for Democratic Prosperity of Albanians. As everybody knows, we succeeded in winning the local elections in the most important constituencies of western Macedonia, that is in Tetovo and Gostivar and the other new municipalities that were born out of these centres. We also won in Struga and in Kicevo. We legitimized a new political mainstream and a new political option in this year. ("Leader of ethnic Albanians outlines demands after local election victory", BBC Summary of World Broadcasts, 10 January 1998)

From its very inception in 1994, the PDPA sought a more assertive role against the Slavic political majority. The term "Slavic" implied an equalization of the Serb repression against Kosovo Albanians with the Slavic Macedonian repression felt by the Macedonian Albanians. As early as 1996 (the year in which the UCK publicly presented itself), at the unification congress, which amalgamated the PDPA and NDP into the DPA:

> The congress resolution referred Albanian Cause and expressed appetites for creating a state within the state with ministries and departments that will be complementary to the Macedonian government, an all-Albanian parliament for the implementation of Albanian policies, where important decisions pertaining to all Albanian regions will be made and which will be aimed at rationalizing Albanian projects. According to testimonies, a group of about 30 uniformed individuals in black clothes with black berets and insignia, who were supposed to represent some kind of security staff, were present at the conference. ("Commentary: Irina Stojkovska slams speech by leader of new ethnic Albanian party", *Nova Makedonija*, 10 July 1997)

This statement clearly shows the initial effect of Kosovo on the radicalizing politics of the DPA. The "state within a state" clearly implies the initial wish to inaugurate parallel state institutions, similar to those that existed in Kosovo. As matter of fact, despite the fragile yet still impressive unity and integrity of the new FYR Macedonian state, and the absence of shadowy parallel state institutions, a "state within a state" existed since its inception. In practice, considerable isolation, segregation, lack of interaction with the state authorities (including the judiciary and police) and endemic tax evasion had virtually created a separate state of existence for the Albanians, especially for those inhabiting the country's rural areas. After the controversial DPA conference, and given the militant statements,

President Kiro Gligorov accused Arben Xhaferi of being an irresponsible radical fomenting extremism. Xhaferi responded in kind:

> This attitude conceals an aversion to the Albanians as being problematic, and implies that Albanian demands are creating instability, that Albanian demands must be eliminated, and that the Albanians themselves must be banished from the political stage. His project is one of marginalization, robbing the Albanians of their identity, and banishing them to the fringes of society ... I think President Gligorov has a problem with his political and intellectual upbringing because he has little knowledge of the past of these territories, and that comes from ideological textbooks. ("Leader of ethnic Albanians outlines demands after local election victory", BBC Summary of World Broadcasts, 10 January 1998)

Furthermore, Arben Xhaferi, in a statement that was to become a self-fulfilling prophecy, predicted a worsening political climate due to the worsening conditions in Kosovo:

> I think that this year [1998] will see a deterioration of the crisis in Macedonia, because the crisis is moving from the north-west of the former Yugoslavia to the southeast, i.e. to Macedonia and Kosovo. I think that the conception of the state that Milosevic is trying to build is similar to the kind of state that Gligorov is trying to build, and that these two concepts are both anachronistic and so do not coincide with global trends or the internal structure of the population. The crisis follows from this objective situation. (ibid.)

In this statement, Xhaferi and the DPA obviously tried to equate the severe grievances and far-reaching demands of the Albanians in Kosovo with those of the Albanians in FYR Macedonia. Apparently, the DPA tried to maximize their own people's demands and sufferings in order to mobilize their supporters against the state and trigger the state's counter-reaction. Of course, the ulterior aim was to gain political power and access in government through the political radicalization of the Albanians. Nevertheless, the differences between the Albanian grievances in the two countries were substantial, and the DPA faced a political dilemma: while the Kosovo Albanians almost unanimously asked for independence, the Albanians in FYR Macedonia generally preferred to cooperate with and in the government in order to resolve their minority issues. The resolution of these issues required systematic consultation and compromise, rather than the confrontational path chosen by the Kosovars. Serbia's actions were soon to release the DPA from its quandary.

After the Serbian crackdown against local militants and their families in the area of Likosane and Cirez in the Drenica area of western Kosovo (28 February–1 March), violent demonstrations erupted in Kosovo towns resulting in twenty deaths and more than 300 injuries in Kosovo. The first Kosovo Albanian refugees from the areas around Decani started arriving in FYR Macedonia, staying with local Albanian friends and relatives. DPA-leader Xhaferi warned that if "the situation in Kosovo deteriorates military involvement by Macedonian Albanians is to be expected" (ibid.). Serbia's "Drenica Offensive" and the consequent influx of approximately 14,000 refugees in FYR Macedonia had a profound impact on the local Albanian political elites and parties: their demands became more aggressive, and the proposed means of their realization became more radical, including resort to political violence (Jankulovski, 1999:32).

In March 1998, large demonstrations organized by both the PDP and DPA took place in Skopje and Tetovo in which thousands of Albanians expressed solidarity with their Kosovo brethren by holding Albanian flags, violating the law on the display of national symbols. On 13 April 1998 the Democratic Party of the ethnic Albanians pulled back its ministers from the national and local governments, in protest over the arrest of a mayor who displayed the Albanian flag. The situation started to become more and more tense. Certainly, during the peak of the Kosovo conflict in 1997–1998, incidents involving shootings, riots, arms seizures, bombings and disputed killings multiplied in the country. The UCK relied on safe havens in FYR Macedonia, and reportedly set up parallel structures among Albanian sympathizers there. On 4 January 1998, the UCK announced that its armed struggle for the liberation of Kosovo and its unification with Albania had begun. On 7 January, it claimed responsibility for the bombing of the municipal court building in Gostivar on 16 December 1997, and for the bombings of the police stations in the FYR Macedonian towns of Kumanovo and Prilep on 4 January 1998. On 19 February 1998, another bomb exploded in Gostivar. Many Slav Macedonian politicians and journalists suspected that supporters of radical Albanian parties rather than the UCK were responsible of carrying out the attacks. Serbia's "anti-terrorist operation" in the Drenica region of Kosovo resulted in the death of several dozen people and the near-annihilation of the militant Albanian Jashari clan and its supporters. From March to September 1998, violence in Kosovo reached new levels. Daily skirmishes and bombings by UCK against security forces triggered governmental reprisals and persecution, often resulting in dozens of dead rebels and thousands of refugees.

By July 1998, Rugova's pacifist policy was dead and buried, as an overwhelming majority in the Democratic League of Kosovo (LDK) demanded a continuation of both military and political efforts. The conflict's first repercussions were soon felt in FYR Macedonia. From September to October 1998, FYR Macedonian police had arrested twenty suspected UCK-members and seized large quantities of weapons, ammunition and explosives in several consequent raids that took place in Skopje, Kicevo and Tetovo. On 21 September 1998, Vlado Popovski, the Head of the Macedonian Intelligence service, admitted that the rebel movement had an infrastructure in FYR Macedonia. Popovski, however, believed that the UCK in Macedonia would not get active since the conditions in the country were (still) different from those in Kosovo; the greatest threat came from the smuggling of weapons into the country from Albania or a large influx of ethnic Albanian refugees from Kosovo (Koktsidis and Ten Dam, 2008).

We believe that Lisen Bashkurti's proposition that the instability in Kosovo affected FYR Macedonia is credible. The cause, according to Bashkurti, is found in the close geopolitical links and human ties across both sides of the border between the Albanians of Kosovo and FYR Macedonia. It is characteristic of Albanians that in times of crisis they strengthen their ethnic relations no matter where they are and live (Bashkurti, 2004). Support for the radical camp in FYR Macedonia steadily increased during the height of the 1997–1998 Kosovo crisis. Considering the widespread Albanian dissatisfaction, the radicals of the DPA were eager to equate the situation in their country with that of Kosovo; for them, the problem was the same: Slavic aggression and greed for power. By contrast, the moderates of the PDP believed that:

> The Albanian issues in FYR Macedonia can be settled within the framework of the Macedonian state, independently of the situation in Kosovo. The Kosovo crisis must not be used to poison relations between Albanians and Macedonians nor to exert pressure on the Macedonian government ... the reaction of the Albanians must be limited to national solidarity without political identification. (De Gille, 1998:31)

Prior to the 1998 elections, the PDP denounced the DPA's decision to withdraw all its elected members from all public institutions (parliament and city councils) as a dangerously radicalizing and destabilizing step. Despite such disagreements, the PDP and DPA agreed to form an electoral alliance for the upcoming parliamentary elections. In September 1998, one of the electoral slogans of the Albanian Democratic Party (PDSH) was "Macedonia will either be also the state of the Albanians, or it just will not be" (De Gille, 1998:17). Questioned about the future political action of ethnic Albanians – should the new government fail to do something in favour of the Albanian population – a DPA official stated that: "Other measures will have to be taken, at that point including a new referendum on autonomy, the removal of ethnic Albanians from all institutions, and the establishing of a parallel parliament and government. It could go as far as the withdrawal of Albanians from the political scene and the arrival of new players, like the UCK" (ibid.:38).

The International Crisis Group (ICG) pointed out that "while not advocating secession as a short-term aim, leading members of his party [DPA] have not excluded it as a long-term objective. Xhaferi has constantly demanded more rights for Macedonia's largest national minority, similar to the ones enjoyed by the Kosovars before Slobodan Milosevic stripped this province of its autonomy" (ICG Balkans Report No. 51, "Macedonia: New Faces in Skopje", Skopje–Brussels, 9 January 1999:11). Indeed, the ICG also observed that "the radicalization of ethnic Albanian politics in Kosovo has brought broader changes to Macedonia and PDP, as a long-term coalition partner is losing popularity for not being able to bring about any solutions to long-standing problems of their electorate" (ICG Balkans Report No. 45, "1998 Elections in Macedonia", Skopje-Sarajevo, 9 October 1998:14). The two major ethnic Albanian parties received 214,360 votes (19.26 per cent of the vote) and consequently won fourteen and ten seats respectively (ibid.).

The more reserved PDP still won the majority of Albanian seats. Yet the new government of Georgievski's conservative rightwing VMRO-DPMNE and Vasil Tupurkovski's liberal Democratic Alternative (DA) chose the DPA as their coalition partner. Georgievski argued that by incorporating the radicals could show the international community that Macedonia was a truly democratic state. E.M., a spokesperson for the Democratic Union for Integration (*Bashkimi Demokratik për Integrim*, DUI), the political successor of the National Liberation Army (*Ushtria Çlirimtare Kombetare*, UÇK or NLA), commented on this seemingly awkward partnership:

> The DPA stood for what was the radical political party of the ethnic Albanians in Macedonia. If you look at the way it was formed, the rift that the leadership caused in the PDP, it was clear that they were supposed to become the more radical political option which would articulate and stand more firmly and eventually implement all the demands, the political demands that the Albanian parties stood for ever since Macedonia's independence. However, this was not the case, as soon as DPA became part of government it became moderate, it suddenly shifted its vocabulary, its political discourse took a totally different direction in a way ... (Interview with the author, 15 July 2007, Skopje)

After the elections, in a surprising statement, DPA leader Arben Xhaferi said the emergence of the Kosovo Liberation Army (*Ushtria Çlirimtare ë Kosovës*, UÇK or KLA) helped his party become part of the governing coalition. He claimed that the existence of the KLA made the party's political adversaries look at it in a different light and take the party and its policies more seriously. In an interview published by the Albanian newspaper *Albania*, Xhaferi stated that:

> I think that we should consider this problem from two points, namely, before and after the emergence of the UCK [Kosovo Liberation Army] on the scene. We did have our theses even prior to the emergence of the UCK, which were, however, ignored, because we did not have any power to impose them. After the emergence of the UCK, our adversaries and we ourselves began to adopt a more serious approach. The UCK was a phenomenon that appeared on the scene following the loss of credibility of the Albanian political parties. This fact accounted for our political adversaries looking at us from a new angle and our political movement becoming more acceptable than in the past. ("Xhaferi praises role of Kosovo rebels in party's successes", BBC Summary of World Broadcasts, 18 February 1999)

The new coalition government (VMRO-DPMNE/DA/DPA) was required to prevent a violent spillover from Kosovo. The government had to counter a potential threefold spillover effect: firstly, militant Albanians from Kosovo, with the support of Macedonian Albanians, could engage in fighting within the country; secondly, Kosovo Albanians could step up operations on its soil; and thirdly, Milosevic's Serbia could severely stretch and worsen inter-ethnic relations in the country. Albanians born in FYR Macedonia were known to have fought on the side of UCK in Kosovo. Domestic political tensions rose during 1997–1998, but there was no verified aggression emanating from Kosovo. Numerous incidents were reported and attempts were made to involve the Albanians of FYR Macedonia in the Kosovo conflict, but they all failed thanks to the rising political expectations of DPA's inclusion into the government. Progress on the most crucial Albanian demands was on the horizon, an amnesty to Albanian political prisoners was granted and talks opened to resolve the university and decentralization issues.

However, the conflict in Kosovo took an unpredictable turn, which affected the stability of FYR Macedonia. On 28 May 1998, the Foreign Ministers of the North-Atlantic Treaty Organization (NATO) decided to take military action if necessary to prevent any possible spillover of the Kosovo conflict into Albania or FYR Macedonia. NATO also requested to use the Krivolak military base for potential military operations against Serbia, but Gligorov refused the request so as not to exacerbate relations with Serbia. While Gligorov stressed that FYR Macedonia could not participate in any NATO intervention against any of its neighbours, PDP leader Abdurahman Aliti and DPA's Arben Xhaferi urged the North Atlantic Alliance to intervene in Kosovo.

In October 1998, NATO requested the use of FYR Macedonia's airfields and the establishment of a surveillance mission headquarters in the Kumanovo barracks for launching surveillance missions in Kosovo. NATO officials also requested the deployment of a Rapid Reaction Force in case evacuation of Kosovo's OSCE personnel was required. The new VMRO-DPMNE government, in its effort to help the fragile country integrate into the North Atlantic Alliance, acceded to all requests. NATO officially installed a 1,500 strong extraction force in Kumanovo in December 1998. The government tried to preserve the balance between NATO's pro-

Albanian stance and the Slav Macedonian fears of an Albanian insurgency. Indicative of this controversy was the proposal by Mitre Arsovski, former ARM General and leading VMRO–DPMNE party member of the time to purge the Army of the Republic of Macedonia (ARM) of all Albanian conscripts.

Prior to the NATO air strikes, the refugee flow from Kosovo had been relatively small, and Skopje had adopted a discreet approach (UNHCR, "The Kosovo Refugee Crisis": An independent evaluation of the UNHCR Emergency Preparedness and Response, 2000:106). Of course, a few hundred Kosovo Albanian refugees had gone to FYR Macedonia after the Serbian crackdown began on 28 February 1998. Common sense indicated that if war started in Kosovo it would inevitably cause an exodus of refugees into neighbouring countries. Skopje feared the ways in which Milosevic could react, while Macedonian Albanians desired to see NATO taking action against the Serb forces. From March to April 1999, the total wave of refugees from Kosovo to FYR Macedonia grew to approximately 150,000. Amidst deteriorating conditions, thousands of Kosovo Albanians crowded its borders in an attempt to escape the war zone. For Skopje, the refugee inflow raised fundamental issues of national security (ibid.).

The Slav Macedonian authorities were becoming increasingly reluctant to accept fresh flows of refugees, given the heavily burdened economy, lack of external aid, and fear of a metastasis of conflict from Kosovo to their country. The sudden refugee presence – including the refugees hosted by Albanian families – amounted to some 10 per cent of the country's total population.[5] In many cases, Slav Macedonian soldiers had to push the Albanian refugees back into the Federal Republic of Yugoslavia ("Europe Macedonia using refugees as lever", BBC News, April 1999). Skopje was eager to resettle many refugees in nearby Albania. However, the border

5 The UNHCR estimates there are now 234,500 refugees in Macedonia, a number which takes into account several thousand who were not previously registered. With the addition of 10 per cent Kosovo refugees, the Albanian population in FYR Macedonia rose to approximately 35–40 per cent. Most guesthouse refugees belonged to Kosovo's elite.

closure and the scenes of desperate refugees being denied entry angered the Albanians in FYR Macedonia.

Did the refugee crisis make many Albanians decide to take up arms, and did it make the outbreak of violent conflict in FYR Macedonia more likely? At first sight, the answer seems to be negative. Despite the arrival of overwhelming numbers of Kosovo Albanian refugees, inter-ethnic relations in FYR Macedonia remained calm. Arben Xhaferi believed that "Slav Macedonian authorities' treatment of the Kosovo Albanian refugees reflects their irrational panic and xenophobia about a shift in the demographics of Macedonia but it may have a long-term impact on ethnic relations" (UNCHR, Refugees Daily, April 1999). Kosovo Albanian refugees were more concerned about returning to their homes than stirring up fresh violence in FYR Macedonia. For the Slav Macedonians, the refugee crisis was not just a humanitarian catastrophe as the Albanians saw it, but presented a demographic earthquake threatening to tip the ethnic balance in favour of the Albanians. A few incidents involving the beating of Kosovo refugees – who attempted to escape refugee camps – by Slav Macedonian police officers did endanger relations between authorities and refugees. Be this as it may, the refugee crisis exposed fundamental differences between the Slav Macedonians and Albanians on vital security issues and prospects:

> Macedonians and Albanians are dangerous for the civil peace in Macedonia. The first ones are pessimistic and deprived of faith leading to depression as they do not see any close perspective for a normal development and still less do they see any prospects for their family prosperity and the Macedonian nation as a whole. The second are in the apogee of their optimism for the future and they are filled with enthusiasm and conviction in their abilities, tested and confirmed in the crucial situation caused by the flow of refugees. (Zhelyazkova, 1999)

For the Macedonian Albanians, a positive turn in Kosovo would invigorate their internal demands. DPA circles believed that a responsive international community to Albanian demands in Kosovo could equally benefit Albanian demands in their country. However, Bedredin Ibrahimi, a DPA politician, warned that "a parallel system of life is growing here. It is possible we will get our own version of the Kosovo Liberation Army". However, he added that "Nobody wants this. Nobody wants fighting" (Fleishman, "Battles stirring Macedonia's Albanians", *The Philadelphia Inquirer*, 3 June 1998). Idriz Bajrami, a village leader, warned that "It smells like war. In two hours, war can be here. The young people here have no jobs and no options. They are looking to the radical ways of the KLA. The older ones like me are trying to calm them, but the resistance is building because there is no other solution" (ibid.). Slavs were fearful that any pro-Albanian developments in Kosovo would enhance Albanian demands on their country. Albanian political circles in both Kosovo and FYR Macedonia knew very well that the plight of the refugees was helpful to the KLA's campaign against the Serb forces. By 28 August 1999, almost 95 per cent of Kosovo refugees returned to their homes. Hundreds of Roma refugees and Kosovo Serbs were now entering FYR Macedonia. The way in which the Slav Macedonians handled the crisis exposed the internal dichotomies and fears. However, the infiltration of the KLA presented a more significant, immediate and dangerous spillover effect from the Kosovo war, contributing to the violent mobilization of Albanians in FYR Macedonia.

Geography, Resources and Albanian Insurgencies

In *Theory of the Partisan* Carl Schmitt writes that a partisan rebel is connected "... with the soil, with the autochthonous population and the geographical characteristics of the country – the mountain, forest, jungle, and desert ... land and sea are distinguished as a elemental spaces of human martial engagements ..." (Korf, 2011:2). The nature of the geographic terrain determines the operational tactics employed by guerrilla fighters, and provides the resources and safe havens necessary for sustaining the rebellion. Some major academic studies have employed explanatory models to explicate the causal links between resource abundance and the occurrence or persistence of violent conflict. Considerably fewer studies have attempted to examine the role of geography as a feasibility factor of violent insurgency. Most studies examining the relation of violent conflict and resources focus almost entirely on the intended acquisition, control and preservation of resources by rebel-predatory groups, rather than on the role of political geography and resources in sustaining the viability of conflict (greed and predatory war theory). These studies also tend to treat the territories of small wars as politically homogeneous (O'Lear and Diehl, 2007). These models ignore many factors relevant to the political geography of violence in small wars, including the ethno-spatial dynamics of warfare, and the differentiations of opportunities across different locations (Ballentine and Sherman, 2003; Buhaug, 2007; Dalby, 2007; Flint, 2005; Gregory and Pred, 2007, Korf and Engeler, 2007; Le Billon, 2007; O'Lear and Diehl, 2007; O'Loughlin, 2005; O'Loughlin and Raleigh, 2007).

Yet geographic location and resources (both material and human i.e. finances, raw materials, arms, recruitment and safe houses) shape the opportunities for and feasibility of violent insurgency, and define the propensity of an aggrieved group to violent insurgency. Paul Collier (Collier, 2009:3) has formulated the "feasibility hypothesis", proposing that where rebellion is materially feasible, it will eventually occur. Similarly, Fearon and Laitin (2003:75) have looked at the variables that make insurgency more feasible and attractive. They agreed with Collier that financing is one determinant of viability or feasibility of rebellion; however, finance and opportunity to loot are not the only factors explaining feasibility of rebellion. Geographic location, including regional geo-political arrangements, penetrability of borders, ethnic composition, safe havens and population density, determine the military-operational feasibility of rebellion.

A number of recent studies have attempted to produce a typology distinguishing and categorizing the geography of rebellion according to its different characteristics. Geography is classified into different types of geographic influence, including geography as rough terrain, (relative) location, resource concentration, and resource flow. Rough terrain models recognize mountainous terrain as a locational factor that makes rebellion feasible. This approach analyses the impact of geography from a purely geomorphological point of view (Korf, 2011). Traditionally, guerrilla leaders and military officers believed that the existence of remote, sparsely populated and mountainous areas rendered the eruption of violent conflict more feasible. On the one hand, rough terrain does allow insurgents to conduct guerrilla warfare, but on the other hand, many cases of violent rebellion have broken out in areas where such conditions were absent.

Interestingly, Collier and Hoeffler (2004) do not seem to find a correlation between rough terrain and the incidence of low intensity conflict, whereas Fearon and Laitin suggest that mountainous terrain is significantly related to higher rates of civil war (Fearon and Laitin, 2003:85). In a similar fashion, other analysts claim that higher forest cover increases the likelihood of prolonged conflict (De Rouen and Sobek, 2004). At the same time, the rough terrain indicators have provided evidence for the military feasibility proposition rather than the broader feasibility proposition (political geography). In response to these criticisms, the geography-as-(relative)-location approach adopts a spatially disaggregated approach to terrain and resource characteristics. Together with co-authors, Buhaug has refined the spatial analysis of war dynamics *within* the spatial container of a war, i.e. looking at spatial scales below the state level (Buhaug and Lujala, 2005; Buhaug and Rød, 2006). They run a comparison of "geography" factors on state and "conflict" levels, and conclude that "the amount of mountainous terrain in the country is positively associated with the duration of conflict, whereas densely forested countries tend to have shorter conflicts, *ceteris paribus*" (Buhaug and Lujala, 2005:412, italics in original). In another study, confined to African civil wars, they differentiate between a) territorial conflict, which is more likely in sparsely populated regions near the state border, at a distance from the capital, and without significant rough terrain and b) conflict over state governance, which is more likely to occur in densely populated regions near diamond fields and close to the capital (Buhaug and Rød, 2006).

Relative location models use spatial grid models to disaggregate national territories, to allow for a finer-grained analysis than rough terrain models. Analysts use spatial econometrics to analyse how geographical factors affect the tactics and characteristics of armed conflict, by defining a circular area around the battle zones of a conflict (Buhaug and Gates, 2002:418). They find that the scope of conflict is associated with a number of politico-geographical factors (ibid.:430), such as the total land area of the country, whether or not the conflict zone is adjacent to the border of a neighbouring country, and whether or not natural resources are located in the conflict zone. On top of this, small wars that occur at a distance from the capital are more likely to turn into protracted contests (Buhaug and Lujala, 2005:412).

Other researchers, using ACLED, have applied a "grid square" approach to study the relationship with country size and population numbers (and spatial concentrations), and conclude that conflict events tend to have "frequencies in proportion to the size of the population in a given location [...] where populations cluster locally" (Raleigh and Hegre, 2009:237). They also claim that the grid square approach is also suitable to test hypotheses regarding the availability of "lootable" resources. They explore the link between local levels of wealth and the location of actual fighting in a conflict (Hegre et al, 2009), or identify "hot spot" locations of violence, showing that forested areas have more violent events, while areas with hostile population ratios have less violent events (O'Loughlin and Witmer, 2010).

Resource concentration models conceptualize the link between type and location of resources, technologies of exploitation and incentives, opportunities for and feasibility of insurgency. Le Billon has provided an influential categorization of how the properties of a resource, its location and the required technologies of exploitation impact upon the dynamics of rebellion and warfare (Le Billon 2001, 2004, 2005a). These categories are then translated into a typology that links particular types of insurgency and warlordism with the geographies of "lootable" or exploitable resources. Following the work of Enders and Sandler, there is also growing literature on the economics of terrorism. Moreover, the World Bank is investing many resources to understand and better cure violence.

Collier and Hoeffler, in their work *Greed and Grievance in Civil War* (2001), have singled out three major types of rebel resources: exploitation of raw material resources, financial flows form diasporas living in developed countries and financial assistance offered by third countries. Accumulated physical, human and organizational resources also enable rebellion to occur. If a country has previously experienced a rebellion (e.g. against Soviet occupation in Afghanistan) there will be a residual stock of weaponry, former rebels who know how to use them, and probably a persistent, if quiescent, rebel organization. All these new approaches have made important contributions to understand the role of geography in small wars, but none has been completely convincing on its own terms.

Nonetheless, the present analysis is preoccupied with the feasibility of conflict in and around geographic borderlands and disputed territorial zones. More precisely, we are mainly concerned with the geographical disaggregation of conflict across different areas, allowing us to consider the variations in political geography and transnational factors influencing rebel strategies. For example, we seek to portray how rebel behaviour evolves in cases where insurgents can retreat into neighbouring states, politically contested lands that governments cannot easily monitor or target. Disputed lands, the spatial clustering of weak states, and the subsequent clustering of conflicts in these states, explain why conflicts cross borders, infecting already vulnerable states. For these reasons, the locations of states, their proximity to one another, and whether or not they share borders, are key variables in the study of conflict (O'Loughlin and Witmer, 2005). Clearly, neighbouring wars exacerbate volatile domestic conditions, and these wars can spread into nearby states. As a matter of fact, the salience of borders highlights the mismatch of nation and state. Borders exist in order to protect and nurture identities of nation-states: "If neither identity nor territory is structured and protected by the state, there seems no conceivable reason on why conflict, like people and services, cannot pass through porous boundaries contributing to the diffusion and escalation of civil wars" (O'Loughlin and Witmer, 2005).

After the formal termination of the war in Kosovo, regional security in the southern Balkans deteriorated. Fresh conflict emerged in the Presevo Valley in southern Serbia between Albanian extremists and Serbian security forces. The south Serbian districts of Pcinja and Jablanica are home to the last remaining Albanian enclaves within Serbia's territory. The municipality of Presevo has a clear ethnic Albanian majority of 89.1 per cent and the neighbouring town Bujanovac a 60.09 per cent ethnic Albanian majority, while Medvedja has a clear Serbian majority of 66.57 per cent, with the Albanians constituting a mere 26.17 per cent of the total municipality's population. All three municipal towns have an overall Albanian population of approximately 70,000 people. The municipalities of Medvedja and

Bujanovac border Kosovo, while the municipality of Presevo borders with both Kosovo and FYR Macedonia.

These three Albanian-inhabited municipalities in south Serbia attracted the attention of the international media in 2000 after a series of armed attacks against Serb security forces and local politicians by an extremist Albanian guerrilla formation called Liberation Army of Presevo, Medvedja and Bujanovac (*Ushtria Çlirimtare e Preshevës, Medvegjës dhe Bujanocit*, UCPMB). After the end of the Kosovo war in 1999, a five-mile-deep Ground Safety Zone (GSZ) was established between Kosovo and Serbia. The UN administered GSZ was intended to create a demilitarized buffer zone in order to deter Serbian aggression and prevent further clashes between Serbs and Albanians. Along this buffer zone, a restricted number of lightly armoured Serbian troops were allowed to patrol, thus becoming an easy prey for Albanian extremists who wished to provoke radical border changes in South Serbia ("Sowing Seeds of Change", USAID, 12 December 2002).

The guerrilla formation mirrored the tactics and *modus operandi* of its Kosovo predecessor, the Kosovo Liberation Army (KLA). On 21 November 2000, the rebels infiltrated Serbian territory and attacked a Serb police patrol, killing four officers. In due course they took over authority in villages and dwellings inside the UN Ground Safety Zone (GSZ). As a result, the Serbian police had to stop patrolling the area to avoid being ambushed. Lethal attacks were also made on Albanian politicians opposed to the KLA, including the murder of Xhemail Mustafi the Albanian vice-President of the Bujanovac branch of the Serbian Socialist Party. Many Albanian militants claimed they were fighting for self-defence against Serbian repression, while others suggested they were fighting for the liberation of Albanian territories under Serbian occupation.

On 25 November 2000, the Albanian militants of the UCPMB agreed to a ceasefire, under the auspices of NATO, after the latter threatened that, unless attacks against Serb officers stopped, it would allow the Serbian Army to intervene. Evidence that violence in Presevo emanated from Kosovo, forced a spokesman of the NATO-led Kosovo Force (KFOR) to state that "KFOR will not tolerate Kosovo as a staging area for exporting violence" ("Ceasefire agreed in southern Serbia", BBC

News, 25 November 2000). Nevertheless, throughout December 2000 Albanian rebels engaged in kidnappings, attempts to smuggle weapons into the GSZ, and sporadic shootings occurred with the Serb police. In the same period, an UCPMB attack resulted in the fatal wounding of a Serb soldier. As violence mounted, NATO allowed the Serbian Army to reclaim parts of the demilitarized zone in March 2001, pushing out some 600 to 700 ethnic Albanian rebels from the GSZ. At the same time, NATO gave the rebels the opportunity to turn themselves over to KFOR; NATO promised to take their weapons and note their names before releasing them.

As a result, more than 450 UCPMB members took advantage of KFOR's screen and release policy; all militants were consequently recorded and released. The crisis in Presevo contributed to the rise of the National Liberation Army (*Ushtria Çlirimtare Kombetare*, UÇK – note the same Albanian acronym as the KLA) in FYR Macedonia and the subsequent crisis there. As political analyst Z.D. asserts, "These conflicts in Kosovo and Presevo Valley are related to the extent that some of the leading figures of NLA and a number of its soldiers participated in the previous conflicts" (Z.D., interview with the author, 14 August 2007, Skopje). Government security advisors were convinced that Presevo fighters were entering the country, suggesting that the National Liberation Army (NLA) was a spillover from the Kosovo and Presevo conflicts (National Security Advisor, names encrypted, interview with the author, 15 December 2006, Skopje).

The International Crisis Group (ICG) found that Albanian political leaders in Kosovo and FYR Macedonia supported the insurgencies in the Presevo valley of southern Serbia. The reasons for this support are diverse, and range from parochial protection of political and economic positions to irredentist aspirations and the ambition to rearrange the Balkan map ("Macedonia: the last chance for peace", ICG Balkans Report No. 113, 20 June 2001:5). During the Presevo crisis (November 2000–March 2001), Tanusevci (a village in FYR Macedonia bordering Kosovo and very close to the border with Serbia) became a transit point for weapons bound for Albanian insurgents in the Presevo Valley. The village of Tanusevci would come to the forefront three months later, after the eruption of hostilities in Presevo and as the conflict there was heading towards a settlement. In order to understand the evolution of events in FYR Macedonia it is important to keep in mind that:

> All the localities where the fighting took place are at a very short distance from each other: there are only about 10–15 km between Presevo and Kumanovo and between Tanusevci and Presevo, about 10 Km between Tanusevci and Kumanovo, about 25 km between Aracinovo and Kumanovo. It was very easy for armed groups to move back and forth very rapidly from northern FYR Macedonia to Kosovo or the Presevo valley in southern Serbia, and vice-versa. (Balalovska et al, 2002:8)

The lack of a clearly delineated frontier between Serbia and FYR Macedonia, running through the Presevo valley, constituted a major source of concern for Skopje. The borderlands between Kosovo, Serbia (apart from Kosovo) and FYR Macedonia created a suitable geographic terrain that allowed Albanian militants to act as communicating vessels. KFOR had established a Ground Safety Zone within Serbian territory that stretched along the administrative line with Kosovo. The Serb army and police were subsequently deprived of their jurisdiction to patrol and control this strip of land alongside their border with Kosovo. Similarly, a small part of the borderlands between FYR Macedonia and Kosovo constituted a jurisdictionally disputed area contested by both. This "no-man's land" created a situation in which small villages like Tanusevci, which formally belonged to FYR Macedonia, were nevertheless practically surrounded by Kosovo. Thus the inhabitants of villages bordering with Kosovo preferred to conduct their educational, health and business affairs in Vitina, a town in Kosovo. It comes as no surprise that areas neighbouring with Kosovo, such as Tetovo and Kumanovo, constituted the operational backbone of NLA's 2001 rebellion.

Although the Albanians regarded the insurgency in South Serbia unsuccessful, the Presevo crisis stimulated the anxieties of frustrated Albanians within FYR Macedonia who viewed the political process between VMRO-DPMNE and the supposedly radical DPA as an indefinite political marathon. As Tim Ripley from *Jane's Intelligence* pointed out:

> The NATO decision in February 2001 to hand back the Ground Security Zone (GSZ), or buffer zone, along Kosovo's boundary with Serbia to Yugoslav control further confirmed Albanian suspicions that the international community was set to betray Kosovo to Belgrade. With suspicions that their cause was about to be betrayed, many former KLA members with family roots in Macedonia therefore decided the time was ripe to stage their own revolution. (Ripley, "Who are the NLA?", *Jane's Intelligence Review*, 2001)

Therefore, permissive strategic conditions facilitated the violent transformation of the conflict between the Albanians and Slav Macedonians. Government restrictions on education and language, inequitable representation, weak local self-government and restrictions on the use of symbols constituted much of the Albanian discontent and frustration with the state and the existing political system. On top of these, the generalized economic hardship remained a constant source of discontent (unemployment, low salaries, poor welfare system etc). The outbreak of hostilities, however, cannot be regarded as merely a form of greed (Collier and Hoeffler, 1999), since the impetus for violence already existed among the Albanians due to their grievances about their comparatively disadvantaged status. Yet some elements of criminalization and destructive greed were evident in the post-crisis environment.

In general, violence would be less likely to erupt in organized forms without the influence of strategic factors, since the governing political elites would happily retain the *modus vivendi* reached in 1998 between the Albanian and Slav nationalists. The regional-strategic environment hardly nurtured conditions of peace in fragile states like FYR Macedonia. External actors further undermined the legitimacy of the state, and intensified the antagonisms between the Albanians and the Slavs. At the same time, for almost a decade, Albanian demands on constitutional reform remained unaddressed and discussions on minority rights were put on hold.

There is little doubt that Greece and Bulgaria also threatened the legitimacy of the new state, complicating the ambiguous readiness of the Slavic majority to implement crucial internal reforms. At the same time, Albania's President Sali Berisha supported the more radical factions among the Albanians in FYR Macedonia, while Serbia, especially after the termination of the war in Kosovo, showed little interest in the internal affairs of its neighbouring country. Most importantly, Greek and Bulgarian objections over the name of the new state and the identity of Slav Macedonians caused a tremendous feeling of insecurity among the latter, which ultimately empowered the reactionary forms of nationalism among them. Consequently, the resulting political stagnation sustained a system of protectionism and prevented any meaningful political change from taking place.

The Kosovo-Presevo-FYR Macedonia triangle (1999–2000–2001) displays an interesting chain reaction. The Kosovo conflict failed to immediately or fully mobilize the Albanians in FYR Macedonia. Yet the latter exhibited great ethnic solidarity during the crisis in Kosovo, and anti-Slavic rhetoric intensified. There is little doubt that the outcome of the international intervention in Kosovo inspired the desire for a fast and drastic change among the Albanians in FYR Macedonia. Kosovo provided a tempting paradigm for the fast and efficient resolution of Albanian grievances through the limited and tactical use of organized violence. Ironically, NATO and US support sustained hopes among Albanian militants for a successful imitation of the Kosovo war in FYR Macedonia. Furthermore, Kosovo's metastasis in the Serbian region of Presevo had a direct impact on FYR Macedonia. Kosovo guerrillas fighting in Presevo provided a reservoir of experienced combatants, and ample ammunition, guns and logistical and technological support. These assets contributed significantly to the preparation and conduct of the Albanian insurgency in FYR Macedonia.

CHAPTER 5

Management of the Albanian Insurgency

This chapter explores the evolution and management of the 2001 armed conflict in the FYR Macedonia, in order to analyse the transformation of unresolved ethno-political disputes into violent confrontations. It also examines the important strategic parameters influencing the decision to use violence, and the effectiveness of coercion in the containment of regional conflicts (George, 1991, 1994). The prominent military and diplomatic analyst, Alexander George, claims that coercion is effective only if one matches threats and pressures with rewards and flexibility. The real aim of coercion, according to George, is to help avoid escalation and persuade the opponent to reassess the costs and risks of an action, rather than compelling them by force. This chapter distinguishes three phases in the evolution of armed conflict: emergence, escalation and settlement. In each section, we review and assess the ways in which international and local policymakers exchanged threats and provided incentives as part of a flexible policy intended to terminate hostilities. In this way, we are able to examine the motivations, opportunities and reactions of the conflict participants, understand the exchange between pressure and flexibility, and draw a number of conclusions concerning the effectiveness of strategic coercion in the containment of violent inter-ethnic conflict.

Conflict Emergence

In the first phase, we seek to understand how the opposing sides view the outbreak of hostilities, and examine the government's military and political failure to contain the spread of the crisis in FYR Macedonia. At this early stage, the EU and NATO devised a policy that would facilitate a quick exit from the crisis. In our analysis in this chapter, it becomes clear that without tangible incentives and pressures, international calls for peace and symbolic gestures cannot facilitate durable negotiations and peace settlements among the warring parties.

On 26 February 2001, armed clashes erupted in the border village of Tanusevci between the Slav Macedonian special police forces and armed Albanian militants after the latter had captured a group of Slav Macedonian journalists. The Albanian rebels claimed they acted out of self-defence after police officers shot an Albanian farmer in the village. The police raid in Tanusevci sparked controversy within the Albanian community. The DPA rushed to condemn the violent episodes, yet the opposition Party for Democratic Prosperity (PDP) justified the Albanian resistance in Tanusevci, claiming that the Slavic Macedonian authorities were conducting ethnic cleansing in the area (ICG Balkans Report No. 109, "The Macedonian Question: Reform or Rebellion?" Skopje-Brussels, April 2001).

Officials in the Ministry of Interior believed that the violence in Tanusevci erupted due to government attempts to disrupt profitable smuggling routes, which infuriated the Albanians (Hajdinjak, 2002). From a rather different angle, officials in the Ministry of Foreign Affairs believed that the skirmishes were a response to the bilateral agreement between FYR Macedonia and the Federal Republic of Yugoslavia to resolve an outstanding border dispute. In February 2001, Belgrade granted a strip of land from Kosovo to FYR Macedonia near Tanusevci. This development infuriated the Kosovo Albanians because they were not consulted on the issue, and consequently viewed this territorial agreement as a deliberate provocation against their demand for independence. The *Security Axis Globe* experts also confirm this:

> Serbia transferred 2,500 hectares to Macedonia and thus deprived Kosovo from 1,200 hectares of farmland. The agreement, which was signed on 22 February, was welcomed by every faction in the international community. The Kosovo Albanians were highly dissatisfied to see Serbia having the authority to decide on their behalf. That the terrorist activities of the Liberation Army of Presevo-Medvedja-Bujanovac (UCPMB) in southern Serbia and the National Liberation Army of Macedonia (UCKM) in

> north-western Macedonia started during those years was not a simple coincidence. (Karpat, "Euro-Atlantic Axis in the Balkans: Macedonia–Kosovo–Albania", AIA, *Axis Globe: Information and Analysis*, 2 May 2006)

This agreement increased the determination of Kosovo's Albanian militant forces – mainly from the officially disbanded Kosovo Liberation Army (KLA) – to stir up trouble in the Albanian-populated parts of FYR Macedonia. In fact, law and order issues in Tanusevci were complicated. Slav Macedonian and even Serb police entered the village and its surrounding areas on several occasions, creating confusion as to which country this village belongs. Undoubtedly, the newly established National Liberation Army (NLA) exploited this vexing issue. Due to mounting tensions, the NATO-led Kosovo Force (KFOR; the peace-enforcement mission in Kosovo based on UN Security Council Resolution 1244), decided to allow the Serbian Army to enter the Ground Safety Zone, and KFOR sealed off the Kosovo border with FYR Macedonia. A week later, the Slav Macedonian army and police captured the border village ("Macedonian Forces retake Tanusevci", *Hellenic Resources Network*, 2001).

Following these events, the NLA decided to confront the government openly. On 14 March 2001, the rebels launched an attack in the area of Tetovo. The rebel movement wished to ignite a popular, "spontaneous" revolt and succeeded in doing so. Two days before the attacks in Tetovo, the NLA published a communiqué stating the reasons for their decision to take up arms: "Albanians have for decades been insulted, discriminated against and banned from all civilization traditions in Macedonia … in vain we tried for years to have our rights realized through a change in government" (Huggler, "Macedonian tanks shell Tetovo guerrillas", *The Independent*, 21 March 2002:87). The communiqué succeeded in mobilizing hundreds of people, who rallied in the city carrying Albanian flags and weapons and shouting slogans. It was the first major demonstration of public support for the NLA. However, public calls for a "Greater Albania" raised governmental fears of a pending territorial disintegration. Throughout March, the insurgents attacked the police in a systematic, quick and effective manner. The police and government were caught in a state of panic. Government official N.D. explains:

> Someone could analyse the reasons for this crisis in different ways. The first few communiqués called for getting rid the Slavic population from Albanian majority territories. Therefore, it was more of a fight for territory and for changing the borders. Then the rhetoric gradually evolved into a human rights plea. Some people thought it was a fight for power among Albanians, an intra-ethnic fight. Well, when you analyse the result, you have one Albanian Macedonian political party in government before the crisis and another after crisis. In addition, another theory relates to the grey areas of organized crime and drug trafficking. What criminals want in order to prosper is to have areas without law and without functional institutions. It was beneficial to them to have this disputed border areas between Kosovo and the Republic of Macedonia free of police or army. So yes, the truth is maybe a combination of all these, forming the context of the crisis. (Interview with the author, 16 December 2007, Skopje)

In reality, the state authorities primarily viewed the crisis as a provocation on the part of Kosovo. Prime Minister Georgievski accused the international community of failing to admit its failure in Kosovo and trying to ignore this aggression, which according to him was "carried out by the new Taliban, this time in Europe" ("Lubjco Georgijevski's Address: Macedonia is under attack from Kosovo; if necessary we shall use the army", 19 March 2001). Government official N.D. explains that "the logistic support was provided as a result of the crisis in Kosovo in 1999, people were trained and armed, a number of people basically did not have jobs, and the Kosovo conflict was over, and reforms – and progress – were too slow in Macedonia" (interview with the author, 16 December 2007, Skopje). In an earlier interview, N.D. observes that:

> The State Department Report is clear; it was an invasion from Kosovo, an invasion from a UN protectorate. However, the rebels [of the UCK] were not received with great sympathy by the majority of Albanians in Macedonia. They enjoyed some support in Kumanovo, Lipkovo, and Tanusevci, but there were no signs of support in other Albanian majority cities such as Gostivar and Debar. However, with huge money from Switzerland, America, and Germany they attracted some supporters [from within FYR Macedonia]. They were about 1,700 [combatants], although they claimed to be more, supported by more than two thousand sympathizers. (Interview with the author, 15 December 2006, Skopje)

By contrast, political analyst I.R. takes a rather different approach:

> Some people explain the crisis as aggression from Kosovo. This is perhaps one of the elements, especially having in mind that a lot of Albanians from here were involved in Kosovo. It was obvious that they were Albanians born here. Kosovo, after 1999 was a UN protectorate, it was difficult to prove that the citizens of a UN-controlled area invaded Macedonia. Secondly it was counterproductive for the political forces in Kosovo to destabilize Macedonia, because it undermined the good image of the Kosovars who were cooperative, moderate and so on. So they were real steps taken by Rugova, Hashim Thaci and Hajradinai to prevent the spreading of the crisis, and common appeals to the Macedonian UCK to stop activities and start negotiations. (Interview with the author, 13 July 2007, Skopje)

After the end of the crisis, politicized former combatants (i.e. former NLA rebels who went into politics) were to argue that the rebellion was an initiative by political "outsiders" against political "insiders" in their own community, a struggle between the privileged Albanian political elites and the marginalized yet dynamically rising Albanian rebels.

Origins of the NLA

Organized violence against the state was not a new phenomenon for the security authorities of FYR Macedonia.[1] The NLA claimed responsibility for sporadic attacks in FYR Macedonia during 1998, 1999 and 2000. Earlier statements implicated KLA founding member Fazli Veliu – the FYR Macedonian-born leader of the National (or People's) Movement of Kosova (*Lëvizja Popullore ë Kosovës*, LPK), arguably the founding movement or

1 National Security Advisor, interview with the author, 14 December 2006: "In 1998 small terrorist incidents happened, including attacks against two police stations and the Supreme Court by a small group of Albanian nationalists. Half of that group was arrested; the other half went to Switzerland. Ahmeti [the NLA's leader] was behind these attacks. There was no Albanian rebellion in Macedonia however, because the conditions were absent. In September 1999 the demilitarization of UCK in Kosovo started with Agim Ceku, as a man in charge. There was clear evidence that the quantity of weapons was enormous".

predecessor of the KLA (Koktsidis and Ten Dam, 2008) – in the case of the "Kicevo bombers", when small bombs exploded near several police stations in 1998 and 1999 (Brown, Farisides, Ordanoski, Fetahu, 2002:21). Yet, until 2001, the NLA never really managed to mobilize much support for a full-scale insurgency, and the group's aims remained widely unknown. The most notable incident attributed to the NLA occurred on 11 January 2000 in the Skopje northern suburb of Aracinovo. Three Slav Macedonian policemen lost their lives after a fatal gun attack by a group of Albanians. The NLA claimed responsibility for the attack in a communiqué published on 30 January 2000. On 22 January 2001, the National Liberation Army shelled a police station in the border village of Tearce ("Macedonia: Step back from the abyss", BBC News, 29 December 2001), resulting in the death of one policeman and the wounding of another three. After the attack, the NLA stated that:

> the NLA had been formed after the failure of the Macedonian state to reform itself by legal means and in response to the use of force by the authorities ... this is a warning to the Macedonian occupiers and their Albanophone collaborators. The uniforms of the Macedonian occupiers will continue to be attacked until the Albanian people are liberated. ("Macedonia: Step back from the abyss", BBC News, 29 December 2001; Rusi, 2002:4).

The rebel movement then transmitted a communiqué (No. 4) to the Deutsche Welle Broadcasting agency, which for the first time outlined its demands: full citizenship and repatriation of all Albanians in FYR Macedonia; an internationally monitored census; elevation of Albanians into a constituent nation; official status for the Albanian language; freedom to use national symbols; elimination of discrimination in public administration; change in the political and electoral systems; and international mediation.

In the meantime, dissatisfaction had dangerously accumulated among the youngest, jobless and less well-off segments of Albanian society (especially in rural and mountainous areas). They saw the supposedly radical DPA unable to press forward the political process, and unable to secure them jobs despite receiving their vote in the last elections. Of course, the initial contradictory statements by rebel commanders, ranging from improved community rights to outright secession, suggested strong factionalism and weak central leadership – a typical feature in the other Albanian rebellions of the former Yugoslavia (Kosovo, Presevo in southern Serbia) as well. The NLA initially heralded an "alternative route" to those who believed that a peaceful debate and resolution of their grievances had proven fruitless. The NLA's call to arms galvanized those Albanians who were frustrated by the lack of progress, and who believed that the Slavic majority whose ethnic members were predominantly employed in the public service and the government were to blame for the persistent discrimination and poor living conditions. By April 2001, the NLA outlined the same demands as those expressed by the Albanian political parties: equal status, official status of the Albanian language, new census and higher education in Albanian. Other demands included decentralization, and improved representation in the police service and state media. A considerable portion of the Albanian community supported, justified and defended the NLA's activities as a necessary means to press not just the Slavic Macedonians but also the international community to grant them their longstanding political demands. Zhidas Daskalovski observed that:

> At the onset of the conflict, the organization's goals were unclear. Its communiqués claimed it was fighting against Slavo-Macedonian oppressors and for a "Greater Kosovo" or a "Greater Albania". Later the NLA changed its rhetoric and argued that it was fighting for the human rights of the Albanians in Macedonia and for constitutional reforms. (Daskalovski, 2006:128)

Some analysts feared that frequent remarks of a "Greater Albania", and the NLA's later establishment of territorial zones of control, indicated secessionism rather than autonomy and equal rights ("Greater Albania question", BBC News, 18 August 2001). The state authorities viewed the crisis as a provocation instigated by Kosovar Albanians, boosted by a small number of Albanian ultra-nationalist academics and politicians within the country. It is difficult to determine the precise motivations behind the NLA's activities. B.J. claimed that "there is a lot of contradiction. I am not sure whether they were a movement of human rights. I think the settlement in Kosovo created euphoria among the Albanians, nationalist euphoria. Firstly, they published one communiqué stating that they need their territory back. For me, this conflict was not justified" (interview with the author, 17 December 2006, Skopje). Whatever the actual intentions, the NLA's founders had carefully secured and coordinated the human and financial resources long before the unfolding of the crisis. Some local Albanians who felt financially disenfranchised and politically excluded wished to provoke a speedy political change i.e. access to state assets and resources. Many were associated with extremist circles in Kosovo and the Albanian Diaspora. Public frustration with the slow progress made by the DPA and the controversial delineation of the border between Kosovo and FYR Macedonia also played into the militants' hands. The bottom line is that some people desired to alter the status quo by force, through the NLA. Essentially, the NLA consisted of a mix of KLA-veterans providing the command cadre, and local Macedonian-Albanian volunteers. As Z.D. explains:

> The violence in 2001 was initiated by a small group of Albanians. Led by Ali Ahmeti, the previously unknown "National Liberation Army" or NLA (the acronym of which is ONA in Macedonian and UCK in Albanian), a motley group of former Kosovo Liberation Army (also UCK in Albanian) fighters from both Kosovo and Macedonia, Albanian insurgents from the south-eastern Serbian regions of Preshevo, Bujanovac and Medvedja crossing the border into Macedonia, young Albanian radicals and nationalists from Macedonia as well as foreign mercenaries. They organized a seven-month armed insurrection against the Macedonian government (February–August 2001). (Interview with the author, 14 August 2007, Skopje)

Local men and boys were recruited to provide logistic support, medical help and other administrative tasks. Villagers provided food for the fighters. Diaspora groups linked to localities provided the funds and expertise to buy and smuggle arms to specific brigades. (Ripley, "Who are the NLA?", *Jane's Intelligence Review*, 24 August 2001). The NLA leadership resided in Sipkovica, an isolated mountain village near Tetovo, but the real headquarters resided in Prizren, Kosovo. Ali Ahmeti, a Kosovo-educated Albanian born in FYR Macedonia, initiated, coordinated and led the NLA's activities, and had close links with Ramush Haradinaj, a former KLA commander and leader of one of the main KLA factions during the Kosovo conflict. Ahmeti had taken over the role of the NLA's politico-military representative together with Gezim Ostremi, a senior KLA commander who deserted from his chief-of-staff post in the Kosovo Protection Forces. Fazil Veliu, former editor of a newspaper in Kosovo and a close friend of the Kosovo's Jashari clan, was also involved in the formation of the NLA. Emrush Xhemaili served as an advisor of Thaci, and he was thought to be the real military leader of the extremists in Macedonia and southern Serbia (Ripley, "Who are the NLA?", *Jane's Intelligence Review*, 24 August 2001). S.O., a political analyst working for the UNDP in Skopje, offers a deeper insight into the structure of the NLA:

> The size of the Albanian rebel force never exceeded 1,200 people. They had five brigades so called ... but actually, the fighting force never exceeded several hundred, 30 to 40 per cent were mercenaries from outside. So they did come as mercenaries, but these are mostly people who came from Bosnia and Kosovo, people whose profession was war, who were paid for that, most of them did not bring any idea behind that, they were working for money. So I wouldn't say it was a kind of ideological movement which now we have problem with it, these were mercenaries, they were paid. That's it. The majority of the rest of the Albanians (60–70 per cent) were people who actually took arms in the Kosovo wars in the 1990s and of course some Albanians from Macedonia, some of them were also active in the former Yugoslav territories where fighting were going on but some of them also were native Albanians from Macedonia who've been told it is worth fighting for. (Interview with author, 15 December 2006, Skopje)

Albanian political analyst I.R. also asserts that:

> At the very beginning of 2001, if you take February as the beginning of the conflict [the events in Tanusevci], it was obvious that in February until the end of April the rebels were small groups of people, Albanians born here but in the meantime leaving Macedonia for Western Europe, becoming part of UCK in Kosovo or living in Kosovo being part of different political organizations linked to Kosovo, not Macedonia. They didn't enjoy the special support of the local Albanian population. (Interview with the author, 14 July 2007, Tetovo)

Hence, most analysts tend to agree on the rather limited level of support the NLA received inside FYR Macedonia at its early stages. The rebel movement attracted a relatively high number of mercenaries, former "professional" combatants from Kosovo, Bosnia and the Presevo Valley. Government security advisors in the Ministry of Interior insist that there was clear evidence that Presevo fighters entered the country, and that Islamic fundamentalists from Afghanistan and Pakistan also joined the ranks of the NLA. The mutilation and desecration of eight soldier's bodies at the Skopje-Tetovo highway massacre in August 2001 indicated Mujahedin involvement, as Albanians were not (yet) known for such actions. Arrests of Chechen and Pakistani individuals also raised suspicions. NLA training centres were reported in Tanusevci and the village of Lojane; Halid Zuzaku, an inactive lieutenant-colonel of the Army of the Republic of Macedonia, allegedly handled the training (Kujundzic, "Balkan Fuse", NIN, 8 March 2001).

Contradictory statements have been given on the NLA's size, but it is highly unlikely that the rebel force exceeded 3,000 active combatants at its peak ("How many groups, how many guns?", *The Economist*, 25 August 2001:26–27). Moreover, it reportedly consisted of at least six brigades: the 111th; the "Ismet Jashari" 113th, which operated a strong military police unit; the 114th, based in the Sara Planina region; the "Karadak" 112th, based in Tetovo; the 115th, based around Skopje; and finally the 116th, in Gostivar ("Macedonia's Bitter Divide", BBC News, 27 August 2001).

However, these "brigades" and any other rebel formations seem to have operated autonomously, barely answering to central or even regional command. As Dejan Anastasijevic, an analyst for the Skopje newspaper *Vreme*, reported in 1998: "Long gone is the view that the Albanian insurgency (in Kosovo) had regional commands ..." ("Rebel defeats may be self-inflicted", University at Buffalo Archives, 1998). The same holds true for the insurgency in FYR Macedonia. Radosa Milutinovic, an independent journalist in Belgrade, added that "the Albanians refuse to submit to higher authority. Indeed it is doubtful whether there ever was a single command" ("Rebel defeats may be self-inflicted", University at Buffalo Archives, 1998). State security officials claim that the rest of the NLA consisted of local Albanian fighters who were paid or forced to participate, but this allegation remains contentious. It is no secret that weapons caches located in Kosovo were to form part of the NLA's arsenal. The affluent arms market in Albania also provided a secure flow of weaponry to the rebels. Weapons known to have been held by the NLA include 9M32 Strella-2M, portable surface-to-air missiles (SAMs), 120mm and 82mm mortars, rocket-propelled grenades, light anti-tank rockets and 12.7mm heavy machine guns, as well as assorted light machine guns and AK-type assault rifles (Matveeva, 2003). Estimates on the number of weapons held by the rebels diverge, as FYR Macedonia, just like Kosovo and other neighbouring regions, is a "heavily armed society" with a secretive "gun culture" that transcends ethnic boundaries ("How many groups, how many guns?", *The Economist*, 25 August 2001:26–27).

Military Responses

From 18 March 2001, Slav Macedonian troops started taking up positions inside and around Tetovo ("Macedonia battle rages on", BBC News, 17 March 2001). At the time, Javier Solana, the EU High Representative of Common Foreign and Security Policy (CFSP), asked the government to postpone a military move against the rebels, and requested the National Liberation Army (NLA) to lay down its weapons. The rebel movement ignored Solana's request and continued its offensive. On 21 March, the government issued an ultimatum, calling on the rebels to leave their positions. The rebels rejected the ultimatum, but offered a unilateral ceasefire to signal their readiness for negotiations. The army responded with a heavy artillery barrage against NLA positions in Tetovo. On the one hand, the EU condemned the use of violence by Albanian extremists, and supported the government in combating terrorist acts with proportionate military responses, signalling for the first time that the crisis could not be resolved through diplomatic pressure alone. On the other hand, the EU urged the government to avoid further escalation and to start a dialogue on political reforms with the elected but discredited Albanian parties ("Macedonia accuses west of inaction", BBC News, 17 March 2001).

While the DPA pressed the government and the international community for dialogue and reforms, Lord Robertson, the Secretary-General of NATO described the NLA as "murderous thugs", and endorsed President Traijkovski's position not to negotiate until guerrilla violence stops first

("Macedonia on the brink of abyss", BBC News, 7 May 2001). The US administration claimed that their human and material resources were overstretched in the Balkans because of Kosovo, and political rather than military means must be used for resolving the crisis. In the US Congress, the Republican non-interventionist faction protested at the American presence in the Balkans, while the "Atlanticist" faction was preoccupied with the much more important theatres of the Pacific and Eurasia. The crisis in FYR Macedonia fell into an American policy gap. Responsibility for handling the crisis was therefore transferred to the EU. The passive attitude of the United States encouraged the NLA to believe that the US did not act because they either approved its actions, or did not care. However, American policymakers knew that neither side possessed the necessary operational capabilities to win a potential full-scale war. Briefly, they and other (Western) policymakers regarded the crisis in FYR Macedonia as a theatre of controlled violence, whereby the state would probably continue to survive until a better deal, preferably a territorial one, was found between the ethnic communities.

As the crisis escalated, international pressures against the rebels increased. US Ambassador Michael Einik announced that the US "was helping authorities in Macedonia coordinate an anti-insurgent response with NATO" (Nafeez Mossadeq, 2001). KFOR sealed off the border with Kosovo and provided intelligence. Yet at the same time, Javier Solana, without offering any tangible incentive, jumped in to persuade the two major Albanian parties DPA and PDP to condemn the insurgents and ask them to lay down their weapons in order to create favourable conditions for dialogue with the Slav Macedonians. The political parties had initially agreed with the proposal but after a month, the PDP defected from its commitment. Meanwhile, a new party, the NDP, emerged to exploit the rising pro-NLA sentiments. In late March the army, backed by a lukewarm international support, increased its military pressure. By the end of March, the government declared its operations complete and successful, despite the fact that military and political officials knew they were incapable of defeating the NLA ("The Tetovo Advance", BBC News, 25 March 2001). B.J. explains that:

> Of course, from a military point of view the best scenario would have been, if the Macedonian security system was able, to keep the NLA out of the game and at the same time intensify the process of giving rights to the Albanians. The government should have put these military and radical structures out of the political game and continue to communicate with the existing Albanian political forces. But unfortunately, this did not happen because the security system in Macedonia was not capable of doing so. (Interview with the author, 2006)

The Slav Macedonian parties were increasingly pressed by the EU to pay attention to Albanian demands, at the very moment at which rebels threatened to dissolve the state. For this reason, the government declared its operations successful, allowing for legitimate talks to open. As the then editor of the newspaper *Dnevnik* stated, "If we can isolate these guys in black pyjamas successfully, then President Trajkovski in the next day or two will announce the beginning of negotiations with Albanian representatives" (Erlanger, "Wide offensive by Macedonia presses rebels", *The New York Times*, 26 March 2001). On 2 April 2001, a fresh NLA communiqué (No. 9) stated that the "NLA has successfully resisted the 'torched land' offensive launched by the Macedonian forces. Now we are entering the phase when the NLA struggle for liberation from the Macedonian state domination would continue with combined forms, suitable to the present military and political situation" (NLA Communiqué No. 9, "Party activities and propaganda are banned in the army", *FAKTI*, 2 April 2001).

In reality, the state's armed forces were ill-equipped and ill-trained in guerrilla warfare, and the government was aware of their low retaliatory (counter-insurgency) potential. The army's equipment, including virtually all Main Battle Tanks (MBTs) and artillery, came as external aid from Greece and Bulgaria. Additionally, approximately 22 per cent of the 12,000 army conscripts were Albanians, who were kept in barracks during operations; many of them defected. The Army of the Republic of Macedonia (ARM) lacked adequate supplies and coordination systems, and showed little experience or readiness. For this reason, the ARM's cumbersome counter-insurgency operation relied on artillery and mortar support, leading to accidents including civilian deaths. The ARM never attempted to gain full control of contested areas; it only tried to temporarily push the NLA away. In one instance, about 100 NLA rebels were cornered in the

Gracani area; their staunch resistance in the face of heavy artillery fire embarrassed the Slav Macedonian security forces, whose infantry units seemed extremely reluctant to engage in open battle (Zoran Kusovac, "Macedonian army lacking strength", *Jane's Intelligence Review*, 23 March 2001). Clearly, the army's inability to clear and hold the rebel-held positions prompted Javier Solana and Lord Robertson to arrive in Skopje and urge military restraint and quick political dialogue.

Political Responses

On the false pretext of capitalizing on operational success over the NLA, the government entered a stage of intense political mobility. President Boris Trajkovski made a draft proposal for addressing the Albanian concerns. He called for the four major elected parties (VMRO-DPMNE, SDSM, DPA and PDP) to participate in roundtable talks with the aim to reach a final agreement on certain reforms by June. The NLA reacted to the President's decision in a statement published on 2 April, in communiqué No. 9:

> The NLA stands for negotiations with the Macedonian side. Negotiations are always led between the two conflicting sides. In this case, the conflicting sides are the Albanians and the Macedonians, i.e. the Macedonian government and the NLA armed forces. Therefore, negotiations without NLA participation would make no sense and would be considered as non-valid. (NLA Communiqué No. 9, "Party activities and propaganda are banned in the army", *FAKTI*, 2 April 2001)

On the same day, President Trajkovski presented a basis for all-party discussions; but the Slav Macedonian parties were not prepared to make any concessions regarding changes in the Constitution. Moreover, calls to accord official recognition to the Albanian language were also rejected. Trajkovksi attempted to shift the focus away from constitutional matters, and concentrate on the improvement of economic and social conditions for all citizens. In line with the NLA, the opposition Party for Democratic Prosperity (PDP) attacked President Trajkovski's draft proposal as ignoring the true Albanian national demands, and focusing instead on other political and economic measures. The PDP also demanded the inclusion of NLA representatives in the talks (ICG Balkans Report No. 109, 2001). The PDP denounced the government's military offensive in Tetovo, and in an effort to exploit the increased popular sympathy for the NLA, declared it would not participate in the talks (Casule, "Macedonia starts talks, Albanian party boycotts", *Daily News*, 2001). By contrast, the radical DPA stuck to the EU directives and pressed for multilateral talks.[2]

In an attempt to help the Slav Macedonian side to proceed with limited constitutional amendments without this being regarded as a capitulation, Javier Solana offered the government the chance to sign and join the EU Stability and Association Agreement (SAA). The agreement required the adoption of EU standards in democracy, human rights and the rule of law – and provided a recognizable framework for normalizing inter-ethnic relations. The government desired to take steps towards EU integration and the signing of the SAA could function as a face-saving device for the Slav Macedonian side ("Macedonia to sign EU Association Pact", BBC News, 9 April 2001). By signing the agreement on 9 April, the government demonstrated resolve against the extremists, while agreeing on reforms required by Europe and not by those Albanians who threatened the country. These efforts appeared less successful in diffusing political tensions, as the big question on constitutional amendments remained unaddressed. No Slav Macedonian politician, party, intellectual, or opinion-maker could or dared to agree on a drastic constitutional change that would elevate the status of the Albanians from a minority to a constituent nation. The NLA was frustrated with the political process, and this led to a resurgence of violence, derailing the very same political process. The socialist party's leader demanded the immediate formation of a broad coalition government. Prime Minister Lubcjo Georgievski clarified that he would not accept any

2 The Minister of Labour and Social Policy, Bedredin Ibraimi, and the DPA's vice-president, Menduh Thaci, caused outrage by saying that the NLA rebels were traitors to the Albanian cause in Macedonia, and that any government has the right to exert its authority over the entire territory it governs (Popetrevski and Latifi, 2002:29–36).

talk on constitutional amendments, and invited the SDSM leader for talks on creating an inclusive coalition (Popetrevski and Latifi, 2002:29–36). President Trajkovski, however, exhibited a greater willingness to accommodate Albanian demands.

According to B.J., "The presidential environment was able to understand that there is a problem; there was a need to change the constitution. But the VMRO and the SDSM were engaged in extensive propaganda" (Interview with the author, 2006, Skopje). The EU in coordination with the United States realized the need to find other ways for pressing towards constitutional change. Yet the multi-ethnic government in Skopje was unable to reach consensus on this issue. There was simply deadlock: while VMRO opposed constitutional changes, the DPA pressed for such changes. Government official N.D. explains that because of this divergence of views:

> The main forum to push the political process forward became the office of the President … so the President invited the political parties and drafted the peace plan. The international community shared the objective of resolving this peacefully, while maintaining the nature and character of the country. The other parties had some differences; they did not share the same agenda. Georgevksi was a hardliner, and then the social democrats – the former government – they were a bit more in line with President Trajkovksi. (Interview with the author, 2007, Skopje)

Although the PDP formally sided with the NLA, the DPA leader Arben Xhaferi continued to push for constitutional change as a means of neutralizing the NLA. However, the VMRO leadership still refused to discuss fundamental constitutional reforms with the Albanians. The political picture became one of confusion, disagreement and petty political tactics. On 24 April, the Albanian rebels delivered a letter to the UN Security Council, the EU and NATO, calling for immediate constitutional changes. Ali Ahmeti, the NLA-leader and chief negotiator, argued that the "constitution should state that Albanians and Macedonians are separate peoples, that Albanian is an official language and outlaw all forms of discrimination. A national census must be carried out by a neutral international organization, as well as the return of political refugees and the release of all political prisoners" ("Albanian Rebels Spell out Demands to Macedonia", *European*

Internet, 24 April 2001). He finally demanded that "negotiations must be held between the two sides in the conflict, mediated by the international community" (ibid.).

Four days after Ahmeti's public call for dialogue, Albanian rebels in the area of Vejce ambushed a convoy of Special Forces. The NLA took responsibility for the attack. The Vejce attack marked a definite crack in the relations between the Slav Macedonians and the Albanians. After the attack, the conflict spread from the political domain to the community itself. Riots broke out in Bitola during the funeral of the four soldiers. Large crowds started attacking shops, cafes and houses known to belong to Albanian families. Most Albanian-owned properties were destroyed and 2,000 Albanians fled the city in panic. The "Vejce massacre" demonstrated the NLA's will to use lethal violence in order to press for direct representation in the peace talks, yet this attack only sparked a wider divide between the Slavs and Albanians – and decreased the chances of NLA representatives participating in any talks.

Conflict Escalation

In the second phase of the conflict, international mediators became more actively engaged, amidst rising levels of violence. For the first time, EU and US policymakers tried to establish contacts with the Albanian militants through secret talks. However, as we shall see, uncoordinated efforts to inaugurate these talks proved unsuccessful, and undermined the political partners in the unity government who resisted the legitimization of violence. The conflict escalated after a number of NLA attacks against the police. The army decided to launch a fresh operation to cleanse the areas around Kumanovo of NLA rebels. To the ARM's bombardment, the NLA answered with mortar and rocket attacks. The rebels were determined to hold their positions, although they accused the army of indiscriminately shelling the villages. G.T., a Ministry of Interior spokesperson and current president of a political party, reveals in interview the difficulties of fighting a war in the areas where the rebels were concentrated. G.T. acknowledges the operational dangers, but remains critical of the refugee flow during the counter-insurgency operation in the Kumanovo area:[3]

> Most western countries in that period [and even now] suggested that we cannot simply send tanks and mortars and bomb some villages. Our Special Forces at that period were very poor in their skills and lacked equipment. But at the same time how does the US army operate in Faluja? There you have one house with ten innocent people there, but two people shot from that house or they shot from the nearby mosque ... so if we say that this house or this mosque is a legitimate target we open fire there. (Interview with the author, 2006, Skopje)

The renewed clashes near Kumanovo proved again the army's incapability to flush out the rebels. The VMRO-DPMNE faced a dilemma; Prime Minister Georgievski asked for the declaration of a state of war, while others did not wish to see such a development and pressed for dialogue in spite of the adverse conditions on the battleground. The DPA declared that in case a state of war was declared, the party would leave the coalition. If the DPA left the coalition there would be no conceding Albanian party left to participate in government, while the SDSM would demand immediate elections. As government official G.T. explains, the declaration of a state of war was unlikely because the whole of the Slav Macedonian parliamentary block was internally divided:

> Our constitution says that the only institution in Macedonia that has the right to establish a war condition is the parliament. The President of the republic and the social democratic party were against this process. On the political level, the SDSM was strongly against the ruling party. On the operational level, our military chain command was in an equally chaotic state. (Interview with the author, 2006, Skopje)

3 According to the UNHCR, more than 6,500 villagers of all ethnic backgrounds (Slav Macedonians, Serbs, Albanians, Roma and Turks) from the Kumanovo region have fled across the border to Kosovo since 3 May 2001. Most Albanians in the affected villages found shelter in underground bunkers and storage pits.

Clearly, the army of FYR Macedonia was incapable of penetrating the villages and clearing them of NLA militants and restoring order. Instead, the ARM engaged in risky long-distance assaults against rebel positions. The EU and NATO watched the deteriorating conditions in Kumanovo and the growing political gap between the Slav and Albanian political blocks. If a state of war was declared, the army would engage in all sorts of military operations using all available means – and that could radicalize the entire Albanian population and mark the definite halt of political dialogue. Lord Robertson, realizing that such military operations could end up in an all-out civil war with the risk of spilling over into Kosovo and the Presevo Valley, asked Javier Solana to intensify his peacemaking efforts. The only solution Solana could see was the promotion of a unity government that would prevent the collapse of the government, promote a sense of cohesion, and at the same time include all major parties in discussions. Solana and Robertson made it clear that the international community did not want to see a further escalation of hostilities in FYR Macedonia, as this could destabilize the entire region.

On 8 May 2001, the SDSM, DPA and PDP all agreed to form a unity coalition government with VMRO. Unsurprisingly, the NLA refused to recognize the new coalition government. The Grand Coalition wished to terminate the violence, isolate the NLA, and minimize the repercussions of the conflict. This would facilitate the negotiation of a peace deal with and through the elected parties. However, clashes between the NLA and the army continued, despite DPA threats of leaving the talks in case the army continued its operations. The rebels deliberately sought to sabotage the dialogue by provoking military responses. F.V.K., a political advisor in the FYROM EU Delegation, described the state's powerlessness in detail:

> The Macedonian armed forces never had the capacity to beat the Albanian forces, so there was really no end to this conflict. They always announced that they would do a final push to crash out the Albanians, but most military officers I knew at the time said that if the Albanians wanted it they could have overrun Skopje, they could have kept Skopje, they could have attained Skopje by force. My assessment is that it was a fight between nationalists and rationalists and I think Trajkovksi was a lot more rational than Georgievski. What was the alternative? Peace now or perpetual conflict for the next two years. (Interview with the author, 14 December 2006, Skopje)

At the same time, the Slav Macedonian parties in the unity government regarded Albanian demands to be excessive. It was clear that a compromise could be reached neither by military defeat, nor through dialogue, but only through some type of external enforcement. From 20 May onwards, the NLA and the army confronted each other on almost equal terms. Nevertheless, despite the technical restrictions, lack of coordination and international warnings for restraint, the army managed to occupy areas around Kumanovo. The intention of the NLA was to stretch the ARM forces across several fronts, and thus diminish the already limited capability of the armed forces. Indeed, the rebels managed to stretch the ARM forces from Tetovo to Kumanovo, creating several mini-fronts. It was clear by then that the army could neither eradicate nor capture the rebels.

As the armed crisis intensified, an unexpected incident of unofficial diplomatic intervention threatened to subvert the Grand Coalition. Richard Frowick, then OSCE Special Envoy in FYR Macedonia, contacted a number of Albanian politicians and parties and proposed to hold an intra-Albanian meeting in Prizren, together with the NLA rebel leader Ali Ahmeti. Frowick engaged in talks with Albanian political parties including Xhaferi's DPA and Imeri's PDP, and invited to this forum prominent Kosovo Albanian politicians such as Ibrahim Rugova, Hashim Thaci, Ramush Haradinaj, Agim Ceku and the Albanian Prime Minister. Frowick was clearly on a mission to confront the government with a *fait accompli* and guarantee some type of inclusion of the rebels in political talks. In a revealing interview, Frowick explained:

> I had very high-level support out of Washington to start to promote an end to fighting and to begin a peace process. I was actively involved in pressing hard against the legitimate political leaders on the Albanian side whether in Macedonia or Albania or Kosovo, to stop the fighting and persuade those that were engaged in it under the political leadership of Ahmeti. In that situation I developed extremely strong chemistry with the Albanian political leaders and the idea was to go back and talk with them; use that kind of influence to affect the peace process in Macedonia. (Interview with Robert Frowick, <http://www.beyondintractability.org/audio/ambassador_robert_frowick/?nid=6738>, 2006).

On 23 May, Frowick struck an informal deal that exchanged a ceasefire by the NLA for negotiations with the government. The deal posited a full amnesty for the NLA fighters. The Albanians in Prizren demanded constitutional amendments and unrestricted use of the Albanian language, – as an official language in FYR Macedonia –, ethnic proportionality in state institutions, and enlarged powers for the municipalities. Moreover, they called for consensual democracy in areas concerning ethnic rights, rehabilitation of all of NLA members, and the reconstruction of villages and family economies destroyed during the fighting. The agreement, however, recognized the integrity of the state and encouraged the use of political means to resolve ethnic grievances. In short, Frowick legitimatized the NLA insurgents by talking to them and accepting their demands. The secret multiparty talks in Kosovo granted the rebels a say in the political process, and gave a mandate to the elected Albanian parties of FYR Macedonia to represent the NLA at the negotiating table. The rebel representatives agreed to halt the fighting in exchange for amnesty and the right to gain veto power over future political decisions about the scope of ethnic Albanian rights in FYR Macedonia. When Forwick presented the documents to the unity government, the Slav Macedonian parties were infuriated with his initiative because it undermined the government's stance of refusing to negotiate with the rebels. Government official N.D. describes how the Slav Macedonian parties felt when the agreement came out in public:

> The government's policy of not negotiating with the rebels lasted throughout the crisis from the very beginning to the end. The policy was that the republic will not have any contact with Ahmeti and his people because that would legitimize them as a political player, and that is what Frowick did. Efforts were made to talk with the registered political parties in Macedonia composed of ethnic Albanians. It was too early to have something that has the signature of Ahmeti on it. It was seen as something legitimizing terrorism. (Interview with the author, July 2007, Skopje)

This controversial deal triggered Slavic anger, undermined the impartial role of the United States, and damaged the OSCE's image in the country. The agreement in Prizren equally undermined the EU's position as an impartial, credible and balanced mediator. The EU had granted full support to the government's decision to reject negotiations with the rebels. The EU and NATO failed to *persuade* the conflicting sides without the use of significant threats, other than projecting the benefits of peace and prospects of integration into the Euro-Atlantic organizations. Nevertheless, any realist of the time could see that there could be no political process without encompassing the rebels into that process. Many Slavs, refusing to acknowledge that one eventually had to talk to the rebels, accused the Albanian political parties – with the support of Kosovo politicians – of having created a platform for legitimizing terrorist violence. As a result, the army stepped up its military operations. All Slavic Macedonian parties seemed to be backing its moves, and fears grew for the militarization of politics.

Unfortunately, EU efforts to facilitate political dialogue failed to create conditions conducive to political progress. Lord Robertson requested that the tottering coalition government must exercise firmness with restraint, but flexibility with their politics in order that a way could be found to end the conflict ("NATO to discuss Macedonia issues", BBC News, 21 May 2001). Solana moved to Skopje to back the unity government, and mitigate the Slav Macedonian fears that the talks would include the NLA or a veto by the Albanian parties on behalf of the rebels. Similarly, Solana promised Albanian representatives that a deal with the Slav Macedonians would significantly change the status of the Albanians. For the first time, Prime Minister Georgievski publicly recognized that there might be a need for a change in the Constitution that would give the Albanians improved status as a constituent nation. However, DPA leader Arben Xhaferi insisted that "We can only end the war by negotiating with players in the war, and that includes the NLA" ("Macedonian President offers amnesty", BBC News, 3 June 2001). His statement undermined Solana's efforts to convince the Albanian side to advance their demands without the direct or immediate inclusion of the NLA.

Strategic Coercion and Settlement

The two opposing sides continued their military engagements despite the international calls for political dialogue. In early June 2001, the National Liberation Army (NLA) ambushed and killed five soldiers in Tetovo. Following these killings, most members of the unity coalition lost their hopes for a cessation of hostilities without conceding to the rebels' demands for direct talks. However, as a response to the heightened levels of NLA violence, the hardliner Minister of Interior Vlado Boskovski devised a new plan to eradicate the rebels – while rumours resurfaced that a state of war would be declared. However, declaring a state of war required a two-thirds majority in the 120-member parliament, and Albanian parties would never vote for such a decision. A declaration of war would bring significant risks: firstly, it would polarize and militarize ordinary people along ethnic lines; secondly, it would severely undermine political dialogue; and thirdly, it would hardly change the stalemate on the ground i.e. there was little likelihood for a definite military victory by either side.

Even so, the NLA seemed to be strengthening by the day. In mid June, 300 rebels moved from the northern villages around Kumanovo towards the capital Skopje. They occupied Aracinovo, a village just ten miles away from the capital's city centre (an effective suburb of the latter), and established a fighting force inside and around the village. From Aracinovo, the NLA published a statement claiming that it possessed mortars and rockets that could reach the oil refinery, the airport, the city centre and a motorway vital to the NATO-led forces in neighbouring Kosovo, and called for the government to consider its demand for direct talks ("Rebels threaten Macedonian capital", BBC News, 10 June 2001).

The national unity government refused to concede to the rebels' demands under these conditions, and the Ministry of Interior launched a counter-strike in order to retake and restore order in Aracinovo. The NATO and the EU granted a last chance to the country's national army to capture or remove the rebels from the vicinity of Skopje. The international observers from NATO and the OSCE gave the security forces three days to complete the counter-insurgency operation. During the first armed clashes, the security forces started to count their first casualties, four dead soldiers and many wounded. After three days of fighting (22–25 June) the security forces had hardly made any progress. Political analyst S.O. offers an informative insight on how the failure to retake Aracinovo marked the end of the crisis:

> The Macedonian Slav forces in power wanted to intervene in Aracinovo, hoping that they would liberate Aracinovo in two days. Besides, they had the approval of the EU and Solana, and it took three days for the Macedonian security forces, using everything they had, including helicopters and planes, but they didn't even enter the village. Obviously, the village was not defended by big numbers of NLA soldiers, inside Aracinovo there were 170 people and they were capable to prevent a lot of policemen and soldiers from entering. When Solana and Robertson, the General Secretary of NATO, returned to Skopje, it was obvious that the Macedonian security forces were not capable of resolving the problem because Aracinovo was near Skopje and there was a danger for the conflict to enter into the city. Until then the conflict was mainly happening in some rural areas near Tetovo and Kumanovo, but not inside the cities. So, that was the end of the story. The international representatives demanded to withdraw the police from Aracinovo. They forced the NLA soldiers to withdraw, and then they forced the Macedonian political parties to go into Ohrid and start a real negotiation with the special envoys of EU and NATO. That was the start of the framework agreement. (Interview with the author, July 2007, Skopje)

More precisely, NATO's crisis negotiator, Peter Feith, intervened in Aracinovo and opened talks with the rebels. He promised the NLA a safe evacuation from the village in return for a ceasefire. Indeed, US military personnel escorted 300 to 500 NLA rebels out of the suburb. Government official N.D. explains that:

> A decision was made when they realized that they could not really take over Aracinovo without experiencing casualties. The decision was that a political deal was needed in order to terminate the deadlock, and that deal was brokered by Peter Feith (NATO's special envoy). The deal was that the NLA would leave Aracinovo with their arms and the state would then agree on a ceasefire. That was a *quid pro quo.* It is very controversial how the transport was provided, we tried with two private companies from Tetovo, but when they realized that they would have to enter the village without police escort they refused, so eventually NATO provided the transport ... and then a controversy was created that they [the Albanians] were supported by the Americans. (Interview with the author, 2007, Skopje)

At the same time, Solana pressed the Slav Macedonians to initiate major constitutional changes in return for peace. To dissolve Slav Macedonian resistance, the EU clearly stated that any future financial EU aid to the country would depend on the results of political dialogue with the rebels. After consultations with Solana and Robertson, President Trajkovski prepared a package of proposals that included a partial amnesty for all FYR Macedonian-born NLA militants and provided for NLA's disarmament under NATO supervision. NATO troops would only come into the country if a durable ceasefire and an agreement between all parties were achieved ("NATO warns of Macedonian civil war", BBC News, 23 June 2001). Hence, the preconditions for the termination of the crisis were clearly set: an immediate ceasefire would be followed by a political agreement. However, the scenes of Albanian militants leaving Aracinovo unscathed, and the government's decision to ask for a ceasefire, triggered angry public protests. Government official N.D. observed that:

> The public reaction varied from ridicule to criticism. We do not see it [the events in Aracinovo] as a huge success. I think the very presence of NATO symbolically helped to calm down the situation. In 2001, for the first time in their history NATO introduced high-level senior diplomats, who were working alongside with European Union diplomats. So, NATO was not just a military organization here, they were present into the political dialogue, in the negotiations of the framework agreement, and brokered the deal in Aracinovo. NATO had a big influence among the NLA because of their role in Kosovo. The confidence of the NLA in what NATO would say was bigger than what the EU representatives would say. (Interview with the author, 2007, Skopje)

The decision by the international bodies to intervene and coerce the conflicting parties was the result of a careful consideration of a wide array of regional-strategic and operational parameters. First of all, NATO and the EU realized that neither the Albanian guerrillas could afford a full-scale war nor the Slavic Macedonian forces could eradicate them without external military assistance. Secondly, the army's clumsy military response generated more recruits to the NLA, and polarized the communities even further. The longer this military campaign went on, the greater the state's fragile social and political fabric was in danger of unravelling. Thirdly, the continuation and intensification of hostilities between the Albanian rebels and the Slavic Macedonian forces threatened to plunge the entire region, including Serbia, Kosovo and Albania, into chaos.

Zhidas Daskalovski explains that the Albanian militants, their supporters and even international representatives were eager to project the crisis in FYR Macedonia as one resulting from a situation in which "Macedonia, although ostensibly democratic and tolerant, has discriminated against and otherwise mistreated its Albanian population. As such, the NLA rebellion was justified and the solution to the crisis required major concessions on the part of the Macedonian government" (Daskalovski, 2004:21). Daskalovksi offers a convincing explanation as to how and why the international community wished to present the crisis to the local communities and the outside public and observers. The "internationals" sought to devise a way to extract major concessions from the resisting Slavic Macedonian leadership, and put an end to the violent conflict without (overly) legitimizing the NLA. They pressed the opposing parties to contain the conflict within the limits of controlled low-intensity warfare, so as to enable a political solution and prevent further escalation and regional destabilization. A political process was required to establish – at the very least – a short-term yet comprehensive compromise before the situation spiralled irreversibly out of control.

These strategic considerations explain why the US Administration put immense pressure on Ukraine to quit arms sales to FYR Macedonia, and why at the same time the US Department of State designated the NLA as a "terrorist organization" so as to counter Slavic Macedonian preconceptions of American bias towards the rebels. In a similar balancing act, the EU promised Skopje financial aid worth 50 million Euros, but only if it accommodated the legitimate grievances of the Albanians ("Macedonia Aid Under Threat", BBC News, 7 December 2001). Furthermore, under the terms of the "Stability Pact", the IMF put a ceiling on FYR Macedonia's military expenditure so as to discourage further military operations in the country (Chossudovsky Michael, "Macedonia: Washington's Military-Intelligence Ploy", *Emperor's Clothes*, 17 June 2001). On top of this, the IMF froze its budgets in the country on civilian and social infrastructure programs, including water, electricity and emergency relief. Finally yet importantly, NATO pressed the government's security forces to withdraw from NLA-occupied areas in return for assistance in peacekeeping and disarmament.

The EU special envoy started talks with President Trajkovski and promised the arrival of a 3,000-strong NATO force to supervise the disarming of the rebels, on the condition that both sides announced and honoured a ceasefire. Despite these efforts, the NLA remained adamant that it would continue to fight until a political agreement was reached. Still, EU's leading legal expert Robert Badinter drafted a constitutional revision plan, and special envoys Pardew and Leotard met with Trajkovski and the Albanian political leaders of DPA and PDP to discuss the start of negotiations. NATO took the next step, by mediating and supervising a bilateral ceasefire on 5 July 2001, agreed and signed by ARM's chief of staff General Pande Petrovski, Police General Risto Galevski, and representatives of the NLA; NATO mediators promised to grant a total amnesty to the NLA fighters, and thus brokered a truce.

The constitutional draft document was to serve as a basis for negotiations. It proposed greater use of the Albanian language in public administration, increased numbers of Albanians in the public service, and devolution of enhanced administrative powers to mayors and municipalities. To the surprise of the international representatives, the Albanian side rejected the plan. The Albanian political parties demanded more provisions. In their view, the plan failed to address the educational and constitutional rights of the Albanians. Two days later, a second draft plan was proposed to include the right to study in the Albanian language, and modified the constitution's preamble ("Macedonians talk peace", BBC News, 9 July 2001). The new Constitution also provided for the appointing of Albanian police chiefs and officers in areas of Albanian majority. Prime Minister Georgievski strongly reacted to the plan, calling it blatant blackmail by external forces who demanded the capitulation of the Slav Macedonians to unreasonable Albanian demands.

During the pre-negotiation stage, Trajkovski attempted to convince the international mediators to return to the previous draft plan that offered fewer concessions to the Albanians. As a result of the President's insistence, the Albanian DPA walked out of the talks. By mid-July, almost one-sixth of the country's entire territory was under rebel control, with approximately 130 villages and hamlets under rebel command. Police checkpoints around Tetovo were deserted and replaced by NLA guards. Almost all Slav Macedonian residents of Tetovo, approximately 20 per cent of the town's population, abandoned their homes. Meanwhile the conflict was spreading to the south-west of the country in the areas around Gostivar. Simply put, the country's leadership was facing a straight dilemma: partition or immediate reform. In an effort to turn the tide, negotiator Peter Feith intervened to persuade the rebels to withdraw from territories under their control, while Javier Solana and Lord Robertson continued to push forward talks on the draft framework proposal. In a gesture to boost the confidence of the Slavic Macedonian side, Washington blocked assets and properties belonging to Albanian extremist groups and individuals, prohibited US payments to these groups and individuals, and barred Albanian rebels from entering the United States. At the same time, the EU and the US decided to impose an informal arms embargo and halt all military supplies to FYR Macedonia. On the political terrain, NATO and EU officials shifted the negotiations from Skopje to the lakeside resort of Ohrid (28 July–9 August). The purpose of this move was to isolate the negotiators and protect them from negative media exposure and popular reactions. Delegates from all coalition parties were invited, as well as EU envoy Leotard and US special Balkans envoy Pardew. The negotiating sides agreed on the need for administrative and fiscal decentralization to strengthen local municipalities, and for a fairer representation of ethnic minorities in public administration.

However, disagreement surfaced on the official recognition of the Albanian language and the local appointing of police chiefs and officers. In early August 2001, negotiations started to bear some fruits, thanks to NATO's guarantees for disarming and disbanding the rebels and the international community's assurances to preserve the unitary character of the state. Albanian representatives made concessions on the status of the Albanian language, which was to be regarded official on a local level and wherever Albanians constituted a minority of at least 25 per cent. Though substantially weakened, DPA leader Xhaferi was still regarded the main Albanian political voice, and together with PDP leader Emir Imeri led the Albanian negotiating team. On 8 August, amidst tough negotiations at

Ohrid, a heavy blow was inflicted on the political process. Albanian NLA dissidents attacked an army vehicle convoy on the Skopje-Tetovo highway, leaving eight soldiers dead and another two heavily injured. Two days later, a landmine between Ljuboten and Ljubanci killed another six army reservists. Despite the incidents, the international mediators compelled the negotiating parties to sign the initial draft of the Framework Agreement. Pardew handed over a pen to the Albanian leaders, who signed the pre-final draft after consulting Ali Ahmeti and the NLA leadership. The Slav Macedonians were psychologically, militarily and politically devastated. They signed the pre-final agreement with great aversion. The planned signing of the official Framework Agreement was set for 13 August 2001.

One day before the official signing of the agreement, on 12 August 2001, the hardliner Minister of Interior Vlado Boskovksi ordered to surround the village of Ljuboten, where suspected NLA rebels were sheltered. Ten ethnic Albanians in Ljuboten were executed by Slavic Macedonian paramilitary forces in revenge for previous killings. Clearly, Boskovski's actions jeopardized the draft framework agreement. Finally, on 13 August, all representatives gathered in the Presidential villa in the Vodno area of Skopje to officially sign the so-called Ohrid Framework Agreement (OFA). Its progress and would be subject to future bargaining. However, it was clear by then that the Slavic Macedonian side would sign the agreement with much resentment, while the Albanian political parties were delighted by their success in forcing the Slavs to accept long-standing demands. Most Slav Macedonian parliamentarians believed that the agreement, which in their opinion rewarded terrorism, could still be amended or resisted on several contentious points at a later stage. The only precondition accepted by the Albanian parties was the Slavic Macedonian demand for an immediate disarmament of the NLA. The two sides, NLA leader Ahmeti and the Slavic parties, agreed on a gradual disarmament process that was to take place parallel with the political process. A third of the weapons would be handed in when the agreement was debated in Parliament, another third would be handed in when Parliament agreed to vote on the agreement, and the final weapons hand-over would occur when the agreement was ratified by (at least) a two-thirds parliamentary majority.

By mid-September 2001, the armed crisis came to an end. The military forces withdrew from their positions, a NATO Task Force arrived, and the NLA fighters were given amnesty. On 16 August, 400 British soldiers arrived in Skopje to coordinate and control the weapons collection/destruction operation "Essential Harvest" (see: NATO, Task Force FOX and Essential Harvest, 16 December 2002). The Slav Macedonian parties maintained that the rebels secretly kept around 50,000 weapons (Matveeva, 2003). Of course, as mentioned before, it is hard to make reliable or precise estimates of hidden weaponries in a society characterized by a widespread "gun culture" (Grillot et al., 2004). Officials regarded NATO's weapons collection operation as a failed and symbolic gesture to force the parties to proceed with the ratification of the peace agreement; Slav Macedonian army personnel were even forbidden to take part in or supervise the disarming process. Antonio Milososki jokingly remarked that the few antique and ill-working weapons collected by NATO should be exhibited in the National Museum of Skopje.

By the end of September, the NATO Task Force announced the operation successful and left the country, while FYR Macedonia succeeded in ensuring an extension of a new small NATO mission called "Amber Fox" (700 troops in strength). Operation "Amber Fox" provided security for international monitors overseeing the re-entry of security forces into former rebel-held areas. NATO's strategic reason to stay in the country was to "demonstrate NATO's continued presence and commitment in facilitating the reconciliation process in order to promote stability by deterring the resurgence of ethnically motivated violence" (NATO, Task Force FOX and Essential Harvest, 16 December 2002). However, Moscow insisted on the replacement of NATO forces with a UN mission that would include Russian troops; a rift in the relations between NATO and Russia was evident. The EU civic-military operation that followed the final withdrawal of NATO provided a crafty compromise on the issue.

Conflict Evaluation

In eight months of fighting, nearly 200 people were killed due to violent clashes and attacks: sixty-three soldiers, police and security officers, sixty-four NLA insurgents, around forty-six Albanian civilians and about sixteen Slav Macedonian civilians ("What do the casualties of war amount to?", AIM, 30 December 2001). Approximately 650 people were wounded and about 140,000 citizens left their homes in forced or voluntary displacement. Many villages in the Kumanovo and Tetovo regions suffered heavy damage due to the army's clumsy artillery bombardments. Many people of various ethnic backgrounds had their properties (shops and homes) vandalized and looted by Slavic Macedonian mobs and NLA militants. The army and police failed to conduct a successful counter-insurgency operation due to their operational weaknesses, lack of experience and insufficient training in urban warfare.

The rebels launched their first major offensive in March. A period of relative tranquillity followed in late March, following a supposedly effective governmental counter-offensive. The real reason for the reduction of violent incidents was President Trajkovski's draft proposal and the opening of talks. The slow progress and perceived inadequacy of the peace proposal indirectly led to the killing of seven Slav Macedonian commandos. Inter-ethnic relations deteriorated in May (the Bitola riots). In the same month, a Grand Coalition including all four major parties was formed after international pressures to avoid a military solution. The NLA succeeded in drawing the international community (NATO and the EU) into the conflict. Ironically, the active involvement of the latter also encouraged the NLA to step up its activity whenever the Slav Macedonians refused to compromise, or whenever it wished to show all involved parties that a peaceful resolution of the conflict was impossible without a say by the rebel movement.

The NLA leadership realized that the internationals recognized the salience of the Albanian grievances in FYR Macedonia, and that these needed to be accommodated in some form in order to stabilize the country and the region. Consequently, the rebel leaders regarded the EU and NATO as impartial, even sympathetic mediators. Moreover, the government was clearly unable to terminate the insurgency through military means. The NLA obviously recognized an opportunity to increase pressure against the government in order to elevate its status and push forward political demands. The fragile situation in Kosovo was used as a counterweight to any NATO action that could go against the insurgent's demands or interests. Hence, the more the EU and NATO intervened in FYR Macedonia, the more pressure the NLA exercised against the Slavs.

In July, the first meaningful negotiations opened with international encouragement, pressure, and guidance. Despite the calling of a ceasefire, the Ministry of Interior recorded a peak in NLA violent attacks during this period. Knowing that the EU and NATO representatives would force the Slavic parties into a compromise, the NLA stepped up its violence in order to increase psychological pressure against the Slavic Macedonian parties. The Slavic Macedonian parties reacted against the renewed wave of hostilities and expressed their objections to certain reforms favouring the Albanians. In response, the NLA ambushed and killed a number of Slavic Macedonian soldiers in a military convoy. At the same time, many villages had fallen under NLA control, threatening the country with partition. In the end, the Slav Macedonians had little choice but to accept most Albanian demands. In mid-August, the Ohrid Framework Agreement was eventually signed.

Assessing the Success of Strategic Coercion

The analysis has so far highlighted the use and influence of strategic coercion in the containment of the violent inter-ethnic conflict in FYR Macedonia. Alexander George was right in suggesting that flexible coercive responses are cost-effective and quick in pressing parties to seek for solutions. By using moderate coercive approaches to conflict resolution (regulation), international policymakers succeeded in doing exactly what facilitation, incentives or persuasion (i.e. diplomacy) alone failed to do. Nonetheless, the low military capacity of the state and the limited operational capabilities of the rebels favoured the effective use of minimum coercion. The government was incapable to resolve the crisis and prevent its escalation due to four basic reasons: i) insufficient technological-military equipment, lack of coordination and operational clumsiness; ii) restrictions of proportional retaliation; iii) fear of increased grassroots radicalization; and iv) lukewarm moral support from the international community. The Albanian insurgency proved successful for another four reasons: i) well–prepared and well-marketed rebellion (human rights etc.); ii) ineffective governmental crackdown; iii) support from NATO and the West; and iv) exploiting the insecurities of the state in the negotiation process.

The EU and NATO policymakers implemented a synchronized formula of coercion that raised the costs of undertaking further military action and lowered the costs of making concessions. The coercing parties exercised different types of pressure and threats, resolving the violent dispute by political-diplomatic means. Therefore, EU and NATO officials succeeded in terminating the crisis for three major reasons, directly related to essential principles of strategic coercion: insurgents were incorporated into the talks and counter incentives were offered to the Slav Macedonians; pressures were proportionally used as signals of disapproval and discouragement rather than punishment; and both the EU and NATO exploited the government's economic and military weakness in order to exercise such pressures more effectively. The entire operation coordinated and assigned different tasks to a number of different international organizations (NATO, EU, OSCE).

Flexibility

Less than a year of low-intensity fighting brought about an unprecedented constitutional and political change in FYR Macedonia. By contrast, two years of heavy fighting between the Albanians and the Serbs in Kosovo resulted in a controversial and costly military intervention. In FYR Macedonia, NATO and the EU condemned the rebellion, but realized that the government was unable to eliminate the militants. Another NATO-led military intervention could enmesh the entire region into renewed warfare, strain the relations between NATO and the Albanians in Kosovo, and radicalize the communities living in the country even further. On top of this, other economic-financial reasons, such as the resources required for NATO's military machine to operate, and the logistical support needed for conducting new military operations, should have affected the decision-making calculus of international military and policymakers. For this reason, flexible coercive methodologies were preferred over rigid, military-based solutions. On the one hand, NATO exercised political pressure against the Albanian insurgents and the Albanian political parties, but never threatened or used any type of military force against them or their opponents. On the other hand, NATO and the EU realized that without the inclusion of the insurgents into the talks there would be little chance for progress.

The Albanian militants and political hardliners in FYR Macedonia were rational extremists, just like many other ethnic militants. In order to gain international sympathy and support, the rebels avoided, to the extent possible, the killing of civilians and quickly lined their rhetoric in accordance to the accepted Western norms, i.e. equality and civil rights. There is little doubt that the objective aim of the rebels was to challenge the political establishment, including the Albanian parties, and participate in a future political agreement by means of tactical violence. The ability to grasp the political ambitions of disenfranchised groups across the ethno-political spectrum accounted for the major success in the strategic management of the armed conflict. As in many other cases of violent conflict, the insurgents were not against any prospect for compromise. In this case, the government showed genuine unwillingness to compromise, but international mediators intervened to break the political deadlock. Instead of assisting the government in suppressing the rebels by force, international mediators pressurized the rebels to give up arms in order to avoid international condemnation – and provided the incentive of political access to the rebels. International mediators established contacts with militant representatives in an effort to secure the rebel's demands, promised them a place at the negotiating table (and thus a recognized role in the final peace agreement), and protected them from government retaliation – all this in return for a ceasefire that would enable both sides to talk. At the same time, NATO provided the necessary guarantees for the safe evacuation of the Albanian rebels from Aracinovo, in order to prevent a dangerous escalation into full-scale war. As a counterweight to the aggrieved Slav Macedonians, international mediators, backed by NATO's military credibility and the EU's financial potential, promised to preserve the state's integrity by introducing non-territorial formulas of conflict management, and by utilizing a range of incentives. The incentives for persuading the Slav Macedonians to accept the NLA's participation in the talks included the granting of financial aid, the provision of EU candidate status, the modernization of the state's armed forces, and future entry into NATO.

Yet many Slav Macedonians regarded NATO and the EU as biased in favour of the Albanian rebels. Some Macedonian Slavs considered the inclusion of former combatants in the agreement as a reward to illegitimate, unjustified and terrorist violence. Even more emphatically, many Macedonian Slavs saw the election and participation of the Albanian militants in the government as an approval of such violence by the Albanian community. The repercussions of this compromise, and the grievances it generated, will be carefully examined in the next chapter.

Pressure

The effectiveness of pressure in strategic coercion is dependent on the ability and strength of the state (or any other actor) to resist them (Pape, 1992; Art, 2003). Strategic coercion works well in cases where resistance is minimal, that is in cases where the receptor of pressures is weak. International policymakers realized that the size and intensity of the clashes signified the state's vulnerability and potential break-up. The consequences of the state's disintegration would transcend the boundaries of FYR Macedonia. On the one hand, the Slavic parties were presented with a nightmare scenario of civil war, inter-ethnic militarization, total polarization and self-destruction. On the ground, things were going badly for the security forces. In our analysis, we have identified the army's inadequacies. However, if the state's armed forces and police had been stronger and more capable, the Slav Macedonians might have been confident enough to hold off a compromise with the Albanians they deem overly beneficial to the latter, irrespective of the international pressure. The active involvement of the international community was largely the result of the state's lack of military power and the fear of disintegration. Faced with this situation, the Slavic parties submitted to the pressures, and accepted compromise. The costs of a futile protracted conflict outweighed the disadvantages of an undesired compromise. International mediators combined incentives with pressures, by exploiting the governmental military and operational weakness. In addition, pressures capitalized on FYR Macedonia's economic destitution. Pressures evolved around a possible reduction in financial aid, blockades in importing military equipment, freezing of subsidies for humanitarian purposes and infrastructure, and diplomatic isolation about the problems with Greece.

In an interview with regional political analyst S.O., he explained:

> The Ohrid agreement was not forged because of Macedonian willingness, i.e. original willingness to seek to negotiate, nor was it forged because of the Albanian willingness to reach a political solution. The international community got involved in the middle of the conflict when they understood that the conflict could destabilize the whole region. It became clear that the Macedonian state as such is not able to defend itself against this kind of thing. Practically, it is very difficult to defend against a rebellion or insurgency, as we can see everywhere around the world, and partly because the state was politically fragile, it's a multi-ethnic state, and it's easy to destabilize multi-ethnic states when you have trained and well-equipped forces to do it ... and then you have unsolved political issues. In my mind, there is no doubt that part of the settlement was a result of pressures. Pressure went to both sides. It is also about processes as well. I would say that a process means that you would have to make many other small agreements for many issues in the future. It is a process, you know, and the process is durable as long as it goes. (Interview with the author, 15 December 2007, Skopje)

Significantly, the international community was unwilling to help the army and security forces to cleanse the rebel-held territories (in part because Albanian grievances were broadly recognized). Perhaps, some NATO military involvement would have been necessary to support the weak Slavic Macedonian forces and discourage – rather than rhetorically isolate – the rebels. Sam Vaknin recognized that:

> The agreement was signed in the wrong circumstances, with a gun to the Macedonian head. The political class in Macedonia – of both ethnicities – is irreversibly discredited by its own venality, corruption and involvement in criminal activities. It does not possess the moral authority to sell the agreement to the people or to preach peace and rectitude. (Vaknin, "Why the Ohrid Agreement Framework in Macedonia will fail", 2002)

The pressure strategy helped to contain the crisis within controllable limits and prevent it from escalating into a full-blown civil war. However, efforts to contain the violence – by restricting governmental activities – were accompanied by a political process set on track to seek a viable compromise before the situation aggravated beyond repair. International policymakers, in collaboration with local politicians, sought a comprehensive compromise to prevent further escalation and ensure future stability. Overall, the Ohrid peace agreement shows the effectiveness of strategic coercion in achieving a quick end to the crisis before it could degenerate into a protracted and bloody conflict.

The Ohrid agreement represents a landmark in the practice of coercive diplomacy for the containment of small and medium-scale conflicts. It provided the Albanians with the desired constitutional, social and political reforms that would improve their lives, and to the Slavic Macedonians it offered in return the preservation of a unitary state. The policy dilemma was resolved by manipulating the operational weakness and fears of the Slavic Macedonian side, while entangling the Albanian rebels into meaningful talks.

Effective Coordination

Teamwork and coordination are critical elements in the efficient application of coercive policies. Three international bodies (NATO, EU and OSCE) were actively involved in facilitating, mediating and ultimately pressing for solutions. All bodies acted in a complementary way to each other. NATO undertook the role of the security guarantor; NATO representatives brokered ceasefires while it promised the NLA's disarmament to Skopje's government. The EU pressed for the political process using incentives (faster integration into the EU, financial aid) and threats (isolation, cut-down of financial aid). The US provided ethical support to the government, by condemning acts of rebel violence and designating the NLA as a terrorist organization. In addition, the US promised military and financial aid, and training for a rapid reaction force in case a political solution was reached. By contrast, Russia kept a low profile but at times sided with those who wanted to terminate the crisis in a military manner. Government official N.D. observed that:

> They [the international representatives] were all speaking in one voice. Therefore, there was not really a difference between the EU, the US, NATO, and the OSCE as well. The international team spoke in one voice. I think it was very important. I think the biggest "carrot" was to avoid a major scale civil war in Macedonia. It was not a case in which the political leadership made concessions in order to gain something else. It is hard to define the involvement in that way. There were differences of course, but I think the overwhelming feeling among the whole public and the political leadership was that we do not want to have a major civil war and we want to keep the country as it is, within these borders. In a way, I think we perceived the international involvement as an ally, with us, in order to reach this objective because of the interest of the internationals to prevent a big problem in Macedonia. (Interview with the author, July 2007)

There is little doubt that the strategic use of coercion by powerful external actors is an effective means to prevent escalation, terminate violence, and force parties to negotiate. In this respect, we agree with Alexander George's framework of forceful persuasion in its effectiveness to manage and resolve (armed) conflicts. We concentrated on the exact conditions and timing under which coercion was applied, and then spotted the reactions of the participants. We have broken down the evolution of the crisis in three parts. In the first phase, parties were unwilling to cooperate, and clearly preferred the path of confrontation. However, the government's unwillingness to proceed with major constitutional changes, the failure to form a solid political front, and the state's failure to suppress the rebels led to an abrupt escalation. Clearly, the lack of substantial incentives and pressures did not help to control the course of violence. In the phase of escalation, important international actors grasped the necessity of intervention, but failed to apply the tools of strategic coercion in a coordinated and meaningful way. The publicizing of secret engagements with the rebels by unauthorized mediators, without positive motivation, security guarantees and tactical pressure, intensified the state's military responses and subsequently increased NLA's activity. The international mediators had so far failed to control the violent explosion of frustration, because they were engaged in sporadic political calls, facilitation without the backing of pressures and uncoordinated interventions. Realizing the conflict's deadlock, international bodies ultimately devised a strategy driven by the classical principles of strategic coercion – or forceful persuasion – as set by George (George, 1991, 1994).

As we have seen, the regional implications of conflict were realistically assessed, and the division of duties and competencies by the international organizations were clearly defined. Pressures were systematically interchanged with attractive financial, political and security incentives. The possibility of military intervention was excluded, and emphasis was put on negotiations and cooperation. Three months after the introduction of coercive methodologies, a ceasefire was brokered, and the conflicting parties sat at the negotiating table. Therefore, we agree with George's theoretical proposition that pressures, incentives and flexibility, if properly used, can produce results that military force usually fails to produce. Following Pape's argument, international mediators succeeded in raising the costs of military action, and lowered the government's confidence in its military potential for suppressing the rebels (Pape, 1992). However, Robert Art's proposition that positive inducements signify less than steely resolve on the part of the coercer is incorrect in cases where the targeted government or other actor is militarily weak and economically needy, and where the rebels realize their own limitations.

CHAPTER 6

Strategic Coercion and the Backlash Effect

Coercive settlements are generally risky, and often fail to produce long-term peace and stability (Jakobsen, 2004; Brown, 2003). We have seen that coercive approaches, when properly applied, may constitute an effective tool for the termination of violence, and generally succeed in bringing about a negotiated end to conflict. Yet analysts regard the use of pressures, an essential part of coercion, as a highly risky method in the resolution of conflicts, and a potential source of renewed conflict and instability (Dugan; 2003; Burgess, 2004; Brown, 2003; Stedman, 2001). This is evident in Jakobsen and Carlson's accounts of the long-term effects of coercion in the resolution of conflicts: the enforcing and pressurizing nature of coercion aggravates inter-ethnic grievances, despite the provision of incentives and guarantees. Systematic external coercion risks producing winners and losers, thereby stimulating revenge and the rectification of perceived injustices, and triggering a dangerous backlash effect. Enforced compromises can produce victors and victims, and help cultivate win-lose perceptions, especially at the grassroots level. In order to highlight the potential dangers of coercive settlements, this analysis will point to the renewed grievances and "negative peace" in FYR Macedonia after the settlement. This chapter explores the crucial indicators of negative peace, and presents the emerging antagonisms in the post-crisis political system between the perceived victims and beneficiaries.

Political Antagonism

The Ohrid Framework Agreement was an enforced settlement, reached with the aim of forcing the government to concede to the rebels' legitimate demands while preserving the territorial integrity and unitary character of the state (Daskalovski, 2002; Hislope, 2004; Vankovska, 2006). The Slavic Macedonian community, which disapproved of the way in which the settlement was reached, felt that their rights were reduced, and resented the increasingly assertive nationalism in the Albanian community. Most Macedonian Slavs believed that the compromise was a result of severe political and economic pressures and their own fear of disintegration. Most people felt that the Slavic political parties and the security forces were systematically manipulated and humiliated throughout the crisis, not only by the Albanians, but also by the international mediators (Brunnbauer, 2002). For this reason, the Slavic political parties had little genuine motivation to compromise over vital issues concerning the national, educational and administrative restructuring of the state.

By contrast, the architects of the Ohrid Framework Agreement (OFA) devised a solution that the Albanians could market as a total, undisputed victory over the oppressive and anachronistic Slavic regime. The only aspect of the agreement that could boost the confidence of the Macedonian Slavs was the formal preservation of the unitary character of the state, whereas the NLA had accomplished all of its important aims and demands. The Albanians, with the help of the NLA's militant pressure, achieved the amendment of the constitution's preamble, formal recognition of the Albanian language (paragraphs 6.1–6.5 OFA), free use of symbols (paragraph 7.1 OFA), and ethnic proportionality in public administration (paragraphs 4.1, 4.2 and 4.3 OFA). Moreover, they successfully pressed for the empowerment of self-government (paragraph 3.1 and 3.2 OFA), the restructuring of the police force (paragraph 3.3 OFA), the full secularization of the state, and finally consensual democracy in areas concerning ethnic rights (double majority and veto powers, paragraph 5.1 and 5.2 OFA).[1] In addition, the NLA succeeded in securing a full amnesty, and public appointments for some of its members. In fact, the rebel movement's limited use or threat of violence attracted international attention, speeded up political change, and neutralized the government's weak resistance.

At the same time, the Slavic Macedonian side was pressed to accept that all proposed changes were in line with the EU's administrative and political requirements, something that is obviously untrue given the multiplicity of administrative systems (ethnic and non-ethnic, territorial and non-territorial) and unrecognized or underrepresented minorities in several European countries. In reality, FYR Macedonia would cease to exist as the national state of the Slav Macedonians. The perceived guest-status given to the minorities by the former Constitution (full equality as citizens and permanent coexistence with the Macedonian people) changed in order to make the Albanians co-owners of the state (Constitution of FYR Macedonia, PE Official Gazette of the Republic of Macedonia. Amendments on the Constitution I–XXX, Skopje 2006). The Slavic Macedonian people would no longer provide equal rights to other ethnic citizens as a gesture of goodwill, as they would become shareholders rather than owners of the state.

In political terms, the Ohrid peace settlement has not succeeded in changing the practices of ethno-political bargaining (Monteux, 2006:162–182). Slavs felt they could resist a settlement that was reached through blunt coercion, while Albanians desired to increase their socio-political status, as designated in the agreement's provisions. Imposed changes by European policy experts, magnified Slavic frustration, and the power-sharing system provided by the OFA sustained the existing win-lose perceptions. As a result, political parties continued to campaign along ethnic lines in order to control human and financial resources according to ethnic and partisan criteria. The entry of the NLA into politics complicated the already fractionalized public arena, and sent a clear message to the Slavic Macedonian side that violence can be graciously rewarded with political gains.

1 See: Ohrid Framework Agreement document, European Commission Enlargement Archives.

Political antagonisms intensified drastically because Albanians came to believe they were entitled to every political benefit previously enjoyed by the majority Slavs, while Slavs believed they were morally obliged to resist or bargain (i.e. demand compensation) for every reform (Zarkovic, 2004). In fact, prior to the 2001 crisis, all governments included an Albanian party in the winning coalition, and Albanians held five ministerial positions in every cabinet. Although there has never been a constitutional provision to compel the winning party to choose a party of a different ethnic background to cooperate with, the inter-ethnic divisions in society necessitated inter-ethnic cooperation in politics, rather than mutually isolating antagonism between Slavic and Albanian parties.

However, the provisions of the imposed framework agreement, in an effort to boost the representation of Albanian parties in parliament, changed the electoral system from majority-proportional into proportional representation with no bonus seats for majority parties. This required the aggrieved Slavs to redraw the administrative map of the country, and change the electoral districts so as to create (more) homogenous or majority Albanian constituencies. Even more importantly, the OFA expanded and institutionalized power-sharing mechanisms into other fields of public life. Thus many public-administration posts had to be filled by ethnic Albanians according to proportionality rather than merit, meaning that the ethnic Albanian party in power could ensure that its supporters would get at least some of these posts. In addition, the increased competencies in local government made the Albanian parties a lot more competitive among each other. The designators of OFA overlooked the realistic competencies of the state, and failed to foresee the political divisions and antagonisms generated by coercive methodologies (Stedman, 2001). The DUI spokesperson M.E. agrees that the system has become more antagonistic, but mainly along intra-ethnic lines. In her words:

> The major topic of contest after 2001, especially after the agreement in the Albanian political campus became the legacy over the agreement, namely who has the highest merit of achieving this agreement, and who has the greatest merits for the political process; this has become the major point of contention or rather conflict between the parties. At the same time, until 2006 the DPA, a signatory of the agreement, claimed

> that the OFA is a failure since it lost the first elections after the conflict – until last year, when it became part of the government and suddenly started to support the Ohrid Agreement. (Interview with the author, July 2007, Skopje)

Proof of this abrupt radicalization can be found in the weakening of the moderate Albanian parties. In the 2002 parliamentary elections, the Albanian moderates in the DPA saw their electorate shrink to 5 per cent while the Democratic Union for Integration (*Bashkimi Demokratik për Integrim*, BDI or DUI), the main political successor of the NLA, received almost 12 per cent of the vote. Disappointment increased among the Slavs with the government's perceived "surrenderism", which led to the fractionalization of the nationalist VMRO-DPMNE. Disappointed Slav voters ousted the VMRO-DPMNE from the government and elected the Social Democrats (SDSM); only to bring back the nationalist VMRO-DPMNE four years later.

After the September 2002 parliamentary elections, from which an incredible coalition emerged between the SDSM (Slav moderates) and DUI (led by Albanian former rebels) the reform process was ready to start.[2] The international community saw this as a chance for creating a *modus vivendi*. As later became evident, the Slavs would not easily allow the SDSM to be controlled by Ahmeti's DUI. Three consecutive NATO missions (Essential Harvest, Amber Fox and Allied Harmony) and the first EU-led police mission, EUPOL Proxima, helped to instil some sense of security among the ethnic communities, and kept the levels of violence down to a minimum. Nonetheless, Biljana Vankovska asserts that domestic and international actors have defined a level of acceptable direct violence as part of normality (Vankovska, 2002:12).

Since the September 2002 elections, every step towards reform was taken after prolonged inter-ethnic negotiations between parties in the parliament, public objections, boycotts and occasional violence. Moreover, the negotiable nature of the Ohrid agreement allowed the political bargaining

2 According to the UNDP EWR 2003, 39 per cent of Slav Macedonians had no confidence or little confidence in the new government, and 58.6 per cent of Albanians declared some confidence or a lot of confidence in the new government.

to expand beyond the parliament to the community itself, and prompted the ultra-nationalist VMRO-DPMNE to obstruct the process and portray every negotiated outcome as treason. The VMRO-DPMNE encouraged an atmosphere of resistance within the Slavic community. Violence appeared again at the forefront in the very first month after the new power-sharing government took office. As a result, the post-agreement environment reflected diminishing trust between the communities. A well-known local Skopje-based political analyst confessed that "the trust level among us is problematic because of various things. In order to discuss peacefully we need someone who can be a facilitator, an American ambassador, or an EU representative, to become a guarantor. Whatever we are bargaining is actually having the seal of NATO and the EU" (Interview with the author, 2007, Skopje).

Overall, FYR Macedonia has made impressive progress in the passing of several new laws guaranteeing equality, representation and promoting a fairer system, but little progress has been marked in the meaningful implementation of reforms. Of course, the Ohrid agreement itself is no panacea: it cannot resolve the long-standing problems the country faces, neither can it ameliorate the antagonisms over who gets what in such a post-conflict environment (Zarkovic, 2004). It is more appropriate to ask ourselves whether the peace agreement, and the way it was reached, have laid the basis for a functional inter-ethnic coexistence on a communal level.

Communal Frustration with the Settlement

One year after the crisis, a public opinion poll survey conducted by Colin Irwin revealed that the two communities held diametrically opposing views on the aetiology of violent conflict and its potential solutions. The survey revealed that most Slav Macedonians (85 per cent) believed the conflict was generally a result of the activities of Albanian paramilitary groups still operating in Macedonia, whereas most Albanians (80 per cent) believed that ethnic discrimination in employment, education and language rights was the principal source of conflict and the impetus for violence (Irwin, 2002:62–74). Indeed, Albanians and Slav Macedonians are miles apart concerning their association and loyalty to the state. Slavs believe that the Ohrid Framework Agreement (OFA) gave the disloyal Albanians excessive rights and access to the state administration, while reducing the existing rights of the Slavs. Significantly, only 13 per cent of Slav Macedonians see the full implementation of the OFA as essential. Clearly, the Slavic side resents the way in which the agreement was reached, and believes that the government was forced to concede to the Albanian demands. For this reason, most Slavs were enraged with decisions to insert thousands of Albanians into the police and public services. Slav Macedonians were generally convinced that EU policymakers pressed the Slavic parties to elevate the status of the Albanians in order to incorporate the Albanians in the public administration. They regarded this as a formal act of state infiltration by disloyal elements.

The March 2005 Early Warning Report (EWR) of the United Nations Development Program (UNDP) revealed the unwillingness of large portions of the Albanian community to identify themselves with the state, while approximately 50 per cent of Albanians always feel citizens of FYR Macedonia, 20.1 per cent Albanians never feel citizens of the country and 12.4 per cent feel citizens of it only when in a foreign country. In contrast, the EWR of June 2006 found that 78 per cent of the Albanians say they always feel citizens of FYR Macedonia. However, the June 2006 EWR reveals that 74 per cent of Albanians do not know the lyrics of the national anthem. There is little doubt that the Albanian perception of state-ownership by the Slavs has reinforced a sense of disloyalty to the state. Indicatively, we elaborated on the Slavic attitudes towards the enhancement of equitable-proportional representation and the inclusion of ethnic minorities into the public services (police, ministries, etc.). This single indicator examines whether Slav Macedonians are happy to see the fair representation of Albanians and other minorities in the public administration.

The results show that Slav Macedonians do not wish to see the equitable representation of ethnic minorities in public institutions, despite what their political representatives were forced to sign. This almost total rejection of equitable representation has several explanations. Some analysts portray the problem as one of partisan favouritism and corruption, arguing that civil servants in FYR Macedonia are recruited through party lines (Van Hal, 2005:4). In reality, the formula for equitable representation of the communities serves as an alibi for the partisanship of the state administration with people whose only credentials are in their party belonging (Vankovska, 2006:14).

Private discussions with many ordinary Slav Macedonians reveal the widespread belief that ethnic minorities are equally represented in their localities, while some others do not seem to trust the inclusion of Albanians into the public administration. Antagonistic perceptions are evident, as most Macedonian Slavs would agree, to different degrees, on the suspicion that Albanians seek for territorial autonomy and the ultimate disintegration of the state. For their part, Albanians understand that they have been discriminated against and maltreated by the majority of Macedonian Slavs, and they believe that they have a right to participate in the decision-making processes of the state as a constituent nation rather than a minority.

A discouraging picture emerges on the post-agreement quality of inter-ethnic relations. Macedonian Slavs regard the Albanians as major beneficiaries, and regard themselves trapped in their own incapacity to resist acting against their will. They regard the role of the EU and NATO as treacherous, intimidating and overall unfair. Slav Macedonian newspapers and media have explicitly accused NATO of trying to cover up its failures in Kosovo by granting benefits to the Albanians in FYR Macedonia, in an effort to prevent a regional conflagration. In contrast, Albanians believe their demands have been rightfully met and have increased their demands for future concessions. Therefore, one part of the society feels frustrated due to the coercive pressures used in resolving the crisis, while another part is exhilarated by what it considers just responses to Albanian grievances.

In order to measure the degree of frustration generated after the settlement, we elaborated on the UNDP EWR indicators of inter-ethnic relations from March 2005 until June 2006. Of course, the short period under investigation (2005–2006) cannot determine the overall quality, or make reliable predictions on the future of inter-ethnic relations. Moreover, a special event could have triggered an abrupt or abnormal negativity in this short period. Nevertheless the EWR indicators for this period clearly indicate a wide gap in the perceptions of the Slav and Albanian communities.

The majority in both ethnic groups believes that inter-ethnic relations are either bad or very bad. However, there is a sizable and growing minority in both groups which believes that inter-ethnic relations are good (an average of approximately 12 per cent). Those who say that inter-ethnic relations are excellent are very few, however. Previous analysis of statistical data shows that the total cumulative average of those who answered very bad and bad is much larger than those who answered good or excellent; still, an optimistic trend can be seen in the growing belief that inter-ethnic relations are good.

In the 2004 EWR, people were asked whether ethnic minorities in FYR Macedonia have greater, equal or less rights. The results are strikingly inconsistent: 45.1 per cent of Slav Macedonians believed that ethnic minorities had greater rights (in comparison with their own community's rights or with their proportionate numbers, etc.) while 46.8 per cent of Slavs believed that they had equal rights; by contrast, 67.7 per cent of Albanians believed they had fewer rights, and only 23.7 per cent believed they had equal rights (EWR UNDP, November 2004:6). This discrepancy of views regarding equitable representation and ethnic rights has a deeper socio-economic reason, expressed by the majority of Slavs: in order for Albanians to occupy their proportional positions in the administration, many Slavs would have to be dismissed from their current posts. For example, if the administrative staff in a given public service – located in an area where Albanians make up 70 per cent and Slav Macedonians 30 per cent of the population – consists of 95 per cent Slav Macedonians, many of the latter will necessarily be fired if that public service seeks to reflect ethnic proportionality.

In 2004, the year in which veto rights and increased ethnic percentages would be introduced for the Albanians, inter-ethnic trust in the power-sharing model and the reformed institutions was to be seriously undermined on a community and regional level. However, the proposition that ethnic communities do not understand each other underestimates the intelligence and analytical capabilities of both ethnic groups (Sebek, 2002). Ethnic communities know what is fair and unfair, but they also know what is advantageous and non-advantageous for their ethnic survival. Below, we illustrate a paradigm of frustration resulting from the Ohrid agreement's dictations in reforming the state despite the unwillingness of the Slavs. This case helps to demonstrate the emergence of new grievances and the sustaining of permanent frustration because of an imposed peace deal (Brunnbauer, 2002).

Negative Peace and New Deprivation

In this part, we illustrate how negative forms of peace set the ground for renewed forms of deprivation. As we have seen in the analysis above, resentment over the Ohrid peace agreement and perceptions of humiliation and injustice have prompted political parties and communities to resist change, entrench their positions and become even more antagonistic and nationalistic. Based on fieldwork evidence, we pinpoint a number of structural and political problems that help a conflict to perpetuate along ethnic lines in the post-armed-conflict phase (Mehmeti, 2007; Ramadani, 2007; Georgieva, 2004). The partial or long-term failure of strategic coercion is reflected in the inability of imposed settlements to ameliorate perceptions of injustice, rectify structural deficiencies, address vital security concerns, and above all remove the stimulants that sustain structural violence (Georgieva, 2004; Stedman, 2001; Harris, Fisk and Rank, 1998). McGinty successfully pinpoints the implications of enforced settlements, stating that in many cases, an imposed settlement runs the risk of freezing into a negative peace, a situation of permanent impermanence in which the peace process becomes protracted and produces a new set of grievances (McGinty, 2002). Through an examination of a number of structural problems that help conflict to perpetuate, we complete our argument that coercive settlements fall short in creating the conditions for addressing the structural sources of conflict (Georgieva, 2004; Stedman, 2001).

Failure to Coexist

The failure to invest in the genuine willingness of parties to seek mutually beneficial solutions is a major weakness in coercive settlements (Stedman, 2001). Besides, strategic coercion is a tool used in the absence of genuine willingness among local parties to resolve intra-state conflict. In the case of FYR Macedonia, third-party coercion worked as an alternative to partition (ICG Europe Briefing No. 143, "The Make or Break Dilemma: Macedonia: Make or Break?", 3 August 2004). The unwillingness of Slavs and Albanians to live together peacefully, while recognizing each other's demands and insecurities, increased since the end of the crisis. Instead of cultivating an atmosphere of cooperation and solidarity, ethnic communities have moved further apart. Since the signing of the Ohrid agreement, minority Slav populations started to depart from their original settlements in a fast pace, after threats and public intimidations by some Albanians who saw an opportunity of "getting even" with their former oppressors ("Tetovo Divided River Pena Border between Ethnic Macedonians and Albanians", *Dnevnik*, 18 March 2002).

The city of Tetovo is a major example. From the city's approximately 20,000 Slav Macedonians, few have remained in their original settlements while many have moved away to Bitola or Skopje. In Gostivar – a city with approximately 55,000 Albanians and 15,000 Slavs – citizens were confronted with publicly displayed UCK (NLA) posters and flags, which were often raised at the city centre to celebrate important dates (Dejan, 2002). According to reports, local ethnic-Albanian TV stations kept broadcasting footage of NLA fighters in action, and built monuments commemorating NLA fighters. Residents claimed that the local authorities refused to raise Macedonian state flags on official holidays, while Albanian state flags could be seen all the time (ibid.). The Albanian flags were allegedly placed to provoke the local authorities, which in turn did nothing because Albanians headed them. Higher authorities peopled with both Macedonian Slavs and Albanians did not intervene in the name of multi-ethnic harmony (ibid.). This situation prompted the constitutional court to cancel all rules concerning the right of using the Albanian flag as the ethnic symbol of the Albanians in FYR Macedonia. Two Albanian members of the court resigned, and all seventeen (16 DUI and 1 DPA) Albanian mayors stated that they were going to disregard the court's decision. This makes one wonder whether Albanians can really become part of FYR Macedonia since "they deny and cannot respect even the simplest of symbols, such as the national flag" ("Macedonian Alliance", 22 July 2004).

At a first glance, the capital of Skopje is a typical example of an ethnically divided city, separated by the Vardar river, which exists as a natural border between the Albanians and the Macedonian Slavs. The recent relocation of many *nouveau riche* Albanians in areas previously inhabited exclusively by Slavs has caused an intense fear among the latter. The Albanians, with the financial assistance of Diaspora relatives, have achieved a faster socio-economic growth, and have outnumbered the Slavs in all major cities of the west: Gostivar, Tetovo and Debar have more than 85 per cent Albanians, while Kicevo and Struga have large Albanian majorities (around 60 per cent). The demographic boom among Albanians, in combination with their social advancement, alarms the Macedonian Slavs, who deem it a geo-strategic threat. It is true that Slav Macedonians understand the ethno-graphic picture of the country in competitive, almost military terms. They talk of Albanians invading and multiplying, with many of them building, buying and moving into places where Slav Macedonians reside. Slavs see this as a subtle way of altering the cultural outlook of specific areas, and an indirect way of depriving them of their ethno-cultural space while forcing them out.

The Ohrid agreement has done little to appease the Slavic Macedonian fears about the high birth rate and consequent population increase of the Albanians. Slav Macedonians believe that increased proportionality has strengthened and institutionalized Albanian dominance in certain areas, and in many job appointments, the principle of merit has been sacrificed to that of proportionality. Fears increased when the Economic Institute of FYR Macedonia suggested that if the Law on Naturalization of 100,000 ethnic Albanians were to pass, Albanians would become a national majority by 2015. Indeed, the period from 1994 to 2002 is marked by very large differences in the increase of the population by nationality. The number of Slav Macedonians increased only by 2,017 persons (0.2 per cent) and the average annual increase rate was 0.02 per cent. The highest increase has been that of the Albanians

(67,979 persons or 15.4 per cent), whose population increased annually by 1.79 per cent. As a result, as much as 88.7 per cent of the total population increase in Macedonia came from persons who declared themselves as of Albanian nationality ("Socio-economic disparities among municipalities in Macedonia", Data and Indicators of Municipalities in Macedonia, UNDP and Ministry of Local Self Government, November 2004:31).

Part of this ethno-cultural competition rests on the fact that there is no mainstream culture that binds the ethnic groups to one other. The two major ethnicities, Albanians and Slav Macedonians, adhere to separate historical traditions, customs and lifestyles, and they are used to living next to each other rather than with each other. There is little common ground to be shared by the two ethnicities, and an almost total lack of a common value-system for the creation of civic type of society. As we examined at the start of our analysis, the country has long been largely divided between a majority of Orthodox Macedonian Slavs, and a considerable minority of Muslim Albanians, two groups characterized by different cultural practices, and a different ethos. The designers of the OFA envisaged that a representative and inclusive model of liberal democracy, as well as market economics, privatization and consumption could transcend ethnic lines and create some shared identity. However, the deep ethno-cultural divide, exacerbated by poor socio-economic conditions and lack of joint inter-ethnic businesses, have so far frustrated the rather naive expectations of Western policymakers. Group-identity becomes a reason of hatred of the "other" when related to competing ethno-nationalist designs and perceived security threats. Ethnicity in FYR Macedonia is largely based on culture, and cultural expressions are often viewed as signs of domination, nationalism and antagonism (Mitrovic, 1999).

Crime and the Rule of Law

The Ohrid Framework Agreement (OFA) designated that a significant number of Albanians (approximately 2,000) must be inserted into the police force. The Macedonian Slavs were pressed to accept changes in policing. These reforms would allow the indirect appointment of Albanian police chiefs through a selection system and the insertion of hundreds of Albanians into the police. However, Slavs were increasingly distressed over the fact that many former NLA combatants with mafia ties were absorbed into the police ("Strategy for the Police Reforms", Republic of Macedonia Ministry of Interior, Skopje, February 2004:57–60, document acquired through the EU Delegation FYR Macedonia, Skopje). At the time, Albanians controlled many regional criminal networks. Moreover, major Albanian parties recruited former rebels to create private armies (usually presented as bodyguards). Hence, former combatants became part of state institutions just after a few months of typical training or induction. Slav Macedonian policemen working in Albanian or ethnically mixed municipalities are too afraid to enter Albanian areas for any purpose.[3] In short,

> Multi-ethnic patrols fail to bring a sense of law and order to much of the former crisis areas. Kidnappings, bombings, spates of murders and armed robberies are frequent occurrences, with the culprits evading capture … many people feel that official law-enforcement structures are not capable of providing adequate protection from crime and that they have to take the law into their own hands. (Matveeva, 2003:157)

In the second period of fieldwork, in 2006, we acquired a confidential report on the objectives and progress of the police reform produced by the Ministry of Interior of FYR Macedonia. The document verified that high-level professionalism characterized new forms of (Albanian) criminality. Police representatives and EU policy advisors underlined the increased numbers of repeat offenders and the decreased number of crimes detected by the police. They also stressed that a significant number of crimes by unknown perpetrators reduced the level of general safety among people in all areas of life ("Strategy for the Police Reforms", Republic of Macedonia Ministry of Interior, Skopje, February 2004:2).

3 Police commanders note that it remains difficult to police Albanian rural areas, as even a multi-ethnic police service cannot enter villages. Large areas around Tetovo remain effectively beyond police control. As a result, armed groups move freely in places where they feel more secure, and they are sometimes supported by the locals, who are reluctant to cooperate with the police (Matveeva et al., 2003:157).

The ethnic aspect of crime distribution cannot be ignored; it is widespread and heavily concentrated in the western parts of the country and in the border villages (Matveeva, 2003). The north-western parts of FYR Macedonia, Kosovo, Albania and southern Montenegro have become the crossroads for the illicit trafficking of arms, drugs, women, cigarettes, alcohol and textiles. The heroin trade in FYR Macedonia is almost entirely controlled by citizens of Albanian origin. This is an almost inevitable and unfortunate result of the virtual exclusion of ethnic Albanians from the lawful and shrinking labour market in the country. Having little alternative, many Albanians turn to the black economy, illegal trade, drugs, arms smuggling and trafficking of women for forced prostitution. Clear indications also exist that the heroin smugglers have close connections to the country's Albanian political parties, whose budgets seem partially funded by profits from the drug trade (Hanjdiak, 2002:30).

Furthermore, Albanian criminal gangs often use ethnic symbols and uniforms while carrying out their illicit activities. At the same time, many members (approximately 900) of "Lions", the former Slavic paramilitary group, were recruited into the Border Police in 2003 (Matveeva, 2003:157). Indicative of this divide is the deadly incident that occurred on 7 November 2007, during which six Albanian paramilitaries were attacked and killed by the Special Army Forces in the hills overlooking Tetovo ("Macedonia Special Forces clashed earlier today with a group of armed men near Tetovo", B92, 7 November 2007). All members of the group wore Albanian UCK badges, while the Special Forces exclusively consisted of Slavic Macedonian commandos. Official reports portrayed the dead paramilitaries as common criminals. Not surprisingly, this military operation was carried out after the killing of three Slav Macedonian police officers in the village of Vaksince in October 2007. According to media sources, the police raids in the Albanian village of Brodec revealed an amazing number of weapons and ammunition, described by Interior Minister Gordana Jankuloska as the largest amount of heavy weaponry seized thus far in Macedonia, sufficient to equip a battalion of 650 soldiers (Fotiadis, 2007). It is no secret that common criminals and their police-collaborators use the pretext of ethno-nationalism to justify their unlawful activities (Matveeva, 2003:157).

Nevertheless, the informal economy has become the meeting point of ethnicities. Albanians and Slavs often cooperate in the illicit trafficking of goods. Albanians control the supplies and the Slavs control access (Customs Office). Slavs were pressed through the OFA to accept a reduction of their privileges, and were subsequently forced to seek alternative ways to make a living. Many Albanians were convinced they could utilize their political rights in a way that facilitates further illicit practices. The fruits of corruption, when evenly distributed, help to build a peculiar type of interest-based coexistence among criminals of all ethnic backgrounds. Indeed, in deeply divided societies, where political consensus is thin and the state is weak, corruption can provide a much-needed adhesive for political stability: "By promoting a policy of zero-tolerance for corruption, the international community may in fact undermine frail states by eliminating the only political mechanism that stands between politics-as-bargaining and politics-as-war" (Hislope, 2005:2).

However, illicit inter-ethnic collusion, as an alternative to genuine peace, increases the vulnerability of eroded state structures and corrupted economies (Mandaci, 2003). Firstly, grievances are generated by those who feel excluded from illicit benefits, such as opposition political parties and their supporters. Secondly, tax evasion weakens the welfare state, and therefore causes even more resentment, especially among the poorest parts of society. The creation of win-lose perceptions means that any law designed to improve the standard of living and reduce tax evasion, is viewed as a contest between the Albanians and the state. The state is often unwilling to prosecute Albanians who do not pay their taxes, because it is still very much afraid of local community reactions and accusations of anti-Albanianism, and when it does, it usually results in confrontations between Albanians and the police. This competitive, antagonistic state-minority interaction creates fresh grievances, or sustains old ones.

The Extremist Threat

Reports indicate that paramilitaries continue to thrive in some majority Albanian areas ("FYROM: Armed Albanians terrorizing Macedonians in

Tetovo", BBC Monitoring Europe, 18 February 2003; "Albanian National Army reportedly recruiting in Macedonian crisis regions", BBC Worldwide Monitoring, *Dnevnik*, 22 February 2003:1). Many Slav Macedonians fear the continued existence of armed Albanian guerrillas ("Former Yugoslav Republic of Macedonia Post-Conflict Confidence Building: Programme Report", International Legal Alliances, 2002:1–39). It is no secret that the Albanian mafia flourishes in areas with little government control. Violent incidents continued throughout 2002, including several kidnappings and sieges of villages. A militant faction of the Albanian National Army (*Armaj Kombetare Shqiptare*, AKsh or ANA), "Avni Bexhiri Drenica", took responsibility for the shooting of two soldiers in Tetovo and the killing of two police officers in Gostivar in August 2002 ("Albanian Terrorism and Organized Crime in Kosovo and Metohia", BIA Report, Security Information Agency, Belgrade, September 2003). Directly after the attacks, a grenade was thrown at the DUI's headquarters in Skopje, and the political office of a DPA MP was destroyed by angry mobs. The Albanian National Army (ANA) was, and still is, the only active militant Albanian group in the region, revived by a few die-hard Albanians who seceded from the KLA and NLA. The group has developed a loose regional network of militant-criminal Albanians who mobilize on a periodic basis. Illiterate and marginalized individuals, usually from rural areas, often seek an alternative career in such activities.[4]

The ANA has claimed responsibility for a bomb attack in 2001 in the town of Aracinovo that killed four Slav Macedonian police officers,

4 Thirty of the 123 municipalities in FYR Macedonia have an unemployment rate higher than 50 per cent. Most of them are in the Polog and south-west regions, with only a few in the Skopje and Pelagonia regions. Zelino (79.4 per cent) and Topolcani (76.7 per cent) municipalities are at the top of the table in unemployment rates. Most municipalities with high unemployment rates are in mountainous rural areas. It is notable that in municipalities with predominantly Albanian populations, high numbers of employees are classified under the rubric "unknown sector" ("Socio-economic disparities among municipalities in Macedonia", Data and Indicators of Municipalities in Macedonia, November 2004, UNDP and Ministry of Local Self Government, 2004:100).

and it was responsible for the single deadliest attack against the Slav Macedonian security forces in August 2001 on the Skopje-Tetovo highway. On 3 September 2003, this rebel movement re-appeared in the villages of Lojane and Vaksince, after the kidnapping of a Slav Macedonian police officer by a group of gunmen under the direction of a self-proclaimed commander, Avdil Jakupi. The standoff was resolved with the mediation of local Albanian politicians. Notably, if the Albanians feel their hopes are not being fulfilled, and if the moderate forces fail to channel their grievances peacefully, then support for the ANA could increase. It is also possible that a serious backlash in Albanian affairs could re-mobilize many supporters of NLA and the Kosovo Protection Corps (KPC). Therefore, former combatants involved in constitutional politics in FYR Macedonia and Kosovo need to be constantly engaged in dialogue, since a potential loss of their stake in politics may bring dire consequences to the whole region (ibid.).[5]

Political Instability

The 5 July 2006 parliamentary elections brought a new coalition into power, led by the nationalists of VMRO-DPMNE (32.3 per cent of the vote). After failed talks with Democratic Union for Integration (DUI), Prime Minister Nicola Gruevski decided to exclude it from the coalition, even though the DUI received more votes in coalition with the PDP (12.2 per cent), and chose instead to cooperate with the rival Albanian party DPA. Not many people know that the first Albanian party invited to talk with Gruevski was not the DPA, but Ahmeti's DUI. The latter responded to

5 It is very unlikely that the Albanian National Army (NLA or AKsh) have more than a few dozen active fighters spread across different countries. Security experts in FYR Macedonia observe that support for the ANA is very low, and suggest there is no existing militant structure operating in the country. By contrast, Serbian authorities claim the operational forces of ANA in Kosovo and southern Serbia are composed of about 650 "terrorists", most of them situated in the region of Kosovska Kamenica and Gnjilane. Furthermore, the ANA's political representation remains obscure.

the Prime Minister's decision to invite the rival DPA to the coalition by organizing demonstrations and boycotting parliamentary sessions, including the session on the passing of the new police reform bill. Political representatives of DUI argued that the new law was aiming at centralization by removing competencies from municipal police to newly designed regional authorities ("Albanians in Macedonia: EU Warns Macedonia on Minority Rights Deal", 15 September 2006). They also threatened that they will use guns unless the DUI joins the government. The party's mayors agreed to block roads in protest and enact their own executive powers. The plan was later abandoned, but the DUI continues to engage in a political power struggle at the expense of the peace process. The party tried to distance itself from violence, but pressures were mounting because many Albanians believed the DUI could have done more: "the Albanians were unhappy because they expected the peace deal to produce swift improvements in their economic situation" (Stojanovska, 2003). However, public frustration increased with DUI's complacency in the preceding government coalition. The following comment by Fami Bajrami illustrates the DUI's vulnerability yet indispensability:

> This weakness on the ground underlines criticisms that the DUI remains top-heavy, poorly organized and politically immature. Analysts in Macedonia say the party has only a handful of experienced officials, no proper party structure and no visible presence on the ground … it is too reliant on its leader Ali Ahmeti, a charismatic figure whom one diplomat pointedly described as the man who keeps Macedonia together. For some observers, the DUI's weak points are outweighed by its steadfast refusal to allow talk of ethnic partition, a positive factor which has played well with Macedonians. (Baijrami, "Macedonia: Albanian Party Dominates by Default in Skopje", IWPR, No. 476, 2004)

Evidently, the pressure to implement the reforms had a tremendous impact on both Slav and Albanian political forces. A remarkable repetition of the pre-crisis conditions seems to be unfolding again. Albanians are starting to believe that the DUI is incapable of improving their status. Many Albanians have again turned to the DPA, a party that professes speedier change and tangible progress. The nationalist backlash is even more evident in the Slavic community. The VMRO-DPMNE, in an effort to divert attention from the country's real inter-ethnic problems, and resist the meaningful application of reforms, has raised its nationalist rhetoric against the Greeks. This nationalist reaction has hampered progress on inter-ethnic matters. To this day, ethnic communities have voted for parties that can either push or resist the implementation of reforms. The enforced compromise imposed through the Ohrid Framework Agreement (OFA) in August 2001, a direct result of coercive diplomacy, continues to obstruct the normal evolution of post-crisis politics. The inter-ethnic competition, sustaining the win-lose perceptions instituted by the OFA, has been aggravated by the country's non-acceptance into NATO, a result of a sterile nationalist attitude towards Greece's legitimate objections to the state's adopted name. Furthermore, the EU, the major sponsor of the Slavic Albanian compromise, considered progress in FYR Macedonia as slow and unsatisfactory. This aggravating, rigid (Slav Macedonian) nationalism perpetuates exclusion from the EU and NATO, which can only place the country at new risk.

In all cases where conflict exists, one must avoid solutions that produce clear winners and losers. Our findings demonstrate that strategic coercion – as a crisis management tool – resulted in a peace agreement that halted the fighting and prevented the country from disintegrating – yet ultimately produced a negative, "frozen" peace. We agree with the theoretical suggestions made by McGinty, Dugan and Burgess, as presented in the theory section (McGinty, 2004; Dugan and Burgess, 2004). Coercive methodologies sustain the antagonisms between the opposing parties. One should use these methodologies only to terminate violence, not to construct agreements that determine the future of a country.

Peace agreements need to be products of inter-ethnic consultation, long-term dialogue and mutual incentive, rather than indefinite and risky peacekeeping ventures. Sometimes, it is even better to generate agreed solutions by which no one can claim to be the winner – or loser. However, when solutions are imposed on the disputing parties, there always will be disappointments, possible dichotomies and structural side effects (Georgieva, 2004). In sum, "coercive strategies fail to produce a peaceful conflict resolution, and therefore coercion is a high-risk strategy" (Jakobsen, 2003:27–40).

The extended overreliance on pressures and positional bargaining makes the Ohrid Framework Agreement (OFA) a bad and unstable solution. As we have seen, the conflict between the Slavs and the Albanians was transferred from the military to the political arena, and consequently simmered inside the ethnic communities themselves. The Slavic parties fiercely resisted the implementation of reforms, since they viewed most OFA provisions as products of illegitimate pressure. The agreement did little to provide incentives for building trust between the communities and integrate them into a common domain. Every reform issue has been a subject of debate due to the resentments held by the Slavic community. Petty political alliances survived and intensified, while the stakes of holding power, rather than building positive peace, became significantly higher.

This type of enforced peace relies on an inter-communal synergy of interests without any genuine willingness to accommodate each other's grievances and aspirations. Finally, the symptoms of such peace arrangements are evident in the generation and preservation of resentments and fresh grievances (Brunnbauer, 2002; Stedman, 2001). The backlash effect is observable in the demographic changes and in the unwillingness to help regulate relations between the state and the minority. In addition, the lack of progress is evident in the proliferation of criminal-militant networks, electoral violence, and the vindictive and polarizing attitudes of parties. In this way, we have shown that coercive diplomacy by international policymakers can help to stop, curtail or prevent violence, but ultimately fails to address the insecurities among the parties of intrastate ethnic conflict.

Conclusion

The question of ethnic strife has preoccupied numerous theorists and policymakers. The study of ethnic conflict contains many schools of thought, and depending on which one we subscribe to, we might get different answers to our questions. Despite the growing accumulation of knowledge, and the increased sophistication of methodological approaches, new debates continue to emerge. This study provides a thorough strategic analysis of the emergence, management and security implications of intra-state violent ethnic conflict through the prism of relative deprivation and strategic mobilization. The analysis has concentrated on the dominant theoretical debate between advocates of greed-based conflict accounts and supporters of grievance-based explanations of the origins of ethnic conflict (Gurr, 1970; Woodward, 2005; Collier, 2004; Fearon and Laitin, 2003). Supporters of the deprivation theory argue that violent conflict is the result of real or perceived social, economic and political grievances (Gurr, 1970, 1993; Gurr and Moore, 1997; Davis, 1999; Woodward, 2005). The theory claims that ethnic groups encounter discontent because of the perceived discrepancy between their expectations and capabilities (Gurr, 1970). The gap between what ethnic groups get and what they think they deserve creates a feeling of frustration. As a result, disgruntled ethnic groups may become aggressive. The theory emphasizes that the level of aggression and violence is determined by the levels of discontent. Thus, economic, social and political grievances instigate the psychological mechanism of frustration-aggression, in order to produce ethno-political conflict.

The theory of relative deprivation has spawned a number of variants, and many theorists have focused on the important role of grievances, along with other factors, in order to explain conflict. Horowitz's theoretical interpretation of ranked ethno-social structures is probably the most prominent contribution in the quest to explain what type of grievances produce conflict, and how these grievances can be institutionally contained. In his work *Ethnic Groups in Conflict* (Horowitz, 2000), Horowitz emphasized the competitive social patterns formed by ethnic divisions and the impact of inter-ethnic comparison, and regarded the existence of ethnic competition in ranked systems as a major source of discontent. Ethnic groups determine their social position and form their collective self-esteem influenced by comparing their own group to other groups (ibid., 1998, 2000). Ethnic groups realize their social position and often attribute their disadvantages to the existence of oppressive structures, which are put in place by dominant groups (ibid., 1998, 2000).

This process creates an underlying antipathy of one group towards another, encourages perceptions of collective threat, and empowers perceptions of deliberate discrimination. As explained by Horowitz, "ethnic conflict arises from the common evaluative significance accorded by the groups to the acknowledged group differences and then played out in rituals of affirmation and contradiction" (Horowitz, 2000:227). As in the original theory of relative deprivation, the existence and severity of grievances is subject to comparison, and relative to a group's expectations (Gurr, 1970). Comparisons reveal the deliberate injustice that is inflicted on a subordinate group in order to deter a perceived threat associated with the opponent group. As a result, intra-group loyalty strengthens and prospects of confrontation increase. This approach is an essential supplement to the core deprivation theory because it specifies the social patterns that stimulate perceptions of deprivation. Recent accounts highlight new and lay an emphasis on older aspects of deprivation and conflict including qualitative analyses on economic inequality and large-N studies on religious grievances and ethno-religious militancy (Woodward, 2005; Fox, 2004).

However, early empirical analysis exposed remarkable contradictions as to whether relative deprivation is sufficient for explaining the outbreak of violence (Connor, 1994; Lichbach, 1995). Empirical observations suggest that not all deprived groups act violently (Olson and Pearson, 2003). This development encouraged scholars to seek explanations on the opportunities to act violently (Collier, 1999, 2004). Moreover, rational choice analysis pinpoints the irrationality of engaging in collective violence even in the presence of real grievances (Tong, 1991; Lichbach, 1995). Although group members may realize that if they act collectively they might eventually attain a public good that benefits everybody within the group, they remain sceptical as to the even distribution of goods, and the benefits each member of the group would eventually attain. Furthermore, the degree and value of expected benefits is always measured in accordance to the groups' capacity to trigger change, the feasibility of aims, the longevity of its campaign and the costs of failure. In most cases, using violence for achieving political gains is a high-cost venture that inhibits the undertaking of collective violent action. Moreover, the likely costs of failure and retaliation are major impediments in the decision of rebel groups to resort in organized armed violence (Lichbach, 1995). Potential failure may cause larger group deprivation, or even bring about the groups' total extinction or displacement, while inaction may at least assist the groups' survival. As it appears, the safest decision is to refrain from the use of violence. Nevertheless, armed insurgencies continue to occur.

In order to spot the motivation for violent conflict, advocates of greed have stressed the catalytic role of opportunities in violent collective mobilization (Collier, 1999, 2004; Lichbach, 1995). Greed theorists regard the role of grievances to be minimal, and even when grievances exist they become subjected to the material gains of private entrepreneurs (Collier, 2004). According to greed theorists, violent conflicts are driven by private material gains and rewards and not by genuine grievances. The vanguards in the process of conflict are "the structure of mafias, peasant armies, social bandits, and base areas" (Lichbach, 1995:229). Political entrepreneurs acquire and maximize resources through plundering, corruption and expropriation. These methods allow for the granting of rewards to members of violent groups. As a result, rebellions arise due to the aspirations of rebels to increase their wealth (Collier, 2000). Therefore, conflict is largely the result of material opportunities and incentives rather than genuine public grievances.

We find that both accounts contain some credible elements, which can be verified by statistical tests and empirical observations (Fearon and Laitin, 2003; Gurr and Moore, 1997). Yet both greed and grievance accounts seem to have strong weaknesses. Deprivation theorists sometimes ignore the influence of opportunities, taking for granted that deprivation leads to violence, while greed theorists insist on the wealth seeking opportunities in conflicts. Again, our analysis highlights the fact that some groups engage in violence whereas others remain inactive, and emphasizes that opportunities should not be regarded as mere economic gains since such a generalization conceals the existence of many other factors that enable or disable groups to act violently, including the intensity of deprivation itself. Hence, our analysis has explored whether deprivation is a sufficient explanation for the outbreak of violent conflict, and examined the conditions under which relative deprivation transforms into violent action. We have examined the impact of relative deprivation as part of a wider strategic framework in an attempt to challenge deprivation beyond the standard criticisms of greed. We have formulated a strategic framework, made up of actors, sources and preconditions, that aims to explain the emergence and transformation of violent conflict (Vasquez, 2000; Paquette, 2002; Duffy, 2003). The use of strategic analysis helps to unfold additional aspects, which were previously ignored or downplayed due to the prevalence of alternative accounts on greed. Our analysis treats conflict as a game between two competing ethnic groups; a dominant and a subordinate one, with different priorities, fears, alliances and values. The major objective of the groups is to ensure their ethnic survival, and for this reason, they tend to compete for political access and power within a given area. For reasons of survival and security, dominant groups suppress the inferior ones, while inferior groups seek an opportunity to alter this unfavourable balance. Through a careful elaboration of strategic opportunities, such as the influence of neighbouring states, the ability of the state to sustain repression, and the influence of violent regional spillover effects, we have identified some processes through which elements belonging to the subordinate and deprived ethnic group, in this case the Albanians, may turn violent. In this way, we have outlined how the circumstances produced by the developing and changing regional-strategic environment provide ample motivation for violence and the likelihood of successful rebellion.

The failure to resolve conflicts by removing every residue of dissatisfaction (Lake and Rothchild, 1996) prompted us to examine the role of strategic coercion, a controversial method in the management of violent disputes advocated by mainstream theorists, and employed by international organizations (George, 1991; Art, 2003; Jakobsen, 2003). Moreover, the suggestion that coercive settlements produce a backlash effect, and help the perpetuation of grievances, established an explicit link between pre- and post-conflict deprivation (Dugan and Burgess, 2004; McGinty, 2004).

Strategic coercion is an elaborate form of peace enforcement that considers the value of negotiations and the utility of positive inducements as an alternative to costly military interventions (George, 1991). In its essence, strategic coercion is a moderate variant of brute-force coercion and compulsion (Shelling, 1966). Strategic coercion differs from other forms of conflict regulation such as mediation, facilitation and good offices, as it depends on the enforcing power of the coercer, rather than the genuine willingness of the parties for resolving their differences. Strategic coercion relies on the calculated exchange of pressures, threats and incentives in order to persuade conflicting parties to act peacefully (George, 1991). The aim of this method is to persuade parties to resolve their differences in peaceful ways.

Some analysts have suggested that strategic coercion, no matter how sophisticated it may be, it will eventually produce a backlash effect due to the catalytic use of diplomatic, military or economic pressure (Brown, 2003; Dugan and Burgess, 2004; McGinty, 2004). Sometimes, ethnic groups need to comply with unfavourable decisions under the threat of the use of unbearable pressure. This forced compliance spawns a fresh round of grievances, one revolving around a perceived sense of victimization, and a desire to revenge and rectify an injustice (Dugan and Burgess, 2004). The backlash effect is a post-conflict reaction to the pressures exercised to a conflicting party (ibid.). This development reproduces a feeling of deprivation and loss from one party to another, and helps sustain the grievances and war energy (Harris, Fisk, and Rank 1998). The explicit link between pre-and post-conflict deprivation urged us to investigate whether strategic coercion is successful in resolving violent disputes characterized by severe grievances.

The case study analysis presented in this book does not refute the significant influence of relative deprivation and its variants. The analysis finds that oppressive structures, socio-economic disparities and economic decline have all played a significant part in the emergence, intensification and reproduction of conflict-prone attitudes among the Albanians. Empirical analysis reveals the dissatisfaction of Albanians with their comparatively backward social and economic status. Based on the analysis of selected economic indices, we have explored the Albanian expectations of increased political access and social improvement in relation to their comparative disadvantages within Yugoslavia. We have drawn out the socio-economic connections between FYR Macedonia, Kosovo and the other Yugoslav Republics and highlighted the problem of resolving political issues of ethnic division without economic and social progress. This sets up a well-rounded critique of sterile ethno-nationalist accounts of conflict.

Yet grievances resulting from perceptions of deprivation failed to generate organized forms of violent collective action. That was mainly due to the structural and operational restrictions set by the politico-military strength of the Yugoslav regime, and the absence of regional opportunities that would facilitate the outbreak of violence. Therefore, the existence of a strong military mechanism, backed by a powerful political leadership, reduces the potential of violent action. Our analysis suggests that deprivation may constitute a solid basis for protest and conflict, but little evidence exists to suggest that deprivation alone is capable to produce organized forms of armed violence. Hence, other factors influence the decision of aggrieved groups to engage in violence.

Our analysis moved forward to depict the conditions that allow the violent transformation of deprivation. We have measured the fluctuating levels of relative deprivation among the Albanians in FYR Macedonia and examined whether violent incidents increased in relation to the degree and severity of deprivation. However, similar degrees of deprivation might have existed in the past, and for this reason we examined relative deprivation through the lens of regional-strategic pre-conditions that were not previously present. We found that the absence of the mighty Yugoslav war machine, and the reduction of retaliation fears, facilitated the violent expression of Albanian grievances. More importantly, the analysis suggested that the continuous existence of oppressive and discriminatory governmental policies, combined with external developments to create favourable conditions for violence. The analysis illustrated the negative, if not outwardly hostile, attitudes held by neighbouring countries against the state's legitimacy, and highlighted the state's incapacity to sustain the oppressive policies. Furthermore, the analysis suggested that violent rebellions in neighbouring Kosovo and Presevo influenced and encouraged the emergence of organized armed violence by local militants in FYR Macedonia. Therefore, the decision to act violently could largely depend on regional conditions that help the violent expression of existing grievances and deprivation within a given state.

The problem of targeted marginalization and minority deprivation seems to have little to do with the government's genuine lack of sensitivity but, rather, our analysis points to the objective lack of policy choices when confronting real security considerations. Indeed, we have effectively shown that geo-strategic considerations played a crucial role in the formulation of intransigent and unresponsive governmental policies, and determined the decision of the minority group to use violence in order to alter such policies. Therefore, the answer to the question whether relative deprivation is a sufficient explanation for the outbreak of violent conflict is a conditional yes. Relative deprivation is necessary to explain the origins of ethnic conflict, but it is not sufficient because it does not adequately explain the violent transformation of conflict, since organized violence requires the interplay of favourable geo-strategic conditions in order to erupt.

Notably, greed accounts explain the motivation of violence from a different angle (Collier, 1999, 2004). Greed theorists attribute the outbreak of violent conflict to the private economic goals of militant criminals. However, focusing on the wealth seeking objectives of militants prevents us from understanding the antagonisms between rival ethnicities with different agendas and priorities. Greed assumptions ignore the repeated instances of conflict and the patterns of dominance and subjugation in the history of ethnic groups. These accounts do not seem to appreciate the impact of downtrodden economic conditions driving people to crime, and seem to fail to account for the deliberate implementation of oppressive policies against specific ethnic groups for reasons beyond the immediate material gain. In short, blunt perspectives of materialist motivation in conflict may sometimes obscure the development of internal and external conditions and the strategic opportunities these conditions create for the activation of violence.

Conflict seems to emanate from need and opportunity, rather than greed and opportunity. For instance, criminal networks in the Balkans have a highly distorted "capitalist mentality" and by exploiting situations of conflict due to the lack of real prospects and alternative options, they seek to make substantial profits in relatively short periods of time. However, while greed is identified with a private desire for riches, need is identified with a commonly shared desire for making a living and improving the conditions of life. Notably, we admit that ethnic conflict is a collective venture, and as such, criminal practices may often overlap with political agendas. In reality, it would be almost impossible to find a conflict where looting, extortion and other profiteering practices have not existed. Even if we attribute such practices to pure greed, we must always consider the sources which gave rise to such violent greed, which in our view is the existence of deprivation in conflict.

Our analysis moves beyond the examination of the conditions under which ethnic conflict develops, and explores the implications of coercion in the management of intrastate violent ethnic conflict (George, 1991; Brown, 2003; Carlson, 2005). The effectiveness of strategic coercion in the regulation of violent conflicts is explored with the analysis of the evolution of the armed crisis in FYR Macedonia and the coercive, rather than preventive, intervention of international actors. We find that strategic coercion may be a very effective tool in the arsenal of international policymakers, especially when the coercer is flexible, credible and well-coordinated, and when the coerced party is weak and needy. We demonstrated the potential of strategic coercion to encourage negotiations through pressures and positive inducements, and swiftly terminate a crisis before it escalates into a full-blown war. For this reason, we suggest the limited use of strategic coercion for containing the escalation of conflict, and for terminating violence.

Yet the application of coercive methods i.e. economic sanctions, conditional provision of incentives, diplomatic isolation, military threats etc. suffer from a major drawback: a reliance on pressure for short-term benefits. This feature renders coercion a risky and unstable method in the regulation of sensitive intra-state disputes (Brown, 2003; Jakobsen, 2003; Carlson, 2005). Evidence shows that the exercise of extensive pressures, the exploitation of the coerced party's structural and military weaknesses, the danger of partisanship and the formulation of an imposed settlement created win-lose attitudes. Fears and insecurity among Slav Macedonians were exaggerated, inter-ethnic and intra-ethnic competition intensified, and ultimately a type of negative peace emerged.

We attributed this negative post-conflict development to immediate counter-reactions towards the coercive settlement. The peace settlement, a result of pressures to compromise on decisions taken by third parties, transformed violent conflict into a win-lose political game with frequent violent lapses. The international mediating bodies intended to address the major sources of Albanian discontent by exercising pressure mainly against the dominant Slavic parties, but eventually created new sources of discontent among both Slavs and Albanians. Thus, the dangerous possibilities of a backlash effect quickly emerged and became evident in the preservation of grievances, the perpetuation of structural violence, and the resurgence of the same antagonisms that produced violence in the first place. Peace compromises resulting from pressure encourage the establishment of win-lose attitudes, which in turn discourage parties from cooperating in a harmonious and constructive way. Coercion is largely responsible for the obfuscation of ethnic discontent, the devaluation of security fears and the institutionalization of antagonism in the post-conflict phase. These elements constitute impediments to peace because they promote ethnic entrenchment, post-conflict intransigence, elevated nationalist rhetoric, revenge and the rectification of past wrongs.

Success in coercion seems to be rather short-lived. This counter-reaction raises questions over the long-term success of coercive diplomacy. These questions related to the limited focus on tactical factors which are important in the short term, and the overlooking of situational factors which we believe are crucial in securing long-term success i.e. peace and stability (Bratton, 2009). Therefore, despite the merits of coercion in the termination of violent hostilities, coercive methodologies have so far proven to be extremely unfruitful in the resolution of longstanding inter-ethnic conflicts such as in the case of the Kurds in Turkey, Kosovo, Iraq, Israel and Palestine and Bosnia (Byman and Waxman, 2000).

Coercive settlements reduce the political will of parties to progress with reforms, or conciliate, as in the case of FYR Macedonia and Kosovo.

However, this does not suggest that the use of coercion is solely responsible for the perpetuation of political grievances and antagonisms, or the economic hardship and the structural deficiencies, which are evident in the system. These systemic deficiencies certainly relate to the quality of a peace settlement, but usually extend beyond the immediate provisions of a peace settlement to the actual politico-economic pathologies of a violently divided society. The inability to secure and handle financial resources effectively, lack of social progress and social provisions, or extreme levels of publicly perceived corruption require elements that supersede the presence of political will, such as opportunities, assistance and regional stability.

The outcome of the analysis should be treated as a unified whole, focusing on the role of deprivation and the existence of grievances both before and after the outbreak of violent conflict. We suggest the existence of an explicit link between pre-conflict and post-conflict grievances, and supplement the theory of relative deprivation with a set of strategic factors. The transformation of relative deprivation into violent conflict seems at least to relate to a range of strategic factors. These factors provide opportunities that facilitate the violent expression of grievances by the most militant and impatient elements of a deprived community. Without the existence of favourable strategic factors, it is doubtful whether violence could erupt. However, the existence of relative deprivation plays a significant role in justifying the decision to act violently. Grievances provide the impetus and justification of conflict, while strategic factors provide the stimulants and opportunities that make violence operationally feasible.

The persistence of grievances in the post-conflict phase is a tough bet for academics and policymakers. Deprivation is of central importance to the emergence and violent transformation of conflict, and for this reason, we investigated further the potency of grievances. In our case, we observed that certain methods in conflict regulation, might even exaggerate the existence of discontent. Strategic coercion is one such method. The role of coercion is not to persuade parties to address the sources of conflict, but to force parties to compromise regardless of their fears and insecurities. Coercive approaches, when applied by credible and powerful external bodies, such as NATO and the EU, can successfully put an end to violent conflict, especially when the conflicting participants are weak, needy and disorganized. However, if coercion continues during the phase of dialogue, then chances are that any compromise will be the result of sheer pressure. Therefore, coercion should stop at the stage where violence ends. Forcing parties to concede on important issues to their security, without carefully examining the implications of such decisions, can only generate a fresh round of disappointment, suspicion and discontent. Peace settlements that were built on pressure, power and tactical objectives, carried out by parties irrelevant to the conflict itself, tend to produce fragile results and recycle grievances. A useful reflection of post-conflict grievances exists in the application of reforms in FYR Macedonia. The decentralization reform, as indicated in the peace agreement, encountered problematic local reactions and antagonisms, which, again with the use of pressure, were bypassed. The result, however, is one where self-governing authorities exist only on paper, while in reality they lack all necessary human and financial resources. Pressures to reform the educational system, bypassed Slavic objections on the institutionalization of segregation. Police reforms meant that international political actors had to press for the inclusion of poor combatants to the police ranks, thus failing to break the links of the police with the mafia.

Similar problems continue to occur in other reforms designed to protect the minorities, such as equitable representation and language provisions. The dominant Slavs agreed on reforms without a clear practical applicability under the threat of pressure, and for this reason the social and political system has so far failed to deliver the promised benefits to the deprived Albanians. The result is that both parties are now dissatisfied for different reasons. This hasty approach has clearly failed to eliminate or address the sources of conflict in an effort to terminate a crisis that threatened to plunge the country and the entire region into war. The failure to address the sources of deprivation in a systematic, rational and gradual manner was mainly due to the deliberate lack of consideration for the existing fears and insecurities held by both parties.

Our findings have a strong regional relevance and significance. Relative deprivation exists in the vast majority of conflicts, while the coercive intervention of third parties in the case of FYR Macedonia, Kosovo and Bosnia has failed to consider the long-standing security fears, which gave rise to multifarious forms of deprivation. International policymakers put an emphasis on the immediate objectives i.e. termination of hostilities, repression of violence, elimination of extremism, and try to accelerate the pace of economic development, without calculating the dangerous regional imbalances and security correlations. As a result, the structural economic and social roots produce ethnic unrest, and the security concerns and expectations of the conflicting parties continue to remain largely unaddressed. Partly for this reason, we observe today a number of frozen conflicts that have been settled in ways that left considerable portions of a society unsatisfied. The perpetuation of the conflict in FYR Macedonia, the peculiar partition of Bosnia, the secession of Kosovo from Serbia, and the unsafe political divisions in Montenegro provide evidence of the inadequacy of coercion and the sustainment of deprivation despite the liberalization of these economies and the absence of war. For example, fourteen years after the Dayton agreement, the people of Bosnia and Herzegovina continue to feel economically and politically deprived, and many attribute their deprivation to the existing post-conflict system. Croats desire to see the unification of parts of Herzegovina with Croatia, Bosnian Serbs threaten to conduct an independence referendum, and the majority of all ethnic groups continue to insist that only nationalist parties can effectively protect minority rights. On a global scale, the military intervention in Afghanistan and the fragmentation of Iraq are equal results of policies enacted against the genuine will of many people, under pressurizing conditions, and enforced upon parties with few alternative options. These power-based approaches, no matter how moderate they are, seem to suffer from a lack of vision.

A priority of primary concern is the removal or containment of the strategic correlations that exist in certain areas, so that we minimize the external factors influencing the decisions of aggrieved groups. The conflict in FYR Macedonia suggests that external actors can undermine internal peace in the most critical way. Additionally, external influences force governments to behave irrationally by sustaining the oppressive mechanisms of the state and increasing the grievances of dissenting groups. Deprivation constitutes a solid justification of conflict. Denial of political rights, torture, extrajudicial killings, electoral fraud and many other bad practices have no place in the politics of divided societies. Security fears cannot be allayed in such ways. Neighbouring states and regional actors should seek to benefit from relations of mutual profit, rather than undermine a neighbouring state's political system. It is useful to remember that security correlations in the Balkans are such that facilitate the spread of conflicts from one region to another. There is little doubt that governments, no matter how strong they are, should be able to plan and execute programmes for the sustainable development of areas that suffer most. Policymakers should put an emphasis on breaking up the deadlock of insecurity, which prompts groups to implement oppressive policies against competitors. The equitable and parallel socio-economic development of ethnic groups might ease the security fears by removing the socio-economic justification of conflict and reducing the existence of comparative ethnic disadvantages. This helps to match separate ethno-political objectives for the benefit of common development.

Minorities should be offered incentives to develop ties with the system and cooperate with other ethnic groups, and disincentives must exist for those who wish to incite violence. Ethnic groups in regional states should understand that seeking to accomplish narrow ethno-nationalist objectives might insult the objectives and interests of other groups, and eventually trigger counter-reactions by those whose interests are threatened. In many cases, dominant ethno-political parties abuse the state mechanism systematically, and exclude other competing ethnic groups from the policymaking process. Subordinate groups engage in illegal and extra-constitutional practices as a reaction to this marginalization. It is important that governments and politically active ethnic groups reach a stage of political maturity which can allow them to work independently, and form alliances of mutual benefit. This can be done by increasing social cohesion, avoiding segregation while permitting the expression of difference, providing positive inducements for institutional and administrative cooperation, and setting rules and guarantees which prevent parties from seeking exogenous and potentially harmful alternatives. A convergence of diverse strategic objectives can only occur with the provision of incentives for development, accompanied by rules of political engagement.

The research findings point clearly in certain directions. We should start analysing relative deprivation in combination with security and strategic factors. This will help us to better understand the motivation and opportunities that drive people to violence. Our analysis incorporated factors relating to state strength, external state legitimacy and regional spillovers, but many other factors should be taken into account when exploring the outbreak of violent conflict. Fresh analysis must consider multiple security factors such as the influence of radical ideologies and political parties, the role of organized crime in the transformation of conflict and the role of energy and resources.

Moreover, in this book we were only able to examine one possible method of managing conflict. The different varieties of coercion must be further examined in order to set clear preconditions and define effective combinations. Other methods in the regulation of conflict should be analysed by taking into consideration the important security factors affecting the behaviour of parties in the post-conflict phase, with the aim of producing stable, genuine and durable peace. Finally, it is vital to provide incentives that help ethnic groups to cooperate on a commonly accepted strategic basis. It is crucial for governments to try to avoid inter-group discrepancies, understand the security environment in cooperative terms, and discover those elements that may help ethnic groups to overcome the narrow frameworks of the state without jeopardizing its sovereign rights and integrity.

APPENDIX I

Origins and Profiles of Main Parties and Groups

KLA / UCK

The Kosovo Liberation Army (KLA) / *Ushtria Çlirimtare e Kosovës* (UCK) formed in 1992 (although it first became active in 1996) and operated mainly in Kosovo, Albania and FYR Macedonia as an armed national-separatist formation seeking to achieve Kosovo's independence from the Yugoslav Federal Republic. The KLA's violent campaign triggered a fierce Serbian crackdown, swelling the ranks of the group with new recruits and provoking an external military intervention by NATO. The organization was estimated to have 12,000 to 20,000 active members by the beginning of 1999. After the completion of military operations in Kosovo, KLA disbanded and was transformed into the Kosovo Protection Forces. Many of its members were later integrated in the police force, while others pursued careers in politics.

UCPMB

The Liberation Army of Preševo, Medveda and Bujanovac / *Ushtria Çlirimtare e Preshevës, Medvegjës dhe Bujanocit* is a small separatist militant Albanian group which operated mainly in Serbia and Kosovo in the period between June and November 2000. The group constituted a KLA / UCK offshoot and it was held responsible for a series of violent attacks against Serbian police across the Ground Safety Zone areas. After a NATO-led "screen and release" policy, members of the group turned themselves in to the Kosovar authorities and the group disbanded.

NLA / UCK

The National Liberation Army / *Ushtria Çlirimtare Kombëtare* is an Albanian militant group which operated mainly in the northern parts of

FYR Macedonia and Kosovo. The NLA was closely associated with the KLA/UCK in Kosovo and it was held responsible for instigating an armed rebellion against the Slavic Macedonian authorities in 2001. After the signing of the peace agreement, the group disbanded and many members of the group were integrated in the police and other public services, while others pursued political careers.

ANA / AKSh

The Albanian National Army (ANA) / *Armata Kombëtare Shqiptare* is a small, loosely organized Albanian ultra-nationalist militant group, active in the border areas between Kosovo and FYR Macedonia. The group, which grew out of the insurgent Albanian groups who battled Slavic Macedonian troops in 2001, seeks to promote the irredentist project of "Greater Albania". The group has been active on a number of occasions, some of their activities resulting in deadly armed clashes. The group's motives are thought to be more criminal than political.

IMRO-DPMNU / VMRO-DPMNE

The Internal Macedonian Revolutionary Organization – Democratic Party for Macedonian National Unity / *Vnatrešna Makedonska Revolucionerna Organizacija – Demokratska Partija za Makedonsko Nacionalno Edinstvo* is a major Slavic Macedonian nationalist political party in FYR Macedonia. The party describes itself as Christian-democratic with a post-nationalist European integrationist agenda. The party's name derives from the historic "Internal Macedonian Revolutionary Organization", a Slavic Macedonian rebel nationalist movement that operated in the region of Macedonia from 1893 until the end of the Second World War. The party has won a series of presidential and parliamentary elections in FYR Macedonia.

IMRO-PP / VMRO-NP

The Internal Macedonian Revolutionary Organization – People's Party / *Vnatrešna Makedonska Revolucionerna Organizacija – Narodna Partija* is a conservative nationalist party which emerged out of a split with the much larger VMRO-DPMNE, because of an internal political rift with VMRO-DPMNE leader Nicola Gruevski.

SDUM / SDSM

The Social Democratic Union of Macedonia / *Socijaldemokratski Sojuz na Makedonija* is the successor party of the League of Communists of Macedonia and presents itself as a modern social-democratic political party. The party ruled from 1992 to 1998 and from 2002 to 2004. The party suffered a number of schisms and is currently undergoing reform.

DUI /BDI

The Democratic Union for Integration / *Bashkimi Demokratik për Integrim* is the largest ethnic Albanian political party in FYR Macedonia, founded by the NLA's leader Ali Ahmeti. Many former NLA combatants have been included in its ranks. The party has supported the peace process in FYR Macedonia and participated in ruling coalitions. In some instances, DUI delegates have abstained from their ordinary parliamentary duties because of political disputes.

DPA / PDSh

The Democratic Party of Albanians / *Partia Demokratike Shqiptare* is a formerly radical Albanian political party in FYR Macedonia. The DPA originates from the merger of the Party for Democratic Prosperity of Albanians (PDPA) and the People's Democratic Party (NDP) and constitutes the second largest Albanian political force in FYR Macedonia. The DPA – led by the Albanian intellectuals Arben Xhaferi and Meduh Thaci – entered government in 1998 and 2006 and it has run in several municipal elections with considerable success.

PDP / PPD

The Party for Democratic Prosperity / *Partia për Prosperitet Demokratik* was a moderate Albanian political force in FYR Macedonia. The party participated in government from 1992 to 1998 but in recent years support for the party has eroded.

LDK

The Democratic League of Kosovo / *Lidhja Demokratike e Kosovës* was the first nationalist conservative political party, founded by moderate nationalist politician Ibrahim Rugova in Kosovo. The LDK has been a major driving force in pushing for Kosovo's independence. Rugova's moderate and peaceful approach to the problem of Kosovo, and the rising popularity of the KLA, decreased the party's strength. The party came into power as a minor partner in a coalition government in 2004 and again in 2007.

KPC

The Kosovo Protection Forces emerged from the transformation of the Kosovo Liberation Army into a civilian emergency service (interim police force) in Kosovo, following the intervention of NATO. The KPC was disbanded in 2009.

APPENDIX 2

Chronology of Major Events: 1991–2007

15 September 1991: The Socialist Yugoslav Republic of Macedonia declares its independence from Yugoslavia.

11–12 January 1992: More than 90 per cent of Albanians in FYR Macedonia approve autonomy in a referendum. The issue hinges on the degree of autonomy sought by the Albanians of FYR Macedonia.

7 April 1992: Representatives of the Albanian population declare the autonomy of the "Albanian Autonomous Republic of Illyria".

11 December 1992: The UN Security Council decides in its resolution 795 to deploy/reassign 700 Blue Helmets to FYR Macedonia.

8 April 1993: FYR Macedonia is admitted to the UN (the 181st member) under the provisional name of the "Former Yugoslav Republic of Macedonia" (FYROM).

16–17 February 1994: Greece imposes an economic blockade on FYR Macedonia

17 February 1995: Violent clashes erupt between ethnic Albanians and Slav Macedonian police. Deputies from the ethnic Albanian Party of Democratic Prosperity begin to boycott parliamentary sessions.

13 September 1995: Greece and FYR Macedonia sign an interim accord in New York which is intended to normalize bilateral relations. The dispute about the national flag is settled.

4 July 1996: More than 10,000 ethnic Albanians rally in Tetovo, protesting against the jailing of Fadil Sulejmani, the Dean of Tetovo University. Demonstrators demand the university's legalization and its integration into the official education system.

9 July 1997: Two ethnic Albanians are killed and many more wounded following clashes between police and hundreds of Albanians in Gostivar.

March–September 1998: Open conflict between Serb police and the separatist Kosovo Liberation Army (KLA). Serb forces launch a brutal crackdown. Civilians are driven from their homes.

1 March 1999: The mandate of the UN Preventive Deployment Force (UNPREDEP) expires and is not extended.

23 March 1999: The Rambouillet negotiations collapse.

24 March 1999: NATO begins seventy-eight days of air strikes against Kosovo and Serbia.

March–April 1999: During the NATO air strikes on Yugoslavia, the wave of refugees from Kosovo increases to approximately 150,000.

June–November 2000: The UCPMB launches an armed campaign against Serbian forces across the Ground Safety Zone separating Kosovo from Serbia.

February–May 2001: Armed uprising by ethnic Albanians. The National Liberation Army emerges, demanding equal rights for ethnic Albanians.

13 August 2001: Government and rebels sign western-backed Ohrid peace agreement, involving greater recognition of ethnic Albanian rights in exchange for rebel pledge to hand over weapons to NATO peace force.

September 2001: NATO carries out the month-long Operation Essential Harvest to disarm rebels, exceeding its target of collecting 3,300 weapons.

16 November 2001: Parliament in Skopje approves new constitution incorporating reforms required by August peace deal. It recognizes Albanian as an official language and increases access for ethnic Albanians to public sector jobs, including the police.

14 September 2002: The Albanian National Army launches a number of attacks in Kosovo and FYR Macedonia.

15 September 2002: The Social Democrats under Branko Crvenkovski become the largest party. Most ethnic Albanian voters back the Democratic Union for Integration, under former rebel Ali Ahmeti.

26 February 2004: President Boris Trajkovski is killed in a plane crash in Bosnia. He was on his way to an investment conference in Mostar.

March 2004: Nineteen people are killed in the worst clashes between Serbs and ethnic Albanians since 1999. The violence starts in the divided town of Mitrovica.

July 2004: Thousands of Macedonians protest against proposals to redraw municipal borders and give minority ethnic Albanians more power in certain areas. The changes are required for the further implementation of the 2001 Ohrid peace agreement.

17 December 2005: FYR Macedonia becomes a candidate for EU membership.

3 June 2006: Following a referendum, Montenegro declares independence. Serbia responds by declaring itself an independent sovereign successor state to the Union of Serbia and Montenegro.

21 February 2007: United Nations envoy Martti Ahtisaari unveils a plan to set Kosovo on the path to independence, which is immediately welcomed by Kosovo Albanians and rejected by Serbia.

16 April 2007: Former interior minister Ljube Boskovski goes on trial at the international tribunal in The Hague, charged with war crimes during the 2001 ethnic Albanian rebellion.

APPENDIX 3

Recorded Interviews

F.V.K., 14 December 2006, Skopje (EU Political Advisor)
B.J., 15 December 2006, Skopje (Journalist)
H.I., 12 December 2006, Skopje (Journalist)
N.D., 15 December 2006 and 16 December 2007, Skopje (Ministry of Foreign Affairs)
S.O., 15 December 2006, Skopje (Chief Editor and Political Analyst)
G.T., 18 December 2006, Skopje (Ministry of Interior)
N.S., July 2007, Thessaloniki (Political Analyst)
I.R., 13 July 2007, Tetovo (Political Analyst)
I.R., 15 July 2007, Tetovo (Journalist/Correspondent)
E.M., 15 July 2007, Skopje (Politician and Party Spokesperson)
I.P., 17 July 2007, Skopje (National Security Advisor)
E.N., 19 July 2007, Tetovo (Politician)
Z.D., 14 August 2007, Skopje (Political Analyst)

Bibliography

Ackerman, A. (1997), "The Former Yugoslav Republic of Macedonia: A Relatively Successful Case of Conflict Prevention in Europe", *Security Dialogue*, Vol. 27, No. 4 (1997), pp. 409–424.
Ackerman, A. (1999), "Managing Conflicts Non-Violently Through Preventive Action: The Case of the Former Yugoslav Republic of Macedonia", *Journal of Conflict Studies*, Vol. 14, No. 1 (Spring 1999).
Ackerman, A. (2000), *Making Peace Prevail: Preventing Violent Conflict in Macedonia*, Syracuse University Press.
Ackermann, A. and Pala, A. (1996), "From Peacekeeping to Preventive Deployment: A Study of the United Nations in the Former Yugoslav Republic of Macedonia", *European Security*, Vol. 5, No. 1 (Spring 1996), pp. 83–97.
Arsovska, J. (2006), "Understanding a culture of violence and crime: the Kanun of Lek Dukagjini and the rise of the Albanian sexual-slavery rackets", *European Journal of Crime, Criminal Law and Criminal Justice*, Vol. 14, No. 2, pp. 161–184.
Art, Robert. (2003), *United States and Coercive Diplomacy*, U.S. Institute of Peace.
Artisien, Patrick F.R and Buckley, Peter J. (1985), "Joint Ventures in Yugoslavia: Opportunities and Constraints", *Journal of International Business Studies*, Vol. 16, No. 1.
Atanasov, Petar (2006), "Post-Conflict Rehabilitation: Lessons from South East Europe and Strategic Consequences for the Euro-Atlantic Community", Austrian Armed Forces Publications. Available at: <http://www.bmlv.gv.at/english/misc/publications.php>.
Babuna, Aydin (2000), *The Albanians of Kosovo and Macedonia* (Publisher Unknown).
Balalovska, Kristina (2004), "Between the Balkans and Europe: A study of the contemporary transformation of Macedonian identity: 1991–2002", *New Balkan Politics*, Issue 6. Available at: <http://www.newbalkanpolitics.org.mk/OldSite/Issue_6/balalovska.beetween.eng.asp>.
Ballentine, Karen and Nitzshke, Heiko (2003), "Beyond Greed and Grievance: Policy Lessons Form Studies in the Political Economy of Armed Conflict", International Peace Academy Policy Report.
Bandura, A. and Walters, R. (1963), *Social Learning and Personality Development*, Rinehart and Winston.

Bashkurti, Lisen (2004), "Political dynamics within the countries in the Balkans: Cases of Bosnia and Herzegovina and Macedonia", Contribution to the Symposium on the Final Status of Kosovo, Chicago Kent College of Law, Chicago, Illinois, USA, 16–17 April 2004. Available at: <http://www.operationkosovo.kentlaw.edu/symposium/bashkurti-simpozium.html>.

Batakovic, Dusan T. (1999), "Kosovo and Metohija: A historical survey", in Petrovic Ruza and Blagojevic Marina, *The migration of Serbs and Montenegrins from Kosovo-Metohija: Results of the survey conducted 1985–1986*, Serbian Academy of Sciences and Arts, Department of Social Sciences, Demographic Studies, Vol. 3.

Baylis, J., Smith, S., and Owens, P. (2007), *The Globalization of World Politics*, Oxford University Press.

Beams, N. (1999), "IMF Shock therapy and the re-colonization of the Balkans", *World Socialist Web*, 17 April. Available at: <http://www.wsws.org/articles/1999/apr1999/imf-a17.shtml>.

Bennett, A. et al (2003), "Do We Preach What We Practice? A Survey of Methods in Political Science Journals and Curricula", *Political Science and Politics*, Vol. 36, No. 3.

Berger, M. (2009), "How Resisting Democracies Can Defeat Substate Terrorism: Formulating a Theoretical Framework for Strategic Coercion against Nationalistic Substate Terrorist Organizations", Doctoral Thesis, St Andrews University.

Berkowitz, L. (1980), "The Frustration-Aggression Hypothesis". In R.A. Falk and S.S. Kim (eds), *The War System: An Interdisciplinary Approach*. Westview Press.

Bieber, Florian (2004), "Institutionalizing Ethnicity: Success and Failures in Post-war Bosnia-Herzegovina, Kosovo, and Macedonia", International Forum Bosnia.

Blum, P. (1987), "Yugoslavia, economy on a bumpy truck", *Financial Times*, 10 June. Available at: <http://www.lexisnexis.com/uk>.

Blumi, Isa (2002), "The Question of Identity, Diplomacy and Albanians in Macedonia: Has the Rain Come?", *International Journal of Albanian Studies*, 14 January. Available at: <http://www.southeasteurope.org/documents/Isa%20Blumi.htm>.

Brown, Keith S. et al (2002), "Ohrid and Beyond: A cross ethnic investigation into the Macedonian crisis", IWPR Lancaster House. Available at: <http://www.iwpr.net/docs/pdf/ohrid_book.pdf>.

Brown, Seyom. (2003), *The Illusion of Control*, Brookings Institution.

Brubaker, R. (1996), *Nationalism Refrained*, Cambridge University Press.

Buck, Thomas (1996), "Fear and Loathing in Macedonia: Ethnic nationalism and the Albanian problem", Institute of East Central Europe, Working Paper. Available at: <http://www.ciaonet.org/conf/iec03/iec03_13-96.html>.

Buhaug, Halvard and Gates, Scott (2002), "The Geography of Civil War", *Journal of Peace Research*, Vol. 39, No. 4, pp. 417–433.

Buhaug, Halvard and Lujala, P. (2005), "Accounting for Scale: Measuring Geography in Quantitative Studies of Civil War", *Political Geography*, Vol. 24 No. 4, pp. 399–418.

Buhaug, Halvard and Rød, J.K. (2006), "Local Determinants of African Civil Wars: 1970–2001", *Political Geography*, Vol. 25, No. 3, pp. 315–335.

Bumci, Aldo (2003), "Regional perspectives for an independent Kosovo – Albania and Macedonia", in Florian Bieber and Zidas Daskalovski (eds) (2003), *Understanding the war in Kosovo*, Frank CAS.

Burgess, G., Burgess H. and Maiese, M. (2004), "Revenge and the Backlash Effect", *Beyond Intractability*, Conflict Research Consortium, University of Colorado.

Byman, Daniel L. and Waxman, Matthew C. (2000), "Kosovo and the Great Air Power Debate," *International Security*, Vol. 24, No. 4, pp. 5–38.

Carlson, Justin (2005), "The Failure of Coercive Diplomacy: Strategy Assessment for the 21st Century", *Hemispheres: The Tufts Journal of International Relations*, 2005 Edition. Available at: <http://www.ase.tufts.edu/hemispheres/2005/Carlson.doc>.

Chichok, Mark (1985), "Revaluating development strategy: Policy implications for Yugoslavia", *Comparative Politics*, Vol. 17, No. 2.

Chiclet, Christopher (1999), "Victim of a new Balkan crisis? Macedonia risks falling apart", *Le Monde Diplomatique*. Available at: <http://mondediplo.com/1999/01/13maced>.

Chima, Jugdep (2005), "What's the Utility of the Case-Study Method for Social Science Research? A Response to Critiques from the Quantitative/Statistical Perspective", Paper for delivery at the 2005 Annual Meeting of the American Political Science Association, 1–4 September.

Choddusovsky, M. (1997), "Dismantling Former Yugoslavia, Re-Colonizing Bosnia: Development in Practice", *Capital and Class*, Vol. 7, No. 4.

Chossudovsky, M. (2001), "Macedonia: Washington's Military-Intelligence Ploy", *Emperor's Clothes*.

Cigar, N. (1995), *Genocide in Bosnia*, A&M University Press.

Clutterbuck, R. (1994), *Terrorism in an Unstable World*, Routledge.

Collier, Paul (1999), "Justice-Seeking and Loot-Seeking in Civil War", International Society for New Institutional Economics. Available at: <http://www.isnie.org/ISNIE99/Papers/collier.pdf>.

Collier, Paul (2000), "Doing Well Out of War", in Mats Berdal and David Malone (eds), *Greed and Grievance: Economic Agendas in Civil Wars*, Lynne Rienner.

Collier, Paul (2006), "Economic Causes of Civil Conflict and their Implications for Policy", Department of Economics, Oxford University. Available at: <http://users.ox.ac.uk/~econpco/research/conflict.htm>.

Collier, Paul and Hoeffler, Anke (2004), "Greed and Grievance in Civil War", *Oxford Economic Papers*, Vol. 56, pp. 563–595.

Collier, Paul and O'Connell. Stephen A. (2007), "Opportunities and Choices", in Beno J. Ndulu et al (eds), *The Political Economy of Economic Growth in Africa 1960–2000*, Cambridge University Press.

Collier, Paul and Sambanis, Nicholas (2002), "Understanding Civil War: A New Agenda", *Journal of Conflict Resolution*, Vol. 46, No. 1, February 2002.

Crawford, James (2006), *The Creation of States in International Law* (2nd edition), Oxford University Press.

Crenshaw, Martha (1992), "Current Research on Terrorism: the academic perspective", *Studies in Conflict and Terrorism*, Vol. 15, No. 1, pp. 1–11.

Dalby, S. (2007), "Geopolitical knowledge: Scale, method and the 'Willie Sutton Syndrome'", *Geopolitics*, Vol. 12, No. 1, pp. 183–191.

Danforth, Loring (1995), *The Macedonian conflict: Ethnic nationalism in a transnational world*, Princeton University Press.

Dannreuther, R. (2007), *International Security: The Contemporary Agenda*, Polity.

Daskalovski, Zidas. (2002), "The Macedonian conflict of 2001: Between successful diplomacy, rhetoric and terror", *Studies in Post-Communism*, Occasional Paper No. 7, Centre for Post-Communist Studies, St Francis Xavier University. Available at: <http://www.stfx.ca/pinstitutes/cpcs>.

Daskalovski, Zhidas. (2004), "Democratic Consolidation and the 'Stateness' Problem: The Case of Macedonia", *The Global Review of Ethnopolitics*, Vol. 3, No. 2, University of Oxford. Available at: <http://www.ethnopolitics.org/ethnopolitics/archive/volume_III/issue_2/daskalovski.pdf>.

Daskalovski, Zhidas (2006), *Walking on the Edge: Consolidating Multi-ethnic Macedonia: 1989–2004*, Globic Press.

Davenport, Christian (1996), "The Weight of the Past: Exploring Lagged Determinants of Political Repression", *Political Research Quarterly*, Vol. 49, No. 2 (June 1996), pp. 377–403.

Davenport, Christian (2003), "Peace by Piece: Towards an Understanding of Exactly How Democracy Reduces State Repression", Center for International Development and Conflict Management, University of Maryland. Available at: <http://mpsa.indiana.edu/conf2003papers/1032021217.pdf>.

Davis, Gareth (1999), "Repression, Rationality and Relative Deprivation: A Theoretical and Empirical Examination of Cross-National Variations in Political Violence", Working Papers Series, George Mason University, Department of Economics.

De Billon, Philippe (2007), "Corrupting Peace? Corruption peace building and reconstruction", Draft manuscript to be submitted to *Singapore Journal of Tropical Geography*, pp. 1–33. Available at: <http://democracy.ubc.ca/fileadmin/template/main/images/departments/CSDI/confences/CorruptionConfLeBillon.pdf>.

De Rapper, Gilles (1998), "Crisis in Kosovo: Reactions in Albania and Macedonia at the Local Level", Ethnobarometer Programme Working Paper No. 3, 1998.

Deboel, Gunnar (1993), "De Makedonische Kwestie", *Tetradio*, No. 2.

Dempsey, Judy (1988), "If Serbia Sneezes, The Balkans Catch A Cold", *Financial Times*, 14 October.

DeRouen, K.R. and Sobek, D. (2004), "The Dynamics of Civil War Duration and Outcome", *Journal of Peace Research*, Issue 41, pp. 305–320.

Dimitrieva, Elka and Verica, Janeska (2001), "Ageing of Population and Labor Force in the Republic of Macedonia", in Micevska et.al. (2002), "Economic Growth of the Republic of Macedonia: Experiences and Policy Recommendations", World Bank Research Project. Available at: <http://www.cerge-ei.cz/pdf/gdn/grp_final_macedonia.pdf>.

Dimitrievska, Vesna (1998), "Poor Household Survey: Changes in Social Structure in the Republic of Macedonia", *South-East Europe Review*, pp. 81–88.

Dollard, John, Doob, Leonard. W., Miller, Neal E., Mowrer, O.H. and Sears, Robert R. (1939), *Frustration and Aggression*, Yale University Press.

Downes, Alexander B. (2004), "The Problem with Negotiated Settlements to Ethnic Civil Wars". *Security Studies*, Vol. 13, No. 4.

Draper, Stark (1997), "The Conceptualization of the Albanian Nation", *Ethnic and Racial Studies*, Vol. 20, No. 1, January 1997, pp. 1–19.

Druckman, D. and Mitchell, C. (1995) (eds), "Flexibility in Negotiation and Mediation", *The Annals of the American Academy of Political and Social Science*, Vol. 542, Sage.

Duclos, J.Y and Philippe, G. (2002), "Absolute and Relative Deprivation and the Measurement of Poverty", *Review of Income and Wealth*, Vol. 48, No. 4, pp. 471–492.

Duffy, Monica (2003), *The Geography of Ethnic Violence: Identity, Interests, and the Indivisibility of Territory*, Princeton University Press.

Dugan, Máire A. (2003), "Coercive Power", *Beyond Intractability*, University of Colorado.

Einstein, Albert and Freud, Sigmund (1939), *Why war?* Peace Pledge Union.

Elsie, R. (2002), *Gathering Clouds: The Roots of Ethnic Cleansing in Kosovo and Macedonia*, Dukagjini Balkan Books.

Engstrom, J. (2002a), "Peace, Stability and Elections: An opinion poll and its implications", *The Global Review of Ethnopolitics*, Vol. 2, No. 1 (September 2002), pp. 62–74.

Engstrom, J. (2002b), "The power of perception: the impact of the Macedonian question on inter-ethnic relations in the Republic of Macedonia", *The Global Review of Ethno-politics*, Vol. 1, No. 3 (March 2002). Available at: <http://www.ethnopolitics.org/ethnopolitics/archive/volume_I/issue_3/engstrom.pdf>.

Enloe, C. (1980), *Ethnic Soldiers: State Security in Divided Societies*, Penguin Books.

Estrin, Saul (1991), "Yugoslavia: The Case of Self-Managing Market Socialism", *The Journal of Economic Perspectives*, Vol. 5 No. 4, pp. 187–194.

Fearon, J.D. and Laitin, D.D. (2003), "Ethnicity, insurgency, and civil war", *American Political Science Review*, Vol. 97, No. 1, pp. 75–90.

Flint, C. (2005), *The Geography of War and Peace: From Death-Camps to Diplomats*, Oxford University Press.

Fisher, R.J. (1997), "Interactive Conflict Resolution", in I.W. Zartman and J.L. Rasmussen (eds), *Peacemaking in International Conflict*, United States Institute of Peace.

Fisher, Gordon (2008), "Relative or Absolute? New Light on the Behavior of Poverty Lines Over Time", Newsletter of the Government Statistics Section and the Social Statistics Section of the American Statistical Association. Available at: <http://aspe.hhs.gov/POVERTY/papers/relabs.htm>.

Galtung, J. (1964), "A Structural Theory of Aggression", *Journal of Peace Research*, No. 2.

Galtung, Johan and Jacobsen, Carl G. (2000), *Searching for Peace: The Road to Transcend*, Pluto Press.

Gaber, Natasha and Joveska, Aneta (2004), "Macedonian census results – controversy or reality?", *South East European Review*, Issue 1, pp. 99–110.

Gavrilis, George (1996), "The Making of a Greater Albania?" in John S. Micgiel (ed.), *State and Nation Building in East Central Europe*, Institute on East Central Europe, Columbia.

George, Alexander L. (1991a), *Forceful Persuasion: Coercive Diplomacy as an Alternative to War*, United States Institute of Peace Press.

George, Alexander L. (1991b), *Avoiding War: Problems of Crisis Management*, Westview Press.

George, Alexander L. and Simons, William E. (eds) (1994), *The Limits of Coercive Diplomacy*, 2nd edn, Westview Press.

Gerges, F. (2005), *The Far Enemy: Why Jihad Went Global*, Cambridge University Press.

Gilbert, A. (1989), *Niccolo Machiavelli: The Chief Works and Others*, Duke University Press

Gomm, Roger (2003), *Social Research Methodology: A Critical Introduction*, Palgrave Macmillan.

Goodrich, Melinda K. (1990), "Yugoslavia Regional Disparities", Library of Congress, Federal Research Division, Country Studies. Available at: <http://lcweb2.loc.gov/cgibin/query/r?frd/cstdy:@field(DOCID+yu0123)>.

Gounaris, Basil (1995), "Social cleavages and national awakening in Ottoman Macedonia", *East European Quarterly*, Vol. 29, pp. 409–426. Available at: <http://www.southeasteurope.org/documents/>.

Gregory, D. and Pred, A. (2006), *Violent Geographies*, Routledge.

Grillot, S. (2003), "Preventing deadly conflict: Learning from the UN experience in Macedonia", *Contemporary Security Policy*, Vol. 24, No. 3 (December 2003), pp. 129–134.

Grillot, Suzette R. et al (2004), "A Fragile Peace: Guns and Security in Post Conflict Macedonia", UNDP, pp. 1–102. Available at: <http://hei.unige.ch/sas/files/sas/publications/spe_reports_pdf/2004-sr4-macedonia.pdf>.

Grossman, Herschel I. (1999), "Kleptocracy and Revolutions", *Oxford Economic Papers*, Vol. 51, No. 2, April 1999, pp. 267–283.

Gurr, Ted Robert (1968), "A casual model of civil strife: a comparative analysis using new indices", *American Political. Science Review*, Vol. 62, No. 4.

Gurr, Ted Robert (1970), *Why Men Rebel?* Princeton University Press.

Gurr, Ted Robert (1980), *Handbook of Political Conflict: Theory and Research*, The Free Press Series on Political Behaviour.

Gurr, Ted Robert (1993), *Minorities at Risk: A Global View of Ethnopolitical Conflicts*, United States Institute for Peace Press.

Gurr, Ted Robert and Moore, Will H. (1997), "Ethnopolitical Rebellion: A Cross-Sectional Analysis of the 1980s with Risk Assessments for the 1990s", *American Journal of Political Science*, Vol. 41, No. 4, pp. 79–103.

Hagmann, Jonas (2004), "Coercion as a tool for third party conflict resolution: Roles, Modes and Use", The Fletcher School. Available at: <http://fletcher.tufts.edu/research/2004/Hagmann-Jonas.pdf>.

Hanjdiak, Marko (2002), "Smuggling in South East Europe: The Yugoslav Wars and the development of regional criminal networks in the Balkans", Centre for the Study of Democracy.

Harris, Ian, Fisk, Larry J. and Rank, Carol (1998), "A Portrait of University Peace Studies in North America and Western Europe at the End of the Millennium", *International Journal of Peace Studies*, Vol. 3, No. 1.

Hashi, I. (1992), "The Disintegration of Yugoslavia: Regional Disparities and the Nationalities Question", *Capital and Class*, No. 48, pp. 41–88.

Hechter, Michael (1995), "Explaining nationalist violence", *Nations and Nationalism*, Vol. 1, No. 1, pp. 53–68.

Hegre, H. (2006), "Population Size, Concentration and Civil War: A Geographically Disaggregated Conflict Analysis", Paper presented at the Meeting for the Environmental Factors in Civil War, Peace Research Institute Oslo, pp. 1–38.

Hislope, R. (1998), "Structure and Strategy in Ethnic Conflict", in B. Pleskovic and J.E. Stiglitz, *Annual Bank Conference on Development Economics*, 1998, World Bank, Washington.

Hislope, R. (2002), "Organized Crime in a Disorganized State: How Corruption Contributed to Macedonia's Mini-War", *Problems of Post-Communism*, Vol. 49, No. 3, pp. 33–41.

Hislope, R. (2003), "Between a bad peace and a good war: insights and lessons from the almost-war in Macedonia", *Ethnic and Racial Studies*, Vol. 26, No. 1, pp. 129–151.

Hislope, R. (2004), "How is Ethnic Peace Possible? Explaining Macedonia's Peaceful Decade", Paper presented at the annual meeting of the The Midwest Political Science Association, Palmer House Hilton, Chicago, Illinois.

Hislope, R. (2005), "When Being Bad is Good: Corrupt Exchanges in Divided Societies", Paper prepared for the conference Post-Communist States and Societies: Transnational and National Politics, Maxwell School of Syracuse University.

Horowitz, Daniel (1998), "Structure and Strategy", Annual World Bank Conference on Development Economics, Washington.

Horowitz, Daniel (2001), *Ethnic Groups in Conflict*, University of California Press.

Irwin, Colin (2002), "Peace, Stability and Elections: An opinion poll and its implications", *The Global Review of Ethnopolitics*, Vol. 2, No. 1, pp. 62–74.

Ivanov, Mihail (2007), "Sofia On the Macedonian Authenticity", *New Balkan Politics*, Issue 6. Available at: <http://www.newbalkanpolitics.org.mk/OldSite/Issue_6/ivanov.macedonian.eng.asp>.

Jakobsen, Peter Viggo (1998), *Western Use of Coercive Diplomacy after the Cold War: A Challenge for Theory and Practice*, Macmillan Press Ltd.

Jakobsen, Peter Viggo (2007), "Coercive Diplomacy: Frequently Used, Seldom Successful", *Kungl Krigsvetenskapsakademiens Handlingar Och Tidskrift*, pp. 27–40.

Jankuloski, Zvonimir (ed.) (1999), "Why Macedonia Matters: Spill Over of the Kosovo Conflict to Macedonia" in "The Kosovo Crisis", RSP Working Paper 1, June 1999.

Jeffries, Ian (2002), *The Former Yugoslavia at the Turn of the Twenty-first Century*: A *Guide to the Economies in Transition*, Routledge.

Johnsen, W. (1994), *Pandora's Box Reopened: Ethnic Conflict in Europe and Its Implications*, Diane Publications.

Judah, Tim (2000), *The Serbs: History, Myth and the Destruction of Yugoslavia*, Yale University Press.

Judah, Tim (2001), "Greater Albania?", Survival, Vol. 43, No. 2, pp. 7–18.

Judah, Tim (2002), Kosovo: War and Revenge, Yale University Press.

Kaldor, Mary (1999), *New and Old Wars: Organized Violence in a Global Era*, Polity.

Kalyvas, Stathis N. (2001), "'New' and 'Old' Civil Wars: A Valid Distinction?", *World Politics*, Vol. 54, No. 1, pp. 524–552

Kaufmann, Chaim D. (1996), "Possible and Impossible Solutions to Ethnic Civil Wars", *International Security*, Vol. 20, No. 4.

Kaufmann, Chaim D. (1998), "When All Else Fails: Ethnic Population Transfers and Partitions in the 20th Century", *International Security*, Vol. 23, No. 2.

Kaufman, Stuart (2001), *The Symbolic Politics of Ethnic War*, Cornell University Press.

Kaufman, S.J. (1996), "Preventive Peacekeeping, Ethnic Violence and Macedonia", *Studies in Conflict and Terrorism*, Vol. 19 (1996), pp. 229–246.

Kees, Klok (1999), "Dutch scholars on the new Macedonian Question (1991–1995)". Available at: <http://www.anistor.co.hol.gr/english/enback/>.

Kemp, Walter (2003), "Profiting from Instability: Crime, Corruption and Inter-Ethnic Conflict" in Yves Victor and Daniel Warner, "New Security Threats and Challenges within the OSCE Region", PSIO Occasional Paper, 1/2003.

Kim, Julie (2001), "Macedonia: Country Background and Recent Conflict", CRS Report for Congress.

King, G. et al (1994), *Designing Social Inquiry: Scientific Inference in Qualitative Research*, Princeton University Press

Kirwin, Mathew (2006), "The Security Dilemma and Conflict in the Cote D'Ivoire", *Nordic Journal of African Studies*, Vol. 15, No. 1, pp. 42–52.

Klimov, Blogoy (2003), "Geopolitics vs. Globalization in the Balkans: The New Rivalries in the Energy and Transport Sectors", Central European University, Budapest. Available at: <http://mpra.ub.uni-muenchen.de/4112/1/MPRA_paper_4112.pdf>.

Kofos, Evangelos (1999), *Greece's Macedonian Adventure: The Controversy over FYROM's Independence and Recognition*. Available at: <http://www.macedonian-heritage.gr/downloads/library/Kofos19990705.pdf>.

Kola, Paulin (2003), *The Search for Greater Albania*, Hurst and Company.

Koppa, Marilena (2001), "Ethnic Albanians in the Former Yugoslav Republic of Macedonia: Between Nationality and Citizenship", *Nationalism and Ethnic Politics*, Vol. 7, No. 4, pp. 37–65.

Korf, B. (2011), "Resources, Violence and the Telluric Geographies of Small Wars", *Progress in Human Geography*, Sage.

Korf, B., Engeler, M. and Hagmann, T. (2010), "The Geography of Warscape", *Third World Quarterly*, Vol. 30 No. 3, pp. 385–399.

Kriesberg, Louis (1992), *The Negotiation of Agreements*, Yale University Press.

Kriesberg, Louis (1998), *Constructive Conflicts from Escalation to Resolution*, Rowman Littlefield.

Lake, David A. and Rothchild, Donald S. (1996), "Containing fear: The origins and management of ethnic conflict", *International Security*, No. 21 (Fall), pp. 41–75.

Lake, David A. and Rothchild, Donald S. (1998), *The International Spread of Ethnic Conflict: Fear, Diffusion, and Escalation*, Princeton University Press.

Le Billon, P. (2007), "Scales, Chains and Commodities: Mapping Out 'Resource Wars'", *Geopolitics*, Vol. 12, No. 1, pp. 200–205.

Levy, J.S. (2008), "Deterrence and Coercive Diplomacy: The Contributions of Alexander George", *Political Psychology*, Vol. 29, No. 4.

Lichbach, Mark Irving (1995), *The Rebel's Dilemma*, University of Michigan Press.

Lijphart, A. (1971), "Comparative Politics and the Comparative Method", *American Political Science Review*, Vol. 65, No. 3, pp. 682–693.

Lorenz, Konrad (1966), *On Aggression*. Harcourt, Brace & World, Inc.

Ludlow, David J. (2003), "Preventive Peacemaking in Macedonia: An Assessment of UN Good Offices Diplomacy", *Brigham Young University Law Review*. Rev.761.

Lunt, Horace G. (1984), "Some Sociolinguistic Aspects of Macedonian and Bulgarian", in Benjamin A. Stolz, I.R. Titunik and Lubomir Dolezel (eds), *Language and Literary Theory*, University of Michigan Press.

Mahnken, Thomas and Maiolo, Joseph A. (eds) (2007), *Strategic Studies: A Reader*, Routledge.

Maleska, Mirjana (2002), "The political and security crisis in Macedonia", *Southeast European Review*, Special Edition, Vol. 9, No. 14. Available at: <http://www.ceeol.com/aspx/getdocument.aspx?logid=5&id=C0C079D0-8E32-42A9-9043-11DA2F9388D8>.

Manheim, J. and Rich, R. (1986), *Empirical political analysis: Research methods in political science*, Longman.

Marks, John and Fraenkel, Eran (1998), "Why Macedonia has not exploded", *Conflict Prevention Newsletter*, Vol. 1, No. 1 (March 1998).

Marshall, G. Monty and Cole, R. Benjamin (2009), "Global Report 2009: Conflict, Governance and State Fragility", Centre for Systemic Peace.

Matic, Babe and Primorak, Emir (1986), "Some causes for the growth of the Yugoslav external debt", *Soviet Studies*, Vol. 38, No 1 (January), University of Glasgow.

Matveeva, Anna et al (2003), "Macedonia: Guns, Policing and Ethnic Division – Small Arms and Security in South-Eastern Europe", Safe World and Bonn International Centre for Conversion, pp. 1–72. Available at <http://hei.unige.ch/sas/files/portal/spotlight/country/eu_pdf/europe-macedonia-2003.pdf>.

McGinty, Roger and Darby, John (eds) (2003), *Contemporary Peacemaking: Conflict, Violence and Peace Process*, Palgrave Macmillan.

Musliu, Alber and Visar, Ademi (2006), "Macedonia: Micro-credit, poverty in ethnic minorities", Association for Democratic Initiatives in Macedonia. Available at: <http://www.minorityrights.org/?lid=942>.

Myhrvold, Ronny (2005), "Former Yugoslav Republic of Macedonia: Education as a political phenomenon", NORDEM Report, NORDEM. Available at: <http://www.humanrights.uio.no/forskning/publ/publikasjonsliste.html>.

O'Loughlin, J. and Raleigh, C. (2007), "Spatial analysis of civil war violence", in K. Cox, M. Low and J. Robinson (eds), *Handbook of Political Geography*, Sage.

O'Lear, S. and Diehl, P.F. (2007), "Not drawn to scale: Research on Resource and Environmental Conflict", *Geopolitics*, Vol. 12, No. 1, pp. 166–182.

Olson, M.L. and Pearson, F.S. (2000), "Policy-making and discrimination: Forecasting ethno-political violence", Presentation of the International Studies Association, Wayne State University.

Olzak, Susan (1994), *The Dynamics of Ethnic Competition and Conflict*, Stanford University Press.

Palmer, S. and King, P. (1971), *Yugoslav Communism and the Macedonian Question*, Archon Books.

Pape, Robert (1992), "Coercion and Military Strategy: Why Denial Works and Punishment Doesn't", *Journal of Strategic Studies*, Vol. 4, No. 15, pp. 423–475.

Paquette, Laure (2002), *Strategy and Ethnic Conflict: A Method, Theory and Case Study*, Prager.

Posen, B. (1993), "The Security Dilemma and Ethnic Conflict", *Survival*, Vol. 4, No. 3 (Spring).

Prevelakis, George (1996), "The return of the Macedonian Question in the changing shape of the Balkans", in F.W. Carter and H.T. Norris (eds), *The Changing Shape of the Balkans*, UCL Press.

Raleigh, C., Hegre, H. and Carlson, J. (2009), "Introducing ACLED: An armed conflict location and event dataset", Peace Research Institute Oslo.

Ramet, S.P. (1992), *Nationalism and Federalism in Yugoslavia 1962–1991*, Indiana University Press. Available at: <http://unpan1.un.org/intradoc/groups/public/documents/nispacee/unpan005871.pdf>.

Regan, P.M. and Norton, T.A. (2003), "Greed, Grievance, and Mobilization: The Onset of Protest, Rebellion and Civil War", *Journal of Conflict Resolution*, Issue 49, pp. 319–336.

Rosen, M. and Wolff, J. (1999), *Political Thought*, Oxford University Press.

Roudometof, Victor (1996), "Nationalism and Identity Politics in the Balkans: Greece and the Macedonian Question", *Journal of Modern Greek Studies*, Vol. 14, No. 2 (1996) pp. 253–301. Available at: <http://www.gate.net/~mango/JHS1.htm>.

Rousseau, D. (2006), *Identifying threats and threatening identities: the social construction of realism and liberalism*, Stanford University Press.

Rummel, R.J. (1977), *Conflict in Perspective*, Sage.

Runciman, W.G. (1966), *Relative Deprivation and Social Justice*, University of California Press.

Sambanis, N. (2001), "Do Ethnic and Non-Ethnic Civil Wars Have the Same Causes? A Theoretical and Empirical Inquiry", *Journal of Conflict Resolution*, Issue 45, pp. 259–282.

Saveska, S. and Brown, R. (1999), "Unemployment in the Republic of Macedonia: Policy options for employment growth", 7th NISPA Conference: Improving Relations between the Administration and Public, Sofia, March 1999.

Schelling, Thomas C. (1967), *Arms and Influence*. Yale Law School.

Shoup, Paul (1968a), *Communism and the Yugoslav National Question*, Columbia University Press.

Shoup, Paul. (1968b), "Yugoslavia's national minorities under Communism", *Slavic Review*, Vol. 22, No. 1.

Sowards, S.W. (1996), "Twenty-five lectures on Modern Balkan History", Michigan State University.

Sullivan, Mark (1995), *The Mechanism for Strategic Coercion: Denial or Second Order Change?* Air University Press.

Tanevksi, Borjan (2002), "The problem between the Macedonian and Albanian ethnic groups in the Republic of Macedonia and its future", *New Balkan Politics*, Issue 9. Available at: <http://www.newbalkanpolitics.org.mk/napis.asp?id=36&lang=English>.

Taras, Raymond C. and Rajat, Ganguly (1998), *Understanding Ethnic Conflict*, Longman.

Ten Dam, Caspar (2011a), "How to feud and rebel: Violence-values among the Chechens and Albanians", *Iran and the Caucasus*, No. 14, pp. 331–366.

Ten Dam, Caspar (2011b), "Histories, Cultures and Grievances of the Chechens and Albanians", *Iran and the Caucasus*, Vol. 15 No. 1–2, pp. 235–273.

Todorovski, Ilija (1999), "Local Self-Government and Decentralization in the Republic of Macedonia", in *Local Self-Government and Decentralization in South-East Europe* (2001), Friedrich Ebert Stiftung, pp. 172–193. Available at: <http://library.fes.de/pdf-files/bueros/kroatien/50257.pdf>.

Ury, William L., Brett, Jeanne M. and Goldberg, Stephen B. (1988), *Getting Disputes Resolved: Designing Systems to Cut the Costs of Conflict*, Jossey Bass Publishers.

Vankovska, Biljana (1997), "Ethnic Conflict in Macedonia: Can There Be Winners and Losers?" *Peace and Security* (September 1997), pp. 39–46.

Vankovska, Biljana (1998), "UNPREDEP in Macedonia: Diplomacy-Security Nexus in the Balkans", *Romanian Journal of International Affairs*, No. 2.

Vankovska, Biljana (2002), "Current perspectives on Macedonia: Part 1, Path from Oasis of Peace to Powder Keg of the Balkans", Heinrich Böll Foundation. Available at: <http://www.boell.de/en/05_world/1733.html>.

Vankovska, Biljana (2006), "The Role of the Ohrid Agreement and the Peace Process in Macedonia", The Transnational Foundation for Peace and Future Research, pp. 1–17. Available at: <http://www.transnational.org>.

Vasquez, J.A. (2000), *What Do We Know about War?* Rowman and Littlefield.

Veselica, Marko (1980), *The Croatian National Question*, United Publishers.

Walker, Connor (1994), *Ethno nationalism: The quest for understanding*, Princeton University Press.

Wannis, Antony (2008), "Peace Processes, Secret Negotiations and Civil Society: Dynamics of Inclusion and Exclusion", *International Journal of Negotiation*, Vol. 13, pp. 1–9.

Woodward, Susan (1995), *Balkan Tragedy*, Brookings Institution.

Woodward, Susan (2005), "The Inequality of Violence: On the Discovery of Civil War as a Threat to the North in the 1990s", APSA Task Force Report on Inequality and Difference in the Developing World.

Yarger, Harry R. (2006), "Strategic Theory for the 21st Century: The Little Book on Big Strategy", Strategic Studies Institute. Available at: <http://www.strategicstudiesinstitute.army.mil>.

Zametica, John (2002), "The Yugoslav Conflict", Adelphi Paper, No. 270.

Zarkovic, Milica (2004), *Economic Decline and Nationalism in the Balkans*, St Martin's Press.

Zhelyazkova, Antonina (1999), "Macedonia and Kosovo after the Military Operations", International Centre for Minority Studies. Available at: <http://www.omda.bg/imir/mk_concl.html>.

Zivojin, Krzalic (1986), "Stanovnistvo Jugoslavije 1921" [Population of Yugoslavia by Religion and Mother Tongue], in Radni dokument 32, Belgrade.
Zravko, Petak (2003), "The Political Economy Background of Yugoslav Dissolution", Workshop in Political Theory and Political Analysis, Indiana University. Available at: <http://www.indiana.edu/~workshop/seminars/papers/y673_spring_2003_petak.pdf>.

Index

NATIONALISMS ACROSS THE GLOBE

Although in the 1980s the widely shared belief was that nationalism had become a spent force, the fragmentation of the studiously non-national Soviet Union, Yugoslavia and Czechoslovakia in the 1990s into a multitude of successor nation-states reaffirmed its continuing significance. Today all extant polities (with the exception of the Vatican) are construed as nation-states, and hence nationalism is the sole universally accepted criterion of statehood legitimization. Similarly, human groups wishing to be recognized as fully fledged participants in international relations must define themselves as nations. This concept of world politics underscores the need for open-ended, broad-ranging, novel and interdisciplinary research into nationalism and ethnicity. It promotes better understanding of the phenomena relating to social, political and economic life, both past and present.

This peer-reviewed series publishes monographs, conference proceedings and collections of articles. It attracts well-researched, often interdisciplinary, studies which open new approaches to nationalism and ethnicity or focus on interesting case studies. The language of the series is usually English, with authors/editors of proposed volumes responsible for meeting the Peter Lang standards of copy-editing. Book proposals for *Nationalisms Across the Globe* and queries should be emailed to either, or both, of the series editors:

Dr Tomasz Kamusella (University of St Andrews, Scotland, UK), tomek672@gmail.com

Dr Krzysztof Jaskułowski (Warsaw School of Social Sciences and Humanities, Poland), krzysztofja@interia.pl

Vol. 1 Tomasz Kamusella and Krzysztof Jaskułowski (eds): Nationalisms Today. 334 pages, 2009.

Vol. 2 Cezary Obracht-Prondzyński and Tomasz Wicherkiewicz (eds): The Kashubs: Past and Present. 307 pages, 2011.

Vol. 3 Sabelo J. Ndlovu-Gatsheni and James Muzondidya (eds): Redemptive or Grotesque Nationalism? Rethinking Contemporary Politics in Zimbabwe. 446 pages, 2011.

Vol. 4 Blessing-Miles Tendi: Making History in Mugabe's Zimbabwe. Politics, Intellectuals and the Media. 304 pages, 2010.

Vol. 5 Pavlos I. Koktsidis: Strategic Rebellion. Ethnic Conflict in FYR Macedonia and the Balkans. 279 pages, 2012.

Vol. 6 Janusz Sawczuk: Turbulentes 1989. Genese der deutschen Einheit. 327 pages, 2011.

Vol. 7 Chris Kostov: Contested Ethnic Identity. The Case of Macedonian Immigrants in Toronto, 1900–1996. 330 pages, 2010.

Vol. 8 Alexander Maxwell (ed.): The East–West Discourse. Symbolic Geography and its Consequences. 237 pages, 2011.

CREATING THE DEPARTMENT OF HOMELAND SECURITY: CONSIDERATION OF THE ADMINISTRATION'S PROPOSAL

HEARINGS

BEFORE THE

SUBCOMMITTEE ON
OVERSIGHT AND INVESTIGATIONS

OF THE

COMMITTEE ON ENERGY AND COMMERCE
HOUSE OF REPRESENTATIVES

ONE HUNDRED SEVENTH CONGRESS

SECOND SESSION

JUNE 25 and JULY 9, 2002

Serial No. 107–113

Printed for the use of the Committee on Energy and Commerce

Available via the World Wide Web: http://www.access.gpo.gov/congress/house

U.S. GOVERNMENT PRINTING OFFICE

80–680CC WASHINGTON : 2002

For sale by the Superintendent of Documents, U.S. Government Printing Office
Internet: bookstore.gpo.gov Phone: toll free (866) 512–1800; DC area (202) 512–1800
Fax: (202) 512–2250 Mail: Stop SSOP, Washington, DC 20402–0001

COMMITTEE ON ENERGY AND COMMERCE

W.J. "BILLY" TAUZIN, Louisiana, *Chairman*

MICHAEL BILIRAKIS, Florida
JOE BARTON, Texas
FRED UPTON, Michigan
CLIFF STEARNS, Florida
PAUL E. GILLMOR, Ohio
JAMES C. GREENWOOD, Pennsylvania
CHRISTOPHER COX, California
NATHAN DEAL, Georgia
RICHARD BURR, North Carolina
ED WHITFIELD, Kentucky
GREG GANSKE, Iowa
CHARLIE NORWOOD, Georgia
BARBARA CUBIN, Wyoming
JOHN SHIMKUS, Illinois
HEATHER WILSON, New Mexico
JOHN B. SHADEGG, Arizona
CHARLES "CHIP" PICKERING, Mississippi
VITO FOSSELLA, New York
ROY BLUNT, Missouri
TOM DAVIS, Virginia
ED BRYANT, Tennessee
ROBERT L. EHRLICH, Jr., Maryland
STEVE BUYER, Indiana
GEORGE RADANOVICH, California
CHARLES F. BASS, New Hampshire
JOSEPH R. PITTS, Pennsylvania
MARY BONO, California
GREG WALDEN, Oregon
LEE TERRY, Nebraska
ERNIE FLETCHER, Kentucky

JOHN D. DINGELL, Michigan
HENRY A. WAXMAN, California
EDWARD J. MARKEY, Massachusetts
RALPH M. HALL, Texas
RICK BOUCHER, Virginia
EDOLPHUS TOWNS, New York
FRANK PALLONE, Jr., New Jersey
SHERROD BROWN, Ohio
BART GORDON, Tennessee
PETER DEUTSCH, Florida
BOBBY L. RUSH, Illinois
ANNA G. ESHOO, California
BART STUPAK, Michigan
ELIOT L. ENGEL, New York
TOM SAWYER, Ohio
ALBERT R. WYNN, Maryland
GENE GREEN, Texas
KAREN McCARTHY, Missouri
TED STRICKLAND, Ohio
DIANA DeGETTE, Colorado
THOMAS M. BARRETT, Wisconsin
BILL LUTHER, Minnesota
LOIS CAPPS, California
MICHAEL F. DOYLE, Pennsylvania
CHRISTOPHER JOHN, Louisiana
JANE HARMAN, California

DAVID V. MARVENTANO, *Staff Director*
JAMES D. BARNETTE, *General Counsel*
REID P.F. STUNTZ, *Minority Staff Director and Chief Counsel*

SUBCOMMITTEE ON OVERSIGHT AND INVESTIGATIONS

JAMES C. GREENWOOD, Pennsylvania, *Chairman*

MICHAEL BILIRAKIS, Florida
CLIFF STEARNS, Florida
PAUL E. GILLMOR, Ohio
RICHARD BURR, North Carolina
ED WHITFIELD, Kentucky
Vice Chairman
CHARLES F. BASS, New Hampshire
ERNIE FLETCHER, Kentucky
W.J. "BILLY" TAUZIN, Louisiana
(Ex Officio)

PETER DEUTSCH, Florida
BART STUPAK, Michigan
TED STRICKLAND, Ohio
DIANA DeGETTE, Colorado
CHRISTOPHER JOHN, Louisiana
BOBBY L. RUSH, Illinois
JOHN D. DINGELL, Michigan,
(Ex Officio)